Local Government and Public Service Reform Initiative

MANAGING
THINK
TANKS

Practical Guidance for
Maturing Organizations

RAYMOND J. STRUYK

The Urban Institute

OPEN SOCIETY INSTITUTE
LOCAL GOVERNMENT AND PUBLIC SERVICE REFORM INITIATIVE

Address

Nádor utca 11.
H-1051 Budapest, Hungary

Mailing Address

P.O. Box 519
H-1357 Budapest, Hungary

Telephone

(36-1) 327-3104

Fax

(36-1) 327-3105

E-mail

lgprog@osi.hu

Web Site

http://lgi.osi.hu/

First published in 2002
by Local Government and Public Service Reform Initiative,
Open Society Institute Budapest

© OSI/LGI and The Urban Institute, 2002

THE URBAN INSTITUTE

Local Government
and Public Service
Reform Initiative

TM and Copyright © 2002 Open Society Institute

ISBN: 963 9419 42 7

Copies of the book can be ordered by e-mail or post from OSI.
Printed in Budapest, Hungary, September 2002.

Contents

The Urban Institute is a nonprofit policy research and educational organization established in Washington, D.C., in 1968. Its staff investigates the social, economic, and governance problems confronting the nation and evaluates the public and private means to alleviate them. The Institute disseminates its research findings through publications, its Web site, the media, seminars, and forums.

Through work that ranges from broad conceptual studies to administrative and technical assistance, Institute researchers contribute to the stock of knowledge available to guide decisionmaking in the public interest.

Conclusions or opinions expressed in Institute publications are those of the authors and do not necessarily reflect the views of officers or trustees of the Institute, advisory groups, or any organizations that provide financial support to the Institute.

Local Government and Public Service Reform Initiative (LGI), as a regional program of the Open Society Institute–Budapest (OSI), is an international development and grant-giving organization dedicated to the support of good governance in the countries of Central and Eastern Europe (CEE) and the Newly Independent States (NIS). LGI seeks to fulfill its mission through the initiation of research and support of development and operational activities in the fields of decentralization, public policy formation and the reform of public administration.

With projects running in countries covering the region between the Czech Republic and Mongolia, LGI seeks to achieve its objectives through various types of activities. LGI supports regional networks of institutions and professionals engaged in policy analysis, reform-oriented training and advocacy. It is involved in policy research and disseminates comparative and regionally applicable policy studies tackling local government issues. LGI delivers technical assistance and provides professional guidance to Soros national foundations. LGI supports policy centers and think tanks in the region, publishes books, studies and discussion papers dealing with the issues of decentralization public policy and lessons learned from the process of transition. They are used for development of curricula and organization of training programs.

Foreword

After a decade of transition in Central and Eastern Europe, the climate surrounding public sector reforms has become increasingly more complex and interconnected. Decision-makers must balance legislative, organizational and management changes in their countries with the demand for rational, effective reforms. Public policy design requires a choice of professional alternatives during the policy process that takes into consideration the multiple actors invariably involved as well as the institutional and financial consequences that are critical to its success.

In order to meet this outstanding demand, advisory and consulting organizations must improve their professional services. Domestic think tanks and policy institutes are regularly involved in policy formulation. Typically, as the scope of their size and activities has increased, their organization and management has been influenced by this growth, whether a detriment or benefit to the organization in question. Beyond professional development, institutional and leadership issues have become essential to their successful evolution.

In a well-run organization, management responsibilities like motivation, quality control, cooperation with boards and external communication are normal elements of day-to-day operations. This book gives a comprehensive review of these and other internal management tasks like creating team leaders, calculating indirect costs and launching new consulting initiatives. Numerous examples are provided to prove the credibility of such ideas for readers in Central and Eastern European countries.

Policy institutes and think tanks were always in the focus of the Open Society Institute's Local Government and Public Service Reform Initiative (LGI). Grants and institutional support to professional networks and advise and training for policy-makers recently was supplemented with a major program on policy institute development. LGI's public policy initiative is targeted on the effective organization of professional advisory activities. The public policy centers that participate in LGI's program for policy centers receive organizational development training, are advised on proposal writing for the European Union and have launched joint policy projects. They have also received considerable and valuable experience through mentorship schemes that connect think tanks from the region with their counterparts from Western Europe. LGI's newly published guidebook—*Writing Effective Public Policy Papers*—is aimed to improve the professional quality of their work.

This publication on managing think tanks fits perfectly into this rubric where management and policy intersect. Ray Struyk, a leading expert on policy development in Central and Eastern Europe, provides practical advice for well-established policy institutes gleaned from his experiences in the region. We hope that this joint publication with The Urban Institute will help our future cooperation in other research and development projects.

Gábor Péteri
LGI Research Director

Preface

My primary inspiration for writing this book was my experience with the Institute for Urban Economics (IUE), a think tank created in Moscow in 1995. IUE's six founders were all members of my staff, which was engaged on a large technical cooperation project in Russia. As the resident advisor for the Urban Institute—an accomplished think tank located in Washington, D.C.—I worked very closely with IUE's management over the next three years to help establish the IUE on a strong footing. During this period I searched for written materials on the management of think tanks. I found that there were none.

From 1990 to today I have visited and worked with more than a dozen think tanks in Eastern Europe and the Commonwealth of Independent States (EE–CIS). Sometimes the collaboration was intense.Often a discussion would turn to particular management challenges, such as how to establish an overhead rate that would be defensible to donor auditors. I wanted to be able to do more than simply provide on-the-spot advice. But, again, I have been frustrated by the lack of written guidance available.

In 1997 the Urban Institute, IUE, and the Metropolitan Research Institute in Budapest founded the Transition Policy Network (TPN). Today TPN is a group of nine think tanks in the EE–CIS region, plus the Urban Institute. The members work together to win and execute policy research and technical assistance projects. In the context of carrying out projects, the Urban Institute does some mentoring on management practices.When the Institute polled TPN members in 2001 about topics for seminars and workshops the network might stage for members management topics were in great demand. In short, casual observations in the EE-CIS region indicate that there is a widespread and persistent need for guidance and financial management.

This demand for—and lack of—management information provided strong motivation for writing a book about good practices in these areas. I decided that the book would be more useful and convincing if I could document actual management patterns with more systematic information about current practices among young think tanks, including examples of good practices. To this end, as time permitted during 2000 and 2001, I have undertaken a series of surveys on specific aspects of think tank management. Most of these involved face-to-face interviews, but one was conducted with a questionnaire via e-mail. This information, plus data on the practices used by exemplary for-profit businesses, nonprofit organizations, and think tanks, forms the basis for the guidelines reported.

I have spent the majority of my working life at think tanks—first at the National Bureau of Economic Research and then at the Urban Institute. I have had the chance to observe the management practices at these organizations and to gather information from 10 other Western think tanks in a survey for a project some years ago. These data convinced me that many Western think tanks were effectively managed in most areas but also that a good share could benefit from improved practices in some aspect of their administrative practices.

This book is directed particularly to younger and smaller think tanks throughout the world, and it may be of the greatest value to those in transitional and emerging economies.Nevertheless, I am convinced that even well-established think tanks in industrialized nations can profit from some of the lessons advanced. This book may also help the foundations and bilateral and mutlilateral aid agencies that work with think tanks everywhere. Sponsors of research and technical assistance projects too often undervalue the productivity of small investments in institutional development. The guidance presented here can alert sponsors to limitations in the management of some of the institutions with whom they work. The information also provides a basis for addressing the problems.

I readily acknowledge that the topical coverage of this volume is not comprehensive. Developing an effective audit strategy and several important governance issues are challenges to think tanks that are not addressed. Over time more chapters will be added on the Urban Institute's web site (http://www.urban.org/r/thinktanks) that will address some of these issues.

I want to thank several people and organizations whose help was pivotal in the preparation of the book. The first vote of gratitude goes to those from some 20-odd think tanks who participated in several surveys on current practices conducted for the book. I benefited enormously from extended discussions on management topics with colleagues at several think tanks, both as part of the formal interviews of the surveys and in other contexts. My greatest debt is to the team at the Institute for Urban Economics—especially its president, Nadezhda B. Kosareva—for sharing the details of several good management practices at the IUE. I am grateful that these think tanks agreed to permit me to publish these materials.

At the Urban Institute, Institute President Robert D. Reischauer was enthusiastic about this project, and offered moral support. Staff from several administrative departments contributed lessons and useful materials. A special thanks goes to Kathleen Courrier for good ideas. Heather Brady capably did the final editing. The Urban Institute supported the writing of this book from its unrestricted funds.

Raymond J. Struyk
April 2002

Raymond J. Struyk

1

Why Pay Attention to Management?

Many directors of think tanks focus squarely on the tasks necessary to fulfill the primary objectives of a private public-policy research organization: expanding the number of policy options considered to address a nation's problems, providing hard facts and analysis to small political parties and advocacy nongovernment organizations (NGOs) to empower smaller players in the political process, and informing the public on key issues of the day. They enjoy the interplay of the policy development process and the challenge of directing good researchers. By and large, think tanks are making a significant contribution to the policy process.[1]

The great majority of think-tank directors come from academic backgrounds—most have Ph.D.s and spend a significant part of their careers at universities or research institutes; a substantial share have served in their national government at senior levels. It is little wonder then that they do not have an abiding interest in management questions.

If this sounds like you or the director of a think tank your organization supports, then be aware that one ignores management issues at one's peril. Consider the following.

- The institute director trusts his senior people to do high-quality research and control the quality of their team's work, so there are no quality control procedures in place to routinely review the quality of

1

products being issued. A report on a high-visibility and urgent problem is sent to the Ministry of Finance with significant flaws in the statistical analysis. These flaws are discovered by an analyst from another organization after the report has been widely distributed. The think tank loses significant credibility with the government and other clients.

- The think tank has adopted informal procedures for determining staff salaries. In practice, management tends to worry about pay increases when they suspect that someone may be looking for another job. Often they outbid potential new employers to retain key staff members. The result is widespread unhappiness among the staff because they believe that no one is really monitoring the quantity and quality of work they do. There is little feedback. The only way to get a raise is to threaten to leave. Low staff morale saps productivity, and several staff actually leave to join other think tanks or commercial firms where they believe their work will be better appreciated.

- There is no law requiring an annual audit in the country where this think tank is located, and the director saves money by not having one done. He trusts his accountant to establish the overhead rate for the organization. The think tank has won a very large contract with a major multilateral donor, and the donor requires an audit to verify the overhead rates before the contract is awarded. The auditors discover that the overhead rates are not justified, and question a number of other financial practices. The donor decides to engage another contractor to do the work.

These are real-world examples, and they are frighteningly common. But there is a more fundamental reason for senior managers at think tanks to make time to address basic administration and financial management tasks: Their organizations will work more efficiently. Dynamic, charismatic leadership cannot offset flawed administrative systems.

Leaders of some think tanks recognize the need for improvement. In the autumn of 1999, the World Bank's Global Development Network (GDN) administered an on-line survey to think tanks about the think tanks' needs for assistance and the services that GDN might provide. One question asked, "how valuable would the following training activities be for your organization?" Respondents were to score the value of each type of training on a scale from one to seven, with seven indicating the greatest value. The 104 think tanks that responded[2] gave an average rating of 5.73 for training directed to "issues related to the management of policy institutes." The same organizations gave a rating of 5.13 to training on "technical issues, qualitative methods, and statistics." This pattern was highly consistent across regions.[3] In short, think-tank directors consider improving their organizations' management to be at least as important as strengthening their analytic capacity. These findings are consistent with the author's work with think tanks outside of industrialized countries.

This book provides guidance for addressing potential problem areas, and as such it fills a yawning void. To be sure, in the past the donor community has worked on institutional development with think tanks, particularly in transitional and developing economies. These efforts have tended to focus on two needs of young institutions. First, donors have provided equipment to support research operations, particularly computers, fax machines, and copiers. More recently, there has been help with Internet access and home pages. Second, donors have organized workshops typically addressing the needs of start-up NGOs more generally. Workshops on the basics of financial management, corporate governance, fundraising, interaction with the media, and policy advocacy have reached a large number of NGOs.[4] These programs provide critical skills to new, comparatively simple operations.

But established think tanks require more sophisticated and more tailored advice. Think-tank leaders seeking guidance and "how to" materials often turn to books and materials written for nonprofit organizations, but the fit is not good.[5] Think tanks have a different mission, staff structure, and clientele from NGOs.

WHO SHOULD READ THIS BOOK?

Leaders of think tanks constitute one primary audience for this book. The number of think tanks, both in and outside of the highly industrialized countries, has continued to expand impressively during the 1990s, building on a surge in the previous decade. One survey shows that there are now over 1,200 think tanks in the United States, up by several hundred from the 1980s. Freedom House (1999) estimates that there are 250 such organizations in Eastern Europe alone.

A recent survey of over 800 think tanks around the world reveals that 62 percent of responding institutions in the former Soviet bloc were founded in the 1990s. In Africa, the corresponding figure is 38 percent; an equal share was created in the previous decade.[6]

The figures for all regions doubtless understate the share of all organizations founded in the 1990s, because of the difficulties in identifying new organizations so that they could be included in the survey. Even so, the overall picture is of an expanding population. At the same time, many longer-established think tanks are expanding and maturing as the value of their analysis and participation in the policy process are more widely recognized by the donor community and by national governments, parliaments, and other participants in the policy arena.

Thus, a significant number of think tanks around the world have or will soon reach what might be termed the "second stage of development." Students of think tanks often use the criterion of ten full-time researchers consistently employed as indicators of think tanks' stages of development. "Second-stage" institutes are at the point where they move from a low and often highly variable level of operations and a small number of sponsors to a higher level of activity—a larger staff, more projects, greater specialization in staff assignments, more opportunities in the policy process and for educating the public on current policy issues.[7] Those in the third stage of development are established, major think tanks in the West, such as the United States' Brookings Institution and the Urban Institute and Germany's Institute fuer Wirtschaft Forschung (Institute for Economic Research, IFO).

As think tanks reach the second stage of development, they must alter their management and financial systems—and probably the way they reach targeted audiences—if they are to be efficient and effective. Managing the transition to a higher level of activity is difficult at best. An excellent policy analyst cannot make up for a primitive financial system that does not permit the institution to control costs or establish a credible overhead rate.[8]

Think tanks at the first and second stages of development are one target audience for this book. But there is a second target audience: foundations and other supporters of think tanks, such as bilateral and multilateral donors—for example, the U.S. Agency for International Development and the World Bank. These sponsors are interested in strengthening the management and capacity of think tanks so that they will become a sustained resource in the country and field in which they operate. Sponsors are also interested in think tanks' management because well-managed think tanks operate more efficiently and are less subject to corruption. At the same time, few project managers at donor organizations have significant experience with think tanks and are often unsure of how to work with them to improve their management. The chapters below provide the necessary guidance in several key areas.

CONCRETE EXAMPLES ARE BEST

In working with think tanks over the years, the author has learned that the best way to communicate an idea is with a specific, relevant, real-world example. Each chapter includes such examples, using information obtained from interviews with tank leaders and materials obtained during visits to think tanks.

The guidance presented here is drawn from four sources: knowledge the author has gained in working at think tanks for 30 years; his considerable experience in studying and mentoring think tanks during the past decade; in-depth interviews on management issues with leaders of 10 leading Western think tanks and more than 12 think tanks in transition economies (see table 1-1); and a close study of superior management practices recommended for nonprofit and for-profit organizations in the same management areas.

Think tanks interviewed for the research underpinning this book included groups located in the United States, Western Europe, and the transition countries of Eastern Europe and the Commonwealth of Independent States. The author came to know numerous think tanks in the transitional economies during the course of interviews done for an earlier book on the performance of think tanks in the policy development process in Bulgaria, Hungary, Armenia, and Russia.[9] Leaders of several think tanks from Asia have indicated to the author that the managerial challenges they face are similar to those confronting think tanks in countries with transitional economies. In other words, the current practices of the think tanks interviewed for this book correspond broadly to those of think tanks in other parts of the world. This would certainly cover "first-stage" and "second-stage" think tanks in all countries, including the United States and Western Europe.

It will be useful to have some general context on the situation for the think tanks in Eastern Europe when reviewing their practices and experiences. Several important points are listed in text box 1-1.

Table 1-1 Think Tanks Interviewed, by Country

Think Tank	Country
Think tanks in the United States and Western Europe	
American Enterprise Institute	United States
Brookings Institution	United States
Center for European Policy Studies	Belgium
Center for Strategic and International Studies	United States
Council on Foreign Relations	United States
The Heritage Foundation	United States
The Hoover Institution	United States
Institute for International Economics	United States
Stockholm International Peace Institute	Sweden
The Urban Institute	United States
Think tanks in EE-CIS countries	
Center for the Study of Democracy	Bulgaria
Institute for Market Economy	Bulgaria
Center for Political Studies and Comparative Analysis	Romania
Institute for Urban Economics	Russia
Institute for the Economy in Transition	Russia
Expert Institute of the Russian Union of Industrialists and Entrepreneurs	Russia
Center for Democracy and Free Enterprise	Czech Republic
Center for Social and Economic Research	Poland
Crakow Real Estate Institute	Poland
Gdansk Institute for Market Economics	Poland
Metropolitan Research Institute	Hungary
TARKI-Social Research Institute	Hungary
International Center for Policy Studies	Ukraine
Viitorul Foundation	Moldova

HOW TO USE THIS BOOK

The remaining chapters address six important management areas that deserve the attention of think tank leaders:

- Motivating staff to be productive and encouraging valuable staff to remain with the organization (essential elements include staff assessment, training, and compensation);
- Controlling the quality of the product presented to clients, particularly through a peer review process;

Box 1-1 Key Points on Think Tanks in Eastern Europe and the Commonwealth of Independent States

- The policy development tradition inherited from the old regimes was a closed process, the range of alternatives considered in addressing most problems was decidedly narrow, and there was little analytic rigor; program evaluation was essentially nonexistent. In the years just before the transition, policy analysts in some countries, such as Russia and Hungary, were stimulated by senior policymakers' interest in a more open and pluralistic policy process. Policy analysis in the Western sense is still somewhat novel in parts of the region, both for practitioners and for public-policy decisionmakers. Think tanks are heavily involved in the policy formulation process in most countries in Central and Eastern Europe, Russia, Ukraine, and Moldova, but less so in other CIS countries.

- Western—particularly American—foundations were instrumental in encouraging the creation of a number of think tanks and had a broad influence on the private policy-analysis industry. The American think-tank model, characterized by very strong independence, has generally served as the standard. Nevertheless, there are examples in the region of think tanks aligned with political parties or unions of industrialists along the "European model." There is also some concern about think tanks' impartiality: A significant share of think tanks have good political connections, and a number of their leaders have held very senior government positions. While this facilitates think tanks' policy development efforts, it raises questions as to whether their positions are truly disinterested.

- Most think tanks are at the first stage of development, although a significant share—perhaps 30 to 35 percent—are in the second stage. Entities in the first stage have a very small permanent research staff (one or two persons), a much larger number of part-time consultants, unstable funding, and primitive financial and administrative systems. The second stage is associated with a larger permanent research staff (5 to 10, at minimum), relatively stable funding, more sophisticated operating systems, and greater staff specialization (e.g., a public relations officer on staff). While most second-stage think tanks evolved from first-stage organizations, a modest number started as larger operations thanks to generous government or donor start-up support.

- National and local governments in Eastern Europe and the CIS have been poor customers for think tanks. Comparatively more contracting has been done in Hungary and Russia, but the volume is still modest. Local philanthropic support is very modest. The current legal and tax environment is broadly adequate, but think tanks generally enjoy no special privileges compared to parallel commercial organizations in the region.

- The donor community has not placed a priority on the institutional development of think tanks. Actually, donors have used think tanks to pursue agendas of their particular interest. Partly as a consequence of weak donor leadership, administrative practices in many think tanks are weak.

- Developing new products and services and identifying new clients and other opportunities;
- Creating strong team leaders—the key middle managers at think tanks who direct projects and have the most interaction with policymakers;
- Working successfully with the Board of Trustees or Board of Directors—getting the most from the Board in the way of advice on strategic issues without Board members becoming too involved in management questions;
- Structuring the research staff, when and why to employ teams of researchers or individual senior researchers supported by a research assistant or two;
- Communicating effectively the results of your research to policymakers and the general public; and
- Determining an overhead rate that is accurate and will withstand the scrutiny of outside auditors.

Each chapter contains a discussion of principles of good practice and provides examples—both positive and negative—of what organizations actually do. Examples of particularly strong practices are highlighted. Chapter annexes contain templates for strong practices, such as a staff assessment form. References to other discussions of the issue at hand are also provided.

Discussions are designed to stimulate the thinking about a management area. While specific examples of how some organizations deal with each area are provided, these examples need not be adopted *en bloc*. It is likely that each organization will want to make adjustments for the particular conditions it faces or for the environment in which it operates. Labor code provisions may affect procedures adopted in the personnel area, and ideas for generating innovations depend heavily on the roster of potential types of clients. In short, the essays in this volume are guides, not recipes.

NOTES

(Complete references can be found in the Reference Section at the end of this book.)

1. See, for example, Johnson (1999), Langsford and Brownsey (1992), McGann (1996), Rich (2001), Smith (2000), Stone, Denham, and Garnett (1998), Struyk (1999), and Telgarsky and Ueno (1996).

2. In addition, 98 private firms and government organizations completed the survey, but the figures in the text are only for think tanks. The questionnaire was directed to 512 research units throughout the world. The response rate was about the same in all regions.

3. A summary of the findings was published at http://www.gdnet.org/ survey2.htm. The results given in the text are based on tabulations prepared by the Urban Institute using a data file provided by the World Bank. Overall, the survey paid very little attention to management issues.

4. An example of a financial management course of this type is the one developed by Centex for International Private Enterprise (CIPE) for think tanks and business trade associations. The course covers the basic elements of budgeting, accounting, and control, but it does not deal with the more sophisticated issues described later in this book. For details, see "Financial Management Handbook" (CIPE, 1998). Some intensive courses for NGOs are now being offered. For example, the Institute for Development Policy and Management at the University of Manchester offers a five-week course, "Managing NGOs." Judging from the published course outline, it would deal with some of the fundamental management issues confronting think tanks, but not in the most useful way. For example, the standard NGO does not need an overhead rate structure or a quality control mechanism of the type needed by think tanks. This particular course is geared to British NGOs; so it would be of limited use to think tanks elsewhere.

5. Thoughtful observers of Western foundations' work with think tanks believe that foundations have generally underinvested in institutional development. Quigley (1996) makes this point emphatically about foundations and other donors working in Eastern Europe.

6. For details, see McGann (1999).

7. A comprehensive 1997 survey of think tanks in Eastern Europe found that about 30 percent of think tanks included met this criterion. The McGann survey cited above asked a simple question about all employees, whether full- or part-time, researchers or support staff. These figures are not used here. The survey is reported in Freedom House (1999). Among CIS countries, only Belarus and Ukraine are covered by the directory.

8. In the United States today there is also pressure for improved management of NGOs in general. See Paul Light (2000).

9. A general presentation of the findings on the Western think tanks is in Struyk (1993). Most of the think tanks from Eastern Europe and the Commonwealth of Independent States listed in table 1-1 were interviewed for an earlier study of think tanks' success in developing public policy; information on these organizations is reported in Struyk (1993).

Raymond J. Struyk

2

Motivating Staff for Higher Productivity and Increased Retention

S taff quality is a key determinant of success for all service organizations, but for think tanks it is fundamental. Senior researchers and policy analysts provide ideas about which problems facing their countries an institute can profitably address, direct the analysis on the problems, and proffer policy responses to meet them. They are also an institute's representatives for convincing policy elites that the course of action the institute proposes will be effective and efficient. As in other service organizations, staff compensation accounts for two-thirds or more of think tanks' costs.

It is not surprising, then, that "motivating staff" ranked first in an Urban Institute survey, conducted in 2001, of what think tanks in nine countries in Eastern Europe and the Commonwealth of Independent States most want addressed in a training session.[1] This rating is consistent with comments from leaders of other think tanks in the region about management issues they would like to be able to confront with greater assurance. Obviously, staff motivation problems can adversely affect an organization's operations, as they are associated with lower productivity and expensive high staff turnover.

In fact, the energy, zeal, and dedication that staff at think tanks bring to their work are the result of a series of personnel management policies and actions. Beyond the personal relations established between the head of the institute or other members of senior management and individual staff members, other important factors include compensation, working conditions, nonmonetary rewards for good work, and the staff assessment system in place, with prominence going to the quality of feedback on performance. Strengths in one area can be offset by weaknesses elsewhere. In analyzing factors such as staff turnover, morale, and productivity, it is essential to go beyond the compensation or performance assessment system and look at the whole array of an organization's interactions with staff.

Despite the importance of staff motivation and satisfaction to the successful operation of think tanks in both industrialized nations and transitional economies, there is little available guidance on the topic.[2] But think tanks and the donors who support them should have a keen interest in staff motivation, given the role that high-caliber, well-motivated staff play in ensuring strong institute performance. This chapter provides think tanks and their sponsors with a perspective on professional (research/policy) staff motivation. It begins by examining the practices generally recommended in human resources management literature, particularly the literature for private organizations (including NGOs). This examination is an essential road map for think tanks designing their ownsystems. It then contrasts these practices with those that six think tanks in the former Soviet bloc use to motivate their staffs.

The author finds that the sample think tanks have addressed the multiple issues of staff motivation with considerable imagination. There are numerous differences, however, from accepted "good practices" used in the West in this field. Indeed, only one of the think tanks reviewed has practices consistent with those generally accepted in "third-stage" organizations. To some extent the differences may result from what might be termed cultural differences (i.e., a somewhat different perspective among Eastern European organizations on how staff will respond to various measures and a preference for a comparatively informal management style). Probably more important, personnel practices have emerged more from think-tank managers' intuition than from exposure to accepted practices.

At the outset, it is worth noting one key difference between NGO staff, including think tanks, and staff in government agencies or for-profit firms which has a fundamental effect on how these different types of organizations may approach issues of motivation and productivity. The spirit of this difference is captured in the following expansive statement from Letts, Ryan, and Grossman (1999):

[Nonprofit-sector staff] are deeply committed to the social causes their organizations address and are inspired by the possibility of "making a difference." Thanks to this asset, the human resources challenge is different from that of most for-profits. Their biggest challenge is not to attract motivated people—they will seek out nonprofit opportunities—but to channel their energy so it advances the organization's mission and goals. (107–8)

GOOD PRACTICES

This section includes an outline of strong practices distilled from the literature on motivating staff. Some points have been interpreted to make them more applicable to think tanks, based on the author's experience in working closely with a dozen think tanks over the years.

Rewards

Theories on motivation can be divided into two groups: motivational structures that rely heavily on external rewards and reinforcements, and those that rely on factors internal to the position.[3] While personnel programs founded on either type of theory can be applied to any job, the nature of policy research suggests that it is more appropriate for think tanks to emphasize factors intrinsic to the job. In general, under this approach staff are given more, rather than less, responsibility in the organization, and the job is made more intrinsically motivating.

A number of personnel specialists argue that motivational factors are intrinsic to the job.[4] What kinds of stimulation are appropriate in think tanks? Note that successful policy analysts need to execute three tasks well: to be strong researchers; to be good managers of research, if they are to rise above the research assistant level; and to be good promoters of the policy recommendations, both in written presentations and, especially, in person. The following is a list of aspects of a policy analyst's job that could be considered sources of motivation.

1. *Achievement.* Analysts want to feel that they are producing high-quality policy research and that they are having a demonstrable impact on the policy process. The level of resources available (computer, Internet connection, research assistance, help from a public relations specialist, etc.) and working conditions at the institute are important for helping analysts pursue their goals.

2. *Recognition of achievement.* Recognition of analysts' efforts is greater if the institution permits analysts to put out papers and publications under their own names (rather than simply the name of the institution) and if the institutions provide more opportunities for analysts to participate in meetings and discussions with policymakers. Beyond this, organizations can recognize specific achievements through awards of various types.[5] At think tanks this could include an allocation of work time (not to a billable project) to prepare a paper for publication in a journal or to complete a book; time and travel funds to attend a conference of particular interest; in-house ceremonies recognizing a specific achievement; or a bonus payment.

3. *Interesting work content.* The more interesting the topic to the analysts, defined in part by the subject's policy relevance in the country at the time, the greater the analysts' motivation.

4. *Opportunity for growth or advancement.* In many think tanks, career ladders are short, often with only three levels of analyst positions defined. Indeed, in many smaller think tanks there is no explicit hierarchy, and promotion is at best ambiguous (the annex to this chapter includes position descriptions for a five-level research ladder from a "third-stage" think tank). Where a career ladder is defined, promotions can be a powerful stimulus. Where one is absent, management must clearly define increases in responsibility and level of work without necessarily changing the job title—for example, by naming an analyst as the principal investigator on a project, providing a research assistant for lower-level tasks, or permitting the analyst more freedom in meeting with clients and policymakers.

Staff can also be kept challenged by giving them high-priority/high-visibility assignments from time to time and by shifting the focus of their work occasionally. Other ideas include adding a senior analyst to the institute's board of directors (management team) or permitting a senior analyst to attend the board of trustees' meetings and mix with the trustees. Also critical is providing research staff with training opportunities—both those for specific skill enhancement (e.g., an econometrics workshop) and those for deepening knowledge on a policy topic (e.g., an international conference on alternative pension-program structures).

5. *Competitive salary.* Without question, salary is a key consideration for all staff, as the level of payment substantially determines analysts' quality of life away from work and represents the value of their work to the organization. Compensation is usually defined as base pay plus

rewards, particularly bonuses, which can be either paid annually or episodically to mark special achievements during the course of the year. Organizations operating under tight budgets often turn to bonuses as part of annual compensation to avoid building the higher payment into the base salary.

Of the factors just listed, the first four are primarily intrinsic to job satisfaction; the fifth (salary) is extrinsic. Clearly, think tanks must employ both kinds of stimulation. A structure for compensation and nonmonetary rewards must be crafted carefully within the organization to maintain equity and to remain within the available budget.

Experts in human resource management of both for-profit and non-profit organizations generally feel that adequate base pay is essential to retaining staff and for basic motivation. But other kinds of rewards, such as those indicated above, are more important in motivating staff to higher levels of achievement. For example, Letts et al. (1999) state that good pay "is more a protection against dissatisfaction than a source of motivation for the long term. Pay cannot substitute for the satisfaction of producing results" (123).[6]

Similarly, explicit pay-for-performance schemes do not get good marks generally in government organizations and have seldom been adopted in nonprofits (Liner et al. 2001, 15–16). A severe limitation is the difficulty in defining goals and achievements with precision.[7] For example, if a senior policy analyst's recommendations for a new program are not accepted by the parliament, how does the evaluator sort out the roles of the myriad actors involved? Researchers working under an incentive system to maximize their income will be motivated to produce work of just-acceptable quality to the client. On occasion the work can be expected to be below the standard of acceptability. Over time, such loose standards could impair the think tank's reputation and cause it to lose clients. Other often-noted problems have been that employees perceive a weak link between performance and pay increments, a lack of integrity in the ratings, and inequities in the resulting pay patterns. In short, these systems seem to have frequently sent more negative than positive signals to staff (Perry 1991). Nevertheless, many companies have improved staff performance by implementing such systems (McAdams and Hawk 1994).

There are numerous types of rewards that think tanks can provide to staff—cash bonuses, time to write articles for professional journals, recognition events, participation in key meetings with policy clients, promotions in the research or administrative hierarchy, training opportunities, and others. For rewards of this type to have their intended effect, they must be

- Awarded consistently to staff with the same achievements,
- Easily identified by the staff as related to specific achievements (which requires a short time between the event and the award), and
- Large enough to be meaningful.[8]

Performance Evaluation

Staff assessment is a subject of some controversy among personnel specialists. A strong appraisal system is one that is used primarily as the basis for discussion between the supervisor and the employee on the employee's record of achievement, the suitability of the employee's goals for the future, and a plan for how the supervisor and organization can help the employee achieve the new goals. As Glen (1990) says,

> It is hoped that data are gathered by systematic observations, not only to accurately measure current performance, but also to reinforce strengths, identify deficiencies, and feed back necessary information of changes in future performance. The purpose is to measure progress, differentiate between levels of performance, pinpoint training needs, validate rewards, and identify promotable employees. (2)

Better systems get substantial employee input on setting goals and description of accomplishments (Lee 1996; Wilson 1994). These assessments are used to inform the salary review process but do not drive it. Stated differently, salary adjustments and other rewards should not be in conflict with assessments, but rewards should not be based exclusively on assessments.[9] Mechanistic "score sheets" that are used to determine salaries are generally viewed as causing more staff problems than they address.[10]

A comparatively new wrinkle in assessments is the rating of the performance of teams rather than individuals.[11] (The annex to this chapter describes the excellent staff assessment system used by a third-stage think tank.) For think tanks with teams executing large projects, such team ratings may be somewhat useful. Individual assessments, however, will clearly remain the rule.

An array of rating systems and procedures is available to think tanks, but describing them is beyond the scope of this chapter.[12] The essential point is that the assessment is critical for generating information on which to base rewards and for developing a program to assist staff with professional development. Increased professional development in turn raises achievement and job satisfaction—and motivation.

Training

Staff training consists of both formal training events and on-the-job training (OJT). The importance of OJT is hard to overestimate, although at most firms and think tanks it is organized haphazardly and therefore fails to realize its potential (Bowsher 1998; Rothwell and Kazanas 1994). The focus here is on formal training because this type of training is more closely related to staff rewards.

Broadly, management can use staff training in two ways. In principle, training needs are identified through analysis of *organizational needs* and *personal assessments.* In the first, staff skills are improved so that employees are better able to do the particular jobs assigned to them, closing a "performance gap." This kind of training can also prepare staff for higher-level assignments in the future or help them take on a different assignment at a similar level of responsibility. This training is usually driven by the organization's future business strategy (explicit or implicit) and the corresponding staff requirements (Bowsher 1998; Ban, Faerman, and Riccucci 1992). In personal assessments–based training, the training is geared more to increasing the human capital of the staff member; the training increases the employee's, skills but the new skills may be only generally applicable to current or future assignments at the think tank. For example, at a think tank that does modest work on banking policy, an employee might take a course on sophisticated bank-risk management. This would be helpful as broad background for the current and expected assignments, but might be more prized by the employee as deepening his human capital. Most third-stage think tanks (and other organizations) understandably emphasize the first type of training. The second type is more often used as a reward for particularly valued employees.

To create and maintain a training program, the organization must make adequate provision for the expense of training in its annual budget and develop a training plan.[13] For think tanks, the presence of an annual training budget will usually signal that there is explicit provision for training as an overhead expense item.[14] Development of the training program can be relatively formal or informal, but the literature indicates that one should definitely be present (e.g., Rothwell and Kazanas 1994). For training to contribute materially to the success of the institution, it should also be directly related to the think tank's implicit or explicit business strategy—including using training to reward some staff for both motivational and staff-retention purposes.[15] The Institute for Urban Economics (Moscow) invested heavily in training in financial analysis for its staff because it understood that it could have a comparative advantage in several topical areas if staff had these skills. At the same time, the core competence in financial analysis gave management more flexibility in assigning staff to an array of projects.

A challenge to think tanks in most transition and developing economies is integrating training opportunities offered by donors, often held at international venues, into the think tanks' training programs. This can be difficult, because the opportunities are offered on short notice and are sometimes not on the highest-priority topics. But their low cost and coverage of topics not addressed by local education programs makes them attractive nonetheless.

PRACTICES AT SECOND-STAGE THINK TANKS

This section covers the same three interlocking topics as the previous section—compensation and rewards, staff assessment, and training—for six think tanks in the former Soviet bloc. It begins by outlining how these think tanks were selected and then describes how they handle these key aspects of the staff function.

The general criteria for inclusion of a think tank were that it have a minimum of 10 full-time researchers and that it had been operating at about this level for the past five years (i.e., sufficient time to address personnel questions of an organization of this size).[16] The six think tanks included in the sample come from two groups. Three are those with which the author has had long-standing working relations; they were selected because each had interesting elements in its personnel system. The other three are institutes that were among those that an Urban Institute team interviewed in 1997 for a prior study of think tanks in the region. Based on information obtained then and recommendations from the first three think tanks, they were invited to participate.

The institutes and the number of full-time researchers in 2000 are shown in table 2-1. (Note the abbreviations for each, as they are used below.) Three Russian think tanks are included, in part because a greater

Table 2-1 Six Think Tanks and Their Staff Size in 2000

Institute	Location	Year Founded	Number of Full-Time Research Staff
Metropolitan Research Institute (MRI)	Budapest	1990	11
Social Research Institute (TARKI)	Budapest	1985[a]	31
Center for Study of Democracy (CSD)	Sofia	1990	20
Institute for Urban Economics (IUE)	Moscow	1995	38
Institute for the Economy in Transition (IET)	Moscow	1990	53
Expert Institute of the Russian Union of Industrialists and Entrepreneurs (Expert)	Moscow	1991	10[b]

a. TARKI shifted its main operations to a for-profit basis in 1997, although it also retains its nonprofit component.

b. Includes the president, executive director, and eight team leaders. All other research staff are contracted for individual projects.

share of Russian organizations have comparatively large full-time research staff (Struyk 1999). Of course, in no way can the think tanks discussed here be considered to be a representative sample. Half-day interviews were conducted with principals and/or staff directors at each of the sample institutes in March and April 2001.

The author relied on a review of the relevant personnel management literature and the practices of several U.S. think tanks to identify those practices viewed as having a positive impact on staff motivation and productivity, and used these materials in developing the interview guide. The guide covered staff compensation systems (both base pay and monetary rewards), staff reward systems, staff structure and criteria for promotion, and the use of training programs.[17]

Environment

Four factors, shown in the first rows of table 2-2, provide a sense of the work environment. Broadly, the included think tanks are quite similar in this area: They rate their office environment and computer support as being at least competitive with similar organizations; authors of reports are listed on title pages; and staff are encouraged to publish. These are all positive factors. On the other hand, only three organizations have formal

Table 2-2 Personnel Environment at Sample Think Thanks

Factor	MRI	TARKI	CSD	IUE	IET	Expert
Rating of research facilities[a]:						
Office quality and space per person	Superior	Superior	Superior	Competitive	Superior	Average
Computer and internet support	Comparable	Comparable	Superior	Competitive	Comparable	Somewhat higher
Authorship policy:						
Names of authors shown on title page of publications?	Yes	Yes	Yes	Yes	Yes	No[b]
Formal classification system for research positions (e.g., junior, mid-level, senior, or project leader)?	No	Yes	No	Yes[c]	Yes	No
Number of levels	NA	3	NA	5	4	NA
Staff encouraged to publish?	Yes	Yes	Yes	Yes	Yes	Yes
Extent of staff turnover in 2000[d]:						
Senior researchers and team leaders	0%	0%	0%	0%	0%	0%
Mid-level and junior researchers	30%	0%	10 to 15%	20%	25%[e]	NA
Management's view of staff productivity	Good; could improve	Good; could improve	Good	Generally good; could improve	Good; could improve	Good

NA = not applicable

a. Compared to similar organizations.

b. Unless the opinions expressed in the publication are those of the author(s) and not those of the Institute.

c. The ranks from lowest to highest are expert, leading expert, project leader, leader of team, and director of department. The last two are primarily management designations.

d. Turnover is defined as a job being vacated and filled. Expansion or contraction is not included.

e. Mid-level: 5 to 10 percent; junior level: 50 percent.

classification systems for researchers, meaning that positions are not explicitly defined at the other three think tanks. Since promotions can be used to reward staff, the lack of career ladders denies management one reward option.

Staff turnover is often used as an indicator of staff satisfaction with working conditions, including salary, but the figures on turnover need to be interpreted with caution since many factors may be at work. The general picture among the six groups studied here is that staff turnover is very low for senior researchers; indeed, there was no turnover among senior analysts at any of the six think tanks. But turnover is more variable at the junior level, with the percentage of middle and junior staff leaving and being replaced ranging from 0 to 25 percent. Respondents attributed the higher turnover rates among junior staff to a combination of young people returning to universities for further education and/or leaving to change the type of work they are doing. A modest share of total turnover at this level was associated with poor performance.

Respondents were asked for their views about the general productivity of the staff—an indicator of management's satisfaction with the researchers. It also provides an indication of the overall environment in the organization: The more frustrated management is with productivity, presumably the greater the pressure on the staff for improvement. While the responses were broadly positive in all cases, room for improvement was noted by five of the six respondents. Principal complaints had to do with analysts "overresearching" issues; the inability of staff to meet deadlines—critical when the work is for "real-time" policy development; and analysts' lack of creativity in approaching their work. "Lack of creativity" means that staff were good at providing technical assistance to clients on familiar topics or using familiar methods but that staff were reluctant to address new topics or pioneer new methods. All these productivity problems concern personal predilections and habits of staff members and may prove resistant to change. The solution likely rests in steady control of researchers' work and in mentoring by think tank leaders.

Staff Assessments

Despite the centrality of formal assessments in providing staff with feedback on their performance and offering a forum in which to discuss employees' future development, only three of the six institutes have any sort of formal assessment (table 2-3). Respondents at institutes without

Table 2-3 Performance Assessment Practices of Sample Think Thanks

Practice	MRI	TARKI	CSD	IUE	IET	Expert
Is there an annual staff assessment process?	Yes	Yes	No	Yes	No	No
Does it include a self-assessment by the staff member?	No	No	NA	Yes	NA	NA
Does the supervisor complete a form or prepare a written statement?	No	No	NA	Yes	NA	NA
Are the results of the assessment discussed with the staff member?	Yes	Yes	NA	Yes	NA	NA
How closely are salary decisions tied to the assessment results?	Generally related	Related	NA	Related	NA	NA
How tightly are various rewards tied to the assessment results?	Very little	Substantially[a]	NA	Substantially	NA	NA

NA = not applicable

a. The year-end assessment is geared primarily to compensation. There are other, less formal assessments during the year that are more directed at performance.

a formal assessment process—CSD, Experts, and IET—stated that their organizations are small and that feedback to staff is more or less continuous, making a formal process unnecessary.[18] These positions were maintained even when questions were asked about possible problems with supervisors who wanted to avoid the potential conflict involved in giving negative reviews. Two of the organizations making this statement each have over 20 researchers.

At two of the three institutes with formal assessments—MRI and TARKI—the assessment consists of a discussion between one or two members of senior management and the researcher. There is no formal staff input into the discussion (e.g., a written statement of accomplishments during the year), nor does the supervisor prepare a written statement.

Only the Institute for Urban Economics (IUE) has a full staff assessment system in place. The process is initiated by the staff member, who completes a written statement about an employee's accomplishments during the year, changes in responsibilities and capabilities, goals for the coming year, and suggestions for how the researcher's supervisor could help the employee achieve them. The evaluator—the department leader—completes a complementary assessment form. The two documents form the basis for the discussion with the employee. The interview covers, among other things, the supervisor's views about what training the analyst needs in order to be more productive or to advance in the organization. After all interviews are completed, a special assessment committee reviews the assessments and the related recommendations for salary increases. Department leaders are invited when their staff is discussed. Institute management gives high marks to the assessment process as a tool for communicating with staff on performance and future development. IUE's process parallels those of third-stage think tanks.

All three of the institutions employing assessment systems use the assessments to inform decisions about payment increases during the annual consideration of staff compensation. On the other hand, only IUE uses the results of the assessments as a primary input for determining who should receive noncash rewards, such as support to attend international conferences (see below).

Compensation and Rewards

A consistent theme across responses was the importance of compensation for staff retention and motivation. Most of the institutes studied see the business community as their primary competitor for staff. While they cannot compete directly on compensation, they try to construct a package of compensation, rewards, interesting work, and quality of environment that can meet this challenge.

Compensation

Three of the institutes—TARKI, Expert, and IET—have compensation programs that provide strong possibilities for very good pay (table 2-4). The main device is for project managers in effect to negotiate fixed-priced contracts with other staff for tasks on a project-by-project basis. Analysts can then increase their earnings by working beyond the normal standards. IET occasionally adds project-specific bonuses. On the other hand, TARKI has a particularly attractive incentive scheme for its team leaders: Net profits on projects are divided according to a formula between the team leader and the organization. Similarly, team leaders at the Expert Institute can design project execution to their financial advantage, as they control decisions on staffing and negotiate contracts with the consultants who work on the project.

The Metropolitan Research Institute (MRI) recently implemented a compensation scheme involving a strong incentive for staff to generate sufficient work to make at least 75 percent of their time billable to projects (rather than overhead functions) over each six-month period. But MRI still retains a traditional annual process for determining full-time equivalent salaries. The new system can add or subtract funds from this amount, depending on performance.

CSD has a remarkably flexible system for determining salaries. In effect, management can increase an analyst's compensation at any time, depending on various factors. But bonuses and incentive payments are rare. On the other hand, IUE has the most traditional salary determination system among the included institutes. It follows an annual review process, under which an individual's salary is determined primarily by a combination of market conditions, changes in the cost of living, increases in the staff member's productivity (broadly defined), and success in marketing. As noted, a committee reviews recommended increases across departments in order to ensure consistency and equity.

In short, the six think tanks demonstrate significant diversity in their compensation strategies. Most embody some sort of incentive payment, consistent with the view of the salary's key role in staff retention and

Table 2-4 Compensation System for Researchers at Sample Think Tanks

Institution	System
MRI	*All staff.* Beginning in 2001, employees receive 75 percent of base pay on a monthly basis. Twice yearly, management assesses the share of time charged to billable projects. If the share is greater than 75 percent over the whole period, then the person receives the other 25 percent of base pay. Staff can bill any number of hours (beyond 40) and receive extra pay for the additional hours worked. But at least 75 percent of time charged must be billable. Researchers are divided into two project teams, each directed by a managing director. Individual compensation depends significantly on the performance of the whole team.
TARKI	*Project directors or team leaders.* Total compensation consists of base salary and bonuses. The bonuses can be substantial—as large or even larger than the base salary. The bonus is determined by the net profit on projects carried out by the project director. Project directors generally negotiate contracts and are responsible for fulfillment. The net profit is split between the organization and the project director based on a formula known to all parties.
	Senior and junior researchers. These employees also have the opportunity for payment beyond the base salary. Project directors negotiate with junior staff for blocks of time within which specified tasks are to be done (e.g., two months to conduct a particular analysis). In effect, staff members are given fixed-price contracts. Staff members are able to take commitments for more-than-nominal full-time work and thereby raise their total compensation.
CSD	*All staff.*[a] Monthly base salary plus the 13th month's payment. Payment rates are changed during the year as needed, in light of both inflation and the need for merit increases (i.e., there is a constant salary review process).
IUE	*All staff.* Salaries are set through an annual salary-setting process associated with a comprehensive staff assessment process.
IET	*All staff.*[b] Compensation is based on three components: a small base salary; principal income, from participation in specific projects, is determined as a fixed-price contract between the project leader and the employee; and bonuses on contracts where funds are available at the end of the contract and the quality of work warrants, as determined by the project leader.

(*continued*)

Table 2-4 Compensation System for Researchers at Sample Think Tanks
(*Continued*)

Institution	System
Expert	*Team leaders.* Payment has two parts: a small monthly salary and payment for directing projects. The team leaders control staffing and execution of the project, including determining the pay for all staff. Team leaders' compensation for a project is agreed upon with the executive director.

a. Excludes the board of directors—president, executive director, and director of research—and the staff in the survey research unit. The latter can receive bonuses largely based on the volume of overtime committed to projects.

b. Excludes senior management.

motivation. Some of the incentive payment plans are designed in part to promote marketing and work acquisition. But these plans also may also create some negative incentives. Staffers at IET and TARKI working on fixed-price contracts have a strong incentive to do the minimum required to fulfill the implicit contract. Team leaders at TARKI and Expert have clear incentives to press clients for a maximum price and to minimize the effort in producing the product contracted for—all to maximize profits and their net pay. Obviously, there is a challenge to senior management to limit such behavior, because clients might not be interested in future contracts if they face a high price for a modest product.

Similarly, the team incentive at MRI to generate enough work for all team members to bill at least 75 percent of their time to contracts could potentially penalize those team members who are not engaged in marketing, if the manager and senior staffers who have the marketing responsibility perform poorly. Failure to reach the goal, and the resulting income reduction, would probably erode the morale of staff who see marketing function as outside their control.

The extremely flexible system used by CSD has some clear advantages but also some significant potential limitations. The lack of a regular across-the-board review of payments opens the door to wider-than-desirable variation in payment for staff with similar assignments and skills. Staff may see evidence of favoritism or arbitrariness. To prevent this, each pay adjustment would need to entail a thoughtful review—a seemingly burdensome task for any organization.

Rewards

Perhaps because of compensation's central role in the personnel strategies of most of the six institutions, nonmonetary rewards do not play a very large role. All of the think tanks do, at some level, help staff prepare publications, attend conferences, and participate in training. But with a few exceptions these activities are not viewed explicitly as rewards; rather, allocation tends to go to the most suitable person. Sometimes, for example, support for writing a paper is given to someone without project coverage for the moment. Some examples of the use of rewards follow.

TARKI awards an annual in-house research fellowship, which provides support for several months of work, on a competitive basis. The fellowship is viewed by both senior management and researchers as an extremely valuable award. An important factor in management's selection of the winning project is the work's likely utility to the overall development of the organization. Past performance is a secondary consideration.

IUE, Expert, and IET use international conferences and training events to reward productive staff, although the set of staff who can participate is limited to those with strong English skills. They also make promotions up the research ladder a reward for past work and improved capabilities. IUE goes further, occasionally rewarding its most productive team leaders by adding them to the IUE council that decides on the future direction of the institute's work and use of discretionary resources. It also rewards certain staff by permitting them to participate in the annual meeting of its board of trustees; a few are asked to make presentations to the board.

All of the think tanks reviewed recognize staff achievements in some way. Most often they do so through an announcement at an institute seminar, working session, or party for a new publication, successful conference, winning of a big contract, or successful policy outcome. IET makes some of these announcements in the bulletin it publishes. At IUE, management and department directors annually select the best analyst in each group (e.g., expert, senior expert) and announce the award at an end-of-year staff gathering.

Retreats

Most of the think tanks studied also have staff retreats designed to build team spirit; sometimes the events have an explicit work element, but sometimes they are purely social. For example, the whole MRI staff and their families go to a recreational area for a weekend in the summer. Similarly, interested IUE staff and their families visit a suburban Moscow rest house for a weekend a couple of times a year during the winter; most staff participate. The Expert Institute reports similar events. These events are primarily recreational for all three organizations. On the other hand, at CSD members of a department go on a Friday-Saturday retreat together once or twice a year to relax and take stock of their work and future directions. IUE has an annual retreat for its "council" (i.e., a special management body to review the work program and to plan for the future). All of these events are subsidized by the think tanks to varying degrees. All the think tanks reporting such events see them as important for building morale.

Training

The importance assigned to training varies widely among the six institutes. CSD, Expert, and TARKI management teams do not assign training a high priority, and a correspondingly small share of staff participate in training outside of the organization in a given year. But Expert and TARKI have substantial in-house training programs (see below). Training expenses are estimated as being under 1 percent of total institute costs. These institutions rely on hiring well-trained staff who have the requisite skills. Senior researchers at TARKI and CSD teach at some of each country's most prestigious universities, so there is a general feeling that they are keeping abreast of developments in their disciplines.

The other three institutes assign greater importance to staff training, and about half of the research staff participate in conferences or formal training events during a year. IUE, for example, spends the equivalent of 3 to 4 percent of its turnover on training, including external and internal funding. Nevertheless, divergence in practices among these three organizations is still evident. IUE and IET come the closest to having a fully defined training plan. In IUE's case, a comprehensive picture of training needs is a product of the staff assessment process and forms the basis for training activities, although a formal plan is not prepared. International opportunities sometimes meet these needs and sometimes supplement the other training; as noted, international travel is often allocated as a reward for staff who will use the training in their work.

Abundant international training activities are available to IET, and a plan for the utilization of these resources is prepared about twice a year.

Table 2-5 Staff Training in the Sample Think Thanks

Training Issue	MRI	TARKI	CSD	IUE	IET	Expert
Importance generally assigned by management to additional training for research staff	High	Low	Marginal	High	High	Marginal
Is there a specific line for staff training explicitly included in overhead charges?	Yes, but not a separate item	No	Yes	Yes	No	No[a]
Is an annual training plan developed?	No	Yes, focused on in-house events	No	No, but needed training is defined[b]	Yes, every six months, for allocation of international opportunities	No
Who participates?	NA	Senior management and team leaders	NA	NA	Senior management	NA
Is the plan developed at the beginning of the fiscal year?	NA	Yes	NA	NA	No	NA

(continued)

Table 2-5 Staff Training in the Sample Think Thanks (Continued)

Training Issue	MRI	TARKI	CSD	IUE	IET	Expert
How is the decision on allocation of re-sources made?	In response to donor offers and staff requests	Little activity; in response to staff requests	In response to staff requests	Needs are defined as part of staff assessment process	In response to opportunities from donors[c]	In response to donor offers
How important are training events sponsored by other organizations?[d]	Very important	Marginal	Marginal	Very important	Very important	Very important
Percent of research staff attending at least one training event or course per year	~50%	5 to 10%	5 to 10%	~50%	~50%	10 to 15%
Are there formal in-house training events?	No, but there are monthly staff seminars on ongoing projects	Yes; internal seminars on methodological topics	Few	Yes; in-house seminars on substantive topics and methods	Yes; internal seminars on substantive topics and methods	Yes; internal project review seminars and brainstorming sessions on methods

a. But there is a line for staff travel; travel typically constitutes most of the cost of attending training events and conferences.
b. The definition occurs as part of the staff assessment process.
c. The department head makes decisions about attendance at domestic conferences and seminars with training content.
d. Includes events sponsored by various donors and foundations.

At both IUE and IET, much of the structured training is accomplished through staff participation in international conferences or explicit training activities. These are funded either as an element in contracts or grants awarded to the organizations or by discrete offers from international sponsors for particular events. IUE also sends staff to local (Russian) training events, and has on occasion contracted with an expert organization for specific training when an existing course could not be identified (e.g., training in the financial aspects of project analysis).

With respect to in-house training events, four institutes—TARKI, IUE, Expert, and IET—conduct a program of seminars on substantive and methodological topics. In all four cases, staff, especially junior and mid-level staff, are strongly encouraged to attend. MRI has monthly staff seminars at which results of ongoing projects are reviewed; these seminars also convey information on technical topics and inform the staff about the range of work going on at the institute.

SUMMARY

How do the personnel practices of these six second-stage think tanks compare with practices generally accepted among third-stage organizations? The record is patchy overall. The following items summarize the situation.

- Staff assessments are a weak point. Only three of the six organizations have an annual review process in place. In only one of these is there written input by both the staff member and the evaluator; importantly, the results of this process feed into training and salary adjustment decisions.
- Compensation structure is diverse, with a surprisingly high number of incentive schemes. Three of the schemes are directed at increasing potential staff payments, while one focuses on generating projects to pay for staff time. One think tank has an extremely flexible approach to salary administration. The incentive plans are little used in the West, and the degree of flexibility in the fifth scheme would draw criticism for possible inequities and abuses. Only one compensation scheme is consistent with normal Western practice.
- Rewards are underutilized compared to what could be done and what the personnel management literature recommends. Five of

the six think tanks studied make explicit use of rewards. While international travel is the most frequent form of reward, other forms are also employed.

- Training is viewed as an integral element in staff development in third-stage think tanks, so the low priority assigned to training by three of the think tanks studied here is unexpected. Two of the other think tanks have substantial training programs, but the allocation of resources appears rather ad hoc. Only one think tank integrates discussion of its training needs into the staff assessment process.

Does the fact that the staff practices of the six think tanks differ in many respects from those generally accepted in third-stage organizations mean that these organizations should revise their personnel management? The leaders of these think tanks generally believe that most of their practices are well suited to their specific organization—its structure, size, and particular operating style. A premium is placed on informality and an atmosphere of democratic collegiality. This attitude, the perceived unequal competition with businesses for their better staff, and the generally low priority assigned to addressing administrative issues may be the principal factors producing the personnel practices observed. Moreover, the think tanks studied are producing high-quality work and succeeding in having it used in the policy process (Struyk 1999).

Nevertheless, the success of the less-developed personnel systems at five of these organizations appears heavily dependent on the particular personalities and styles of key managers. Most think tanks, especially young ones, are very much creatures of their founders. There is a real possibility of a turbulent transition when new leadership eventually comes to these think tanks if staff motivation continues to be so dependent on this type of personalized operating style. These think tanks could adopt the practices common to third-stage organizations without disturbing their essential operating styles.

In short, adoption of more structured personnel practices is likely to yield both short-run and longer-term gains. The short-term benefits are in the perceived equity in treatment among researchers below the team-leader level, and this can certainly influence productivity and retention. The longer-term gain is in a smoother transition when there is a change in top leadership.

NOTES

(Complete references can be found in the Reference Section at the end of this book.)

1. The think tanks, one in each of nine countries in the region, are members of the Transition Policy Network (TPN), as is the Urban Institute. For more on TPN, see *HTTP://WWW.URBAN.ORG/TPN*. There are no known systematic surveys of think tanks that identify areas of administration and financial management that respondents believe need to be strengthened.

2. Exceptions are some of the essays in Struyk, Ueno, and Suzuki (1993).

3. For an overview of these theories, see Rabin et al. (1985, 154–56).

4. See Heneman (2001, 167), Herzberg (1987, 112–13), and Heskett (1987, 121).

5. See Bowsher (1998) and Wilson (1994).

6. See also Herzberg (1987); Heskett (1987); and Wilson (1994, 83). Heskett's support on this point is especially interesting because he is writing about personnel motivation for for-profit firms in the service industry.

7. See McAdams and Hawk (1994, 33) and Stone, Bigelow, and Crittenden (1999, 382).

8. See Wilson (1994, 47–50).

9. This is the system used by several Western think tanks known to the author. In addition, a number of well-managed corporations use the same procedure, including the General Electric Corporation (Glen 1990, 3). Lee (1996) and Ledford (1995), among others, also strongly support separating assessments from the formal salary adjustment process.

10. Fox (1991), Rabin et al. (1985, 183–84), and Wilson (1994, ch. 9) also list problems with the assessment process. Lee (1996) reports that 60 percent of 218 corporations surveyed reported using a narrative evaluation with an overall numeric score; the second most frequently used system was numeric scoring.

11. Heneman (2001, ch. 8).

12. Alternatives are discussed in Rabin et al. (1985, 184–94) and in chapter 7 of Heneman (2001).

13. In the corporate world, the rule of thumb is for training expenditures to equal about 5 percent of payroll (Bowsher 1998, 76).

14. Chapter 5 contains an extended discussion on overhead rates.

15. See Ban et al. (1992, 410 ff.) and Bowsher (1998, ch. 2).

16. Interviews on personnel practices were conducted with two smaller think tanks in the region, and the results confirmed that these practices are very unstructured.

17. Comprehensive treatments of these topics include Bowsher (1998), Dibble (1999), Heneman (2001), Letts et al. (1999), and Rabin et al. (1985).

18. CSD uses its department-level staff retreats at a rest house for this purpose, as described below.

A

Staff Assessment and Salary Administration at the Urban Institute, Washington, D.C.

The Urban Institute is one of the largest and most respected think tanks in the United States, with a staff of over four hundred. Staff work on a wide range of issues, including pension policy, urban housing and community development, health policy, education policy, and social assistance and social services. The Institute works in similar areas in countries outside of the U.S.[1]

This Appendix contains documents from the Urban Institute's personnel administration system. In particular, documents from three areas are present.

1. Position Descriptions for Researchers and Standards for Promotion

The Institute has a five level structure for its researchers: research assistant, research associate I, research associate II, senior research associate and principal research associate. There are formal job descriptions for the first three levels. The qualifications for the senior research associate, principal research associate and senior fellow positions can be inferred from the standards for promotion to these levels. Included here are the job descriptions and standards for promotion for the various positions.

---

[1] A great deal more information on the Institute is available on its web site: www.urban.org.

2. Performance Appraisal—Policy and Forms

The following pages include the Institute's formal state on the staff assessment process and the form used in the process. The form has two parts. The first is completed by the staff member as input into the rating done by the supervisor; it covers accomplishments and goal setting for the coming year. The second part of the form is used by the supervisor. Both parts are the basis for the discussion between the supervisor and staff member.

3. Salary Administration Policy

The final document in the Appendix is the Institute's policy statement for salary determination. Job performance figures in salary increase recommendations but is far from the sole determining factor.

1

Position Descriptions for Researchers and Standards for Promotion

THE URBAN INSTITUTE

Job Description

Job Title: Research Assistant

Salary Grade: R01

Reports To: More experienced researcher

General Summary

Under close supervision by more experienced researchers, assists in the performance of social science research by gathering information and helping to prepare material for inclusion in reports. May administer surveys and/or questionnaires and compile results. May collect, tabulate, and process data using basic statistical methods and statistical analysis software.

Typical Responsibilities and Duties

1. Performs library research on specified topics and synthesizes material in the form of bibliographies, abstracts, memoranda and reports, according to instructions.
2. Tabulates and/or maintains collected data by means of coding or organizing data into tables or graphs.
3. Processes data from tapes or other sources of large data sets using statistical analysis software such as SAS or SPSS.
4. Analyzes primary and secondary data using basic statistical methods.
5. Administers structured surveys (telephone, written, computer-assisted, and in -person interviews) for projects requiring primary data collection.
6. May assign work to junior level administrative staff or temporary staff.

Qualifications

The academic knowledge of a discipline that is generally associated with the comple-tion of a bachelor's degree or an equivalent combination of education and experience or demonstrated ability to perform beginning level research in a social science field. Only those major job duties necessary for proper job evaluation and/or labor market analysis have been included. Other duties may be assigned by the supervisor.

Job Number: 60000   FLSA Status: Exempt

THE URBAN INSTITUTE

Job Description

Job Title: Research Associate II

Salary Grade: R02

Reports To: More senior researcher

General Summary

Responsible for conducting assigned parts of social science research projects under the general direction of more senior staff members. Assists in the development of research approach and data collection instruments and in the selection of statistical techniques. Collects data and applies standard methods of statistical analysis. Reports research findings in writing.

Typical Responsibilities and Duties

1. Reviews and writes critical summaries of research literature and/or public policy.
2. Administers surveys (telephone, written, computer-assisted, and in-person interviews). Makes site visits and conducts surveys and interviews with local public officials and/or private citizens.
3. Analyzes data using such standard statistical techniques as multiple regression and factor analysis; draws conclusions from analyzed data; prepares statistical reports and data presentations.
4. Writes up research results; assists in writing proposals and preparing papers for publication. May be called upon to present results to clients.
5. Supervises and assigns work to research assistants and more junior administrative staff.

Qualifications

The academic knowledge of a discipline that is generally associated with the attainment of a master's degree (usually with a bachelor's degree in a related field) or an equivalent combination of education and progressively more responsible relevant work experience.

Only those major job duties necessary for proper job evaluation and/or labor market analysis have been included. Other duties may be assigned by the supervisor.

Job Number: 62000   FLSA Status: Exempt

THE URBAN INSTITUTE

Job Description

Job Title: Research Associate I

Salary Grade: R03

Reports To: Senior researcher

General Summary

Responsible for planning and independently executing a major segment of a social science research project in consultation with and under the general supervision of a Center Director, Senior Research Associate, or Principal Research Associate. Designs the research approach and selects the appropriate quantitative or other tools of analysis, with consultation from more senior staff. Performs analysis; draws policy inferences; writes and presents reports. May develop and write proposals. May function as principal investigator and project manager for small projects.

Typical Responsibilities and Duties

1. Develops or participates in developing research topics, proposals, and research design.
2. Selects appropriate statistical techniques to analyze collected data.
3. Supervises and/or participates in data collection, and analysis by less senior research staff; participates in interpreting data from a policy perspective.
4. Makes site visits, conducts interviews with public officials, and supervises field research.
5. Maintains budget and manages resources for segments of research project under his/her responsibility; may supervise less senior researchers.
6. Participates in writing final reports and presenting results to clients.

Qualifications

A combination of the quantitative, analytical, and writing skills, relevant substantive knowledge, and social policy research experience needed to perform the duties described above, or the academic knowledge of and research experience in a discipline that is generally associated with the attainment of the Ph.D.

Only those major job duties necessary for proper job evaluation and/or labor market analysis have been included. Other duties may be assigned by the supervisor.

Job Number: 64000   FLSA Status: Exempt

THE URBAN INSTITUTE

Standards for Promotion from
Research Assistant to Research Associate II

Those promoted to RAII must demonstrate the ability to conduct research that is equivalent in quality and thoroughness to work done at the master's degree level. They should be performing at a level that exceeds the level expected of a research assistant. Most importantly, they must consistently demonstrate a high level of *independence* and *initiative* in their work. This requirement applies whether the research assistant's work is largely quantitative or qualitative. In general, it takes a minimum of two to two and a half years of experience as a research assistant to achieve the level of RAII; however, given truly exceptional performance, this standard could be met in a shorter period of time.

The research assistant should be making substantive contributions to research projects by helping to do the following: 1) frame analytic questions; 2) identify relevant measures and data sources; 3) organize the process of data collection and analysis; and 4) interpret the results.

To be promoted, a research assistant must consistently demonstrate at least three of the following:

- Expertise in manipulating and analyzing complex data using statistical programming software, such as SAS or STATA.
- A detailed and thorough understanding of one or more databases (e.g., CPS, SIPP, or NSAF) or programming software. As an expert in these areas, the research assistant serves as a resource to other researchers.
- Strong writing skills, demonstrated through high-quality contributions to reports and articles.
- Substantive knowledge of his or her field(s), including an understanding of key policy issues and an ability to apply that knowledge to research.
- Effective data collection through surveys or site visits. For example, the research assistant will have successfully led site interviews and synthesized information collected in a site visit, identifying key issues raised and questions for follow-up.
- Excellent communication skills and good judgment when working with internal or external collaborators.
- Effective mentoring of new research assistants, including helping to train them.

THE URBAN INSTITUTE

Standards for Promotion from
Research Associate II to Research Associate I

A researcher promoted to RAI must demonstrate a combination of analytic and writing skills, relevant substantive knowledge, and social policy research experience that is generally associated with the attainment of a Ph.D. These skills can be demonstrated while working under the supervision of a more senior researcher. In general, a minimum of four years of research experience at the RAII level is required to achieve the level of an RAI, although not all of this experience must occur at the Urban Institute. In addition, an RAII *must meet four of the following five performance standards* to be promoted:

1. Plays a significant role in the development and design of research projects.

- Designs the approach and methodology for at least one proposal, research project, or for a significant component of a large project.
- Research designs and/or proposal contributions should demonstrate independent expertise in the concepts and methods of social science research (although they may involve the application of pre-existing methodologies and a more senior researcher may participate as an advisor and/or contributor).

2. Independently analyzes qualitative information and/or quantitative data.

- Primary responsibility for implementing statistical techniques and/or other methods for analyzing data in at least one significant research project, *and*
- Demonstrated ability to synthesize results and draw conclusions from empirical analysis.
- These accomplishments should be reflected in one or more written proposals, design documents, or research reports.

3. Authors or co-authors research reports.

- Sole or co-author of at least three project reports, journal articles, or book chapters (see new UI policy on authorship).
- These publications should involve different analytic efforts (not three versions of the same analysis) and demonstrate substantive knowledge of the field and relevant policy issues.
- For publications where the candidate is a co-author, he/she should have lead responsibility for one or more significant components of the analysis and writing.

4. Manages major components of research projects.

■ Takes initiative and works collaboratively with his/her supervisor in the conduct of research projects and their management;

■ Plans and manages research activities, such as data collection, data base development, or statistical analysis; *and*

■ Manages schedule, budgets, and project coordination for at least one funded research project.

5. Presents research methods and findings to clients and other outside audiences.

■ At least two presentations to clients or at academic or policy conferences, *or*

■ Assigned primary responsibility for communication with outside clients, or other users of Urban Institute research.

THE   URBAN   INSTITUTE

Standards for Promotion to Senior Research Associate

Those promoted to SRA must have demonstrated on more than one occasion their ability to conduct research that is equivalent in thoroughness and originality to the completion of a doctoral dissertation. Also, they generally must meet minimum requirements in each of four performance categories:

- Publications—achieve the qualitative equivalent of being the sole author of two articles published in selective refereed journals (e.g., *Journal of Human Resources*);
- Other Dissemination Activities—accomplish the qualitative equivalent of (a) being the primary author of two project reports which achieve wide circulation and attention and (b) presenting six research papers at selective national conferences;
- Fundraising—over a period of time not longer than two years, achieve the qualitative equivalent of raising the funding for three professional-person-years of research activity; and
- Management—over a period not longer than two years, accomplish the qualitative equivalent of managing the budget, staff, schedule, substantive work and external relations for three professional-person-years of research activity.

Substantially exceeding the minimum requirements in one category can offset a shortfall relative to the minimum requirements in another category. A combination of publications and other dissemination activities can be used to satisfy one of the two dissemination requirements. Special experience (e.g., service as a program administrator or as a practicing lawyer) will be considered if relevant.

THE URBAN INSTITUTE

Standards for Promotion to
Principal Research Associate

The fundamental qualification for the PRA designation is a national reputation for policy-related research/analysis. This reputation should be demonstrated through a number of research accomplishments:

■ An extensive publications record including a significant number of articles in top-rated journals and a body of other published work such as policy briefs, contributions to books, and influential project reports;
■ Research leadership demonstrated through the initiation and completion of a number of successful, highly-complex research projects, and the proven ability to mentor junior staff;
■ A substantial fund-raising track record that contributes significantly to their research center's base of financial support.

It is expected that a PRA will meet most, if not all, of these criteria. PRA status generally will require a minimum of 15 years of research experience beyond a PhD or equivalent. Designation of PRA status through promotion or the hiring process only result after consideration by an Urban Institute SRA/PRA-review committee.

THE URBAN INSTITUTE
Standards for Promotion to Senior Fellow

Senior Fellows must have a broad-based national reputation for expertise on major issues on which their views, analysis, and commentary are sought out by the broad public policy world (including academics, political figures, journalists, and private sector individuals/ groups). They will often have held some prominent public/ private-sector position. They will have evidenced an ability to interact competently with that broad public policy making world in a variety of forums and under public pressures. For example, they will frequently engage in the following activities:

- Interactions with the media (often quoted in print, on local and national radio and television);
- Speaking at high quality forums and gatherings focussed on broad public policy— not just academic meetings;
- Writing substantive pieces for the serious popular press such as opinion editorials or articles for national news outlets (such as major newspapers, the *Atlantic Monthly*, *Harpers*, etc.)
- Serving (or having served) on government and private commissions, substantive panels, and/or advisory boards;
- Testifying before the Congress.

Senior Fellows will be responsible for raising funds to support their own activities and those that promote the mission of the Institute. Designation of Senior Fellow status is at the discretion of the Urban Institute President.

2

Performance Appraisal—
Policy and Forms

THE URBAN INSTITUTE

Personnel Policies   Policy and Procedure No. 109
and Procedures   Date: 7/14/00
                                         Supersedes P.P. & P. Date: 10/9/95

Subject   Authorization: _____ per RDR _____

Performance Appraisal

Policy

Performance appraisal is a continuous part of the management process. Throughout
the year supervisors are expected to communicate with employees concerning their
work progress, letting them know what is expected of them and by what standards
they are being judged. Any serious deficiencies in an employee's performance should
be communicated by supervisors in face-to-face counseling meetings with the
employee before such deficiencies are documented in their annual performance
appraisal.

Once a year, usually in the fall, there is a formal review of every regular Institute
employee which consists of a written self-assessment and a written supervisor's
evaluation followed by a performance appraisal discussion.

The purpose of the annual review process is to assess and document the employee's
accomplishments since the last appraisal or hire date; indicate areas where improvement is possible; and define future goals, career objectives, and training needs. Since
performance appraisals affect salary adjustments, transfers, promotions, and other
personnel actions, they should be frank, objective, and specific and should refer only
to job-related criteria.

When the timing of the hire or transfer of an employee, or the transfer or termination
of a supervisor does not coincide with the annual performance review process, an out-
of-cycle appraisal is required as described below. A written appraisal is also required
before the end of the three-month period for each newly-hired nonexempt employee
and at the end of six months for new exempt staff.

Procedures

Annual Performance Review

The personnel office will provide instructions, forms, and a schedule for completing
performance appraisals. The appraisal form consists of two parts: a self-assessment for
completion by the employee and a supervisor's evaluation for completion by the
employee's official supervisor. Appraisal forms are distributed by the personnel office

well in advance of the period scheduled for appraisal discussions. The employee signs and returns the completed self-assessment form to the supervisor by the date indicated on the schedule provided by the personnel office.

The official supervisor reviews the employee's self-assessment and writes an evaluation of the employee's performance for the prior twelve-month period. The supervisor consults with other individuals to whom the employee reports for specific projects or for day-to-day guidance or supervision and incorporates the comments of those individuals, as well as a response to any concerns noted in the employee's self-assessment, into the written supervisor's evaluation. The supervisor's evaluation is given to the employee for review at least 24 hours prior to the performance appraisal discussion, which is scheduled at this time.

Performance appraisal discussion topics should include both the employee's concerns as expressed in the self-assessment and the appraiser's evaluation of the employee's performance. At the conclusion of the performance appraisal discussion, the appraisal form must be signed by the employee, the rating supervisor, and the Center or Office Director (if different from the rating supervisor). The employee must sign to acknowledge having read and discussed the contents of the appraisal. The employee's signature does not necessarily constitute agreement. The employee may express a difference of opinion with the written appraisal by forwarding a separate memorandum, addressed through their supervisor to the personnel office, which will become part of the employee's personnel file along with the written appraisal.

The completed appraisal form must be returned to the personnel office for review and signature by the Director of Personnel and, when appropriate, the Senior Vice President, before being entered into the employee's personnel file.

Probationary Three-month Period for Nonexempt Employees

Nonexempt employees are hired on a probationary basis for the first three months of employment. If performance is not satisfactory during this period, the supervisor may at any time recommend terminating employment without following the progressive discipline process outlined under Policy and Procedure No. 112. If possible, the employee should be given at least one week's notice of termination of employment.

Under extenuating circumstances, the Center/Office Director may make a written request to the Director of Personnel for an extension of the probationary period. The employee must be notified in writing about the extension and its conditions.

Initial Appraisal of Newly-hired Employees

New nonexempt employees will be given an initial appraisal of their performance not earlier than two months nor later than three months from their date of employment. The initial evaluation period for new exempt employees is six months from the date of hire.

Performance of Transferring Employee

Before validating a transfer, the Director of Personnel will make certain that the prospective supervisor knows whether an employee's performance is satisfactory or unsatisfactory and will require that the losing supervisor prepare a performance appraisal if more than six months have passed since the last one.

Change of Supervisor

When a supervisor terminates employment or transfers out of a Center or Office, he or she should prepare a performance appraisal for each supervisee if more than six months have passed since the last appraisal.

THE URBAN INSTITUTE

Annual Performance Appraisal
(Part One) Employee Self-Assessment

Employee's Name: *Job Title:*

Center: *Period Covered: (from/to)*

(If more space is needed, attach additional sheets.)

1. List your major accomplishments during the appraisal period: **Research Staff examples** include: data collection and analysis, literature reviews, research reports/publications, research proposals and other fundraising activities, special external activities (speeches, testimony, briefings); special internal activities (committees, presentations, staff development). **Administrative and Computer Services examples** include: ways you have contributed to the efficiency and performance of your center/office, include special activities such as committee participation, presentations, etc.

2. Did you achieve the objectives set by you and your supervisor during the last year? (Please explain.)

3. During this period did you take on new major responsibilities or expanded supervisory responsibilities? If so, how? If research staff, has the level of your research increased? If so, how?

4. Have you recently acquired new job-related skills or attended courses that will prepare you for additional responsibilities in the future or enhance your skills in your current position? If so, please specify.

5. If you have had budgetary/project management responsibilities during the past year, have you operated within budget and on schedule? Please explain.

6. What steps have you taken to address the career development of those who report to you? (For employees with supervisory responsibility only—others mark N/A)

7. Indicate areas in which you hope to improve your performance and goals you wish to achieve during the coming year.

8. Are there ways in which your supervisor(s) can assist you in improving your performance or achieving your goals? If so, please indicate:

☐ make expectations clearer

☐ provide more frequent feedback

☐ set more realistic work deadlines

☐ provide additional resources such as:

☐ other (specify): _____

9. Are there other aspects of your job that you would like to discuss during the performance review? If so, please specify.

10. Are there other people who have directed your work during the rating period? If so, please list their names and give a brief description of the work done.

Note: Research Staff should attach a current resume to this assessment.

Employee's Signature:_____ Date:_____

THE URBAN INSTITUTE

Annual Performance Appraisal
(Part Two) Supervisor's Evaluation of Employee

Employee's Name: *Job Title:*

Center: *Period Covered: (from/to)*

(If more space is needed, attach additional sheets.)

A. Comment on the employee's self-assessment of job performance for the appraisal period and note any significant omissions. If your view of employee's performance differs from that of employee, please explain.

B. Comment on the employee's goals for the coming year as stated in the self-assessment and any additional objectives you have set for the employee. If you do not concur with the objectives stated by employee, please explain.

C. Identify the employee's strengths. Give examples of exemplary or outstanding performance.

D. Note any areas of performance that need improvement and describe your plan for correcting them.

The following question is for future planning and career development purposes and is not part of the assessment of the prior year's job performance. It should be used as a basis for discussion of the employees long-term career development.

E. Make at least one suggestion that, if followed, could enhance the employee's performance, strengthen skills, or improve the employee's opportunity for advancement or career growth.

F. **General Performance Factor Ratings**: Using the definitions provided below, rate each of the following general performance factors according to the typical level of competency demonstrated by the employee.

E **EXCEPTIONAL** level of performance: Employee accomplishes requirements of the position in an exemplary manner, adding to its depth and breadth by *consistently* working beyond its defined scope and expectations. NOTE: even the very highest-performing employees cannot perform in an exemplary manner all the time. ***Cite specific examples.**

S **SUPERIOR** level of performance: Employee's performance meets all performance criteria and far exceeds several, but not all, other criteria. ***Cite specific examples.**

F **FULLY SUCCESSFUL** performance: Employee has accomplished all normal requirements and *consistently* meets *all* of the Institute's usual high expectations of performance.

I **IMPROVEMENT REQUIRED:** The employee falls short of achieving one or more job requirements or goals. Improvement is required in order to fully meet the requirements of the job. It is expected that some new employees who are still learning aspects of their positions will receive this rating for some factors. ***Cite specific examples where performance needs improvement and provide a plan for achieving improvement.**

D **SERIOUS DEFICIENCY** in approach to or accomplishment of the job: Substantial improvement is required to meet the requirements of the job. ***This rating must be explained fully by the supervisor and unless extraordinary circumstances exist, must have been the subject of a previous face-to-face counseling session with the employee. Such rating constitutes a written warning of a serious performance problem as required in UI Policy 112, Addressing Performance Concerns.**

CA = CANNOT ASSESS   **NA = NOT APPLICABLE**

FOR ALL EMPLOYEES:

General Performance Factors

1. **Quality of Work**/content, accuracy, follow-through, thoroughness, creativity:
   ☐ E*   ☐ S*   ☐ F   ☐ I*   ☐ D*   ☐ CA   ☐ NA

2. **Productivity**/quantity of high-quality work:
   ☐ E*   ☐ S*   ☐ F   ☐ I*   ☐ D*   ☐ CA   ☐ NA

3. **Organizational Skills & Timeliness**/plans and organizes work efficiently; produces results on a timely basis:
   ☐ E*   ☐ S*   ☐ F   ☐ I*   ☐ D*   ☐ CA   ☐ NA

4. **Technical Skills**/competence in performing technical work (please specify*):
   ☐ E*   ☐ S*   ☐ F   ☐ I*   ☐ D*   ☐ CA   ☐ NA

5. **Initiative**/self-starter; works well without detailed instructions:
   ☐ E*   ☐ S*   ☐ F   ☐ I*   ☐ D*   ☐ CA   ☐ NA

6. **Problem Solving**/anticipates or recognizes relevant problems and recommends or applies solutions:
☐ E*   ☐ S*   ☐ F   ☐ I*   ☐ D*   ☐ CA   ☐ NA

7. **Writing Skills**/produces concise, readable written work:
☐ E*   ☐ S*   ☐ F   ☐ I*   ☐ D*   ☐ CA   ☐ NA

8. **Oral Communication Skills**/transmits or presents information articulately, accurately, and in a timely and professional manner:
☐ E*   ☐ S*   ☐ F   ☐ I*   ☐ D*   ☐ CA   ☐ NA

9. **Flexibility**/adapts well to changing priorities and work situations; adjusts easily to new colleagues, ideas, and procedures:
☐ E*   ☐ S*   ☐ F   ☐ I*   ☐ D*   ☐ CA   ☐ NA

10. **Interpersonal Skills**/positive work attitude and ability to work with others to facilitate group performance:
☐ E*   ☐ S*   ☐ F   ☐ I*   ☐ D*   ☐ CA   ☐ NA

11. **Work Habits**/attendance and punctuality:
☐ E*   ☐ S*   ☐ F   ☐ I*   ☐ D*   ☐ CA   ☐ NA

FOR RESEARCH STAFF ONLY:

12. **Policy Understanding**/knowledge of policy issues and the ability to relate them to research and vice versa:
☐ E*   ☐ S*   ☐ F   ☐ I*   ☐ D*   ☐ CA   ☐ NA

13. **Conceptual Ability**/the ability to formulate and design research plans:
☐ E*   ☐ S*   ☐ F   ☐ I*   ☐ D*   ☐ CA   ☐ NA

14. **Professional Involvement**/presentations at professional meetings, articles in refereed professional journals, briefings, testimony, etc.:
☐ E*   ☐ S*   ☐ F   ☐ I*   ☐ D*   ☐ CA   ☐ NA

15. **Raising Funds to Support Research:**
☐ E*   ☐ S*   ☐ F   ☐ I*   ☐ D*   ☐ CA   ☐ NA

FOR SUPERVISORS AND MANAGERS:

16. **Supervisory Skills/**makes timely and effective decisions, provides constructive feedback, develops staff, resolves performance issues appropriately, uses staff efficiently, and keeps staff apprised of Institute policies, practices, and objectives:

    ☐ E*   ☐ S*   ☐ F   ☐ I*   ☐ D*   ☐ CA   ☐ NA

17. **Financial Management/**uses financial resources efficiently and stays within budget:

    ☐ E*   ☐ S*   ☐ F   ☐ I*   ☐ D*   ☐ CA   ☐ NA

18. **Compliance with Organizational Policies and Procedures/**integrates office objectives with those of the Institute:

    ☐ E*   ☐ S*   ☐ F   ☐ I*   ☐ D*   ☐ CA   ☐ NA

19. **Compliance with the Institute's Affirmative Action Program/**meets, and ensures that subordinates meet program objectives; ensures good faith efforts to include underrepresented groups in recruitment and promotion decisions:

    ☐ E*   ☐ S*   ☐ F   ☐ I*   ☐ D*   ☐ CA   ☐ NA

G. Based on all parts of the above evaluation, what is your overall assessment of this employee's performance?

Additional Comments:

Signatures:

Rating Supervisor:_____ Date: _____
  (if different from center/office director)

Center/Office Director: _____ Date: _____

Employee's Signature:* _____ Date of Appraisal Discussion:_____
(*signature acknowledges that employee has read the appraisal)

Executive/Personnel Office Review:

Signature:_____ _____Date:

3

Salary Administration Policy

Policy and Procedure No. 108   Date: **10/17/94**
                                        Supersedes P.P. & P. Dated: 9/ 9/83
                                        Personnel Policies and Procedures
Subject   Authorization: Per W. Gorham

Salary Administration

Policy

The goal of the Institute's salary administration program is to enable the Institute to attract, retain and motivate the number and caliber of employees necessary to achieve its objectives. In pursuing this goal, the Institute has developed a logical structure of job levels and associated pay ranges to compensate employees appropriately for the nature and level of work performed and to provide opportunities for growth.

The pay ranges assigned to each job level within the salary structure were designed and are maintained to be consistent with the financial position of the Institute, internally equitable, and competitive with those paid by other employers for comparable work. The salary review process provides an effective method for evaluating and rewarding individual job performance.

The salary administration policy seeks to comply with relevant federal and District of Columbia laws and to keep employees informed of compensation matters affecting them while protecting the confidentiality of salary information pertaining to other Institute employees.

The Institute considers only job-related factors in making decisions on pay and does not discriminate on the basis of race, color, age, sex, sexual orientation, religion, national origin, disability, matriculation, veteran status, marital status, personal appearance, family responsibilities or political affiliation.

Definitions

Position: Work consisting of responsibilities and duties assignable to one employee. There are at least as many positions within the Institute as there are employees.

Job: A grouping of positions which are essentially the same in terms of the nature and level of work being performed by the position incumbents. Each job has a title, classification and an associated grade level.

Job Description: There is a formal description of the **major** responsibilities, duties, and level of work performed for each job. Such job descriptions are not exhaustive lists of responsibilities.

Job Description Questionnaire: A questionnaire completed by an employee and reviewed by the supervisor which describes the employee's work assignment and lists the skills and abilities normally required to perform it satisfactorily. The questionnaire provides the basis for the personnel office's evaluation and classification of a position and for preparing or updating a job description.

Job Evaluation: The process used to determine the level and appropriate classification and salary grade for each job relative to all other Institute jobs.

Salary Grade: The classification level assigned to a group of similar jobs which, although different with respect to skill and knowledge requirements and kinds of work performed, are similar enough in level of difficulty and responsibility to warrant similar pay.

Salary Range: The minimum to maximum dollar amount payable to incumbents in each salary grade.

Salary Structure: A hierarchy of salary grades and ranges which allows for the appropriate classification of each job.

Job Classification and Salary Structure

There is a job classification and salary structure for each category of Institute employees:

> Research Staff (Grades R01–R05)
> Administrative Staff (Grades A01–A08)
> Computer Services Staff (Grades C01–C05)

The Institute assigns each job to a grade on the appropriate salary structure based on an evaluation of the job's relative worth to the Institute and what other organizations pay for comparable work. The personnel office uses a point-factor system to evaluate the jobs assigned to the administrative structure. Research and computer positions are classified according to standard industry categories at each level.

Along with a salary grade, the personnel office will assign each job an appropriate title and will prepare a standard job description. (See Policy and Procedure No. 101: Establishing a Position.)

Each job is also designated as either exempt or nonexempt from the overtime provisions of the Fair Labor Standards Act. (See Policy and Procedure No. 100: Hours of Work and Overtime.)

Annual Review of Salary Ranges

Once a year, normally in November, the personnel office will review the salary ranges for each of the three structures in comparison to rates of pay by other employers in the various labor markets in which the Institute competes. The director of personnel will obtain or conduct a survey of the outside labor market and will recommend to the senior vice president any changes in each classification structure necessary to remain competitive. The senior vice president will authorize such changes, when they are feasible, on the basis of labor market conditions and not directly on changes in the cost of living.

This process is separate from the adjustment made to individual salaries.

Annual Review of Individual Salaries

Salary Increase Budget: Each fall, the personnel office will distribute to center and office directors historical and comparable salary data for their staffs. Prior to the fall meeting of the Institute's board of trustees, the senior vice president and/or director of personnel will meet with the center and office directors to discuss current staffing considerations and to develop a recommended salary increase budget for the annual review based on competitive labor market data available at the time. The senior vice president will forward a recommendation to the president who, in consultation with the board of trustees, will authorize a salary increase budget.

Salary Review Committee: The salary review committee consists of the senior vice president, the vice president & controller, all center directors, two office directors appointed by the senior vice president, and the director of personnel. The function of the salary review committee is to ensure consistency and fairness of the salary review process and in the salary adjustments approved for staff members. The committee reviews the salary increase and promotion recommendations for all staff below the center/office director level.

Salary Increase Recommendations: At least three weeks before center and office directors make their salary increase recommendations, the senior vice president will issue an all-staff memorandum containing guidelines for the annual review, such as eligibility, the amount of the salary budget approved by the board of trustees, the average percentage increase, and a schedule for submitting recommendations. Center and office directors will base their recommendations on an individual's job performance, level of responsibility, and comparative position in the salary range. Directors will provide a brief written justification for each salary increase recommendation significantly above or below the average increase amount. **Supervisors must not communicate to the employee the amount of the recommended adjustment until it has been formally approved by the salary review committee, since modifications are sometimes made to the original recommendations for equity and other reasons.**

Salary Review Committee Decisions: Center and office directors will send salary increase recommendations to the salary review committee through the director of personnel. The personnel office will review the recommendations for consistency with the most recent performance appraisals and with the goals of the Institute's Affirmative Action Program, and will verify that they are within the established salary ranges. The personnel office will provide the salary review committee with the information it needs to make fair and equitable decisions. The recommendations of the salary review committee shall be reviewed and approved by the president or designate. Approval by the board of trustees is required for salaries at or above the federal government ES-4 level. Since this approval may occur after the salary review committee meets, such increases will be made retroactive to January 1.

Notification to Employees: The personnel office will transmit a notification, through the appropriate center or office director, to each employee who receives a salary increase. In addition, the director of personnel will inform the respective directors of the reasons for a denial or modification of their recommendations. The center or office director will notify each employee who does not receive a salary increase of the reason for such action.

Salary Adjustment Appeals: An employee who wishes to appeal a salary increase decision should forward the appeal through the appropriate center or office director and the director of personnel to the salary review committee. The appeal must be in writing and must explain why the employee feels the salary review committee's decision should be modified. The committee must receive the appeal by the date published in the all-staff memo regarding the annual salary review schedule. The committee will consider the information presented in the written appeal and will make a recommendation to the president for final decision. Modifications resulting from an appeal will be made retroactive to January 1.

Midyear Review of Individual Salaries

The salary review committee meets in June of each year to consider salary increase recommendations for those employees whose dates of hire made them ineligible for consideration during the annual review or whose supervisors elected to defer consideration until midyear. The committee also acts on salary increase recommendations for research assistants whose dates of hire make midyear the appropriate consideration time. The process for making salary increase recommendations is the same as during the annual review, except that no all-staff memo is issued. Center and office directors may meet individually with the director of personnel to discuss current labor market information and internal equity prior to making midyear salary increase recommendations.

Starting Salaries for New Employees

Center and office directors may make recommendations to the director of personnel in connection with the hiring of a new employee, but only the director of personnel has the authority to extend an official offer of employment or to authorize any other Institute employee to extend a verbal offer of employment. Starting salaries will not be set below the minimum or above the maximum of the salary range for the job.

The director of personnel will recommend all starting salaries, basing them on internal equity and outside labor market considerations and may authorize starting salaries for all nonexempt employees and all exempt employees at or below the Research Associate I (R03) level (C03 level on the Computer Staff structure; A07 level on the Administrative Staff structure). All other starting salaries, and those in cases where the center or office director and the director of personnel do not concur, require the authorization of the senior vice president.

Timing of First Salary Review for New Employees

All Employees Except Research Assistants—In general, employees hired between January 1 and July 31 will be eligible for salary adjustment January 1 as part of the annual salary review process.

Employees hired between August 1 and October 31 may be eligible for a January 1 salary adjustment, at the discretion of the center or office director. Alternatively, the center or office director may elect to defer salary consideration until midyear.

Employees hired between November 1 and December 31 are not eligible for salary adjustment on January 1 but their starting salaries will reflect this fact. These employees will be eligible for salary adjustment the following January 1 as part of the annual salary review process.

Salaries for regular employees on term assignments are set for the duration of the assignment. If the term is extended or renewed, the term employee's salary will be considered at that time for adjustment for the duration of the new term. If the employee continues on regular employment status but is no longer subject to a specified term, the salary may be adjusted at that time or deferred until the next annual review cycle. Thereafter, the employee will receive salary consideration during the annual review cycle.

Research Assistants—In addition to the regular salary review cycle outlined above, researchassistants receive a one-time six-month salary review. Since the salary review committee meets only at specified times during the year to consider salary recommendations, some recommendations may be acted upon after the effective date of the increase. In such instances, approved salary increases will be made retroactive to the effective date (the first day of the first full pay period following six months of employment as a regular full- or part-time research assistant).

Following the six-month increase, research assistants will receive consideration during the next appropriate salary review period (midyear or January 1, depending on the length of time since last review) and during the annual review cycle thereafter.

Out-of-Cycle Increase in Salary

There may be circumstances that justify a salary increase at times of the year other than during the annual review period; such as promotion into a vacant position, or the necessity of counteracting an outside offer to an Institute employee. In such cases, associated salary increases will be effective on the date of approval.

Decrease in Salary

Occasionally, because of work schedule requirements, the assumption of fewer or lower levels of responsibility, organizational changes which result in the elimination of an employee's former position, changes in career path, or other reasons, an employee will apply for a vacancy in a position at a lower level. The salary in such circumstances will be set within the new position's range at a point comparable to salaries paid to incumbents in that grade who have similar job responsibilities and job performance levels. An appropriate salary rate will be recommended by the director of personnel in consultation with the appropriate center/office director and approved by the senior vice president.

Promotion

An employee will receive a promotion when he/she fills a vacant position posted at a higher salary grade. A salary increase associated with a promotion will be based on the individual's performance and relative position in the new salary range. The increase will be effective on the first day of the pay period following the date of approval, unless specified otherwise.

Reclassification

A reclassification will occur when an employee's existing position is reevaluated by the personnel office and reclassified into a higher or lower salary grade as a result of discernible and measurable changes in the level of responsibilities and skills required to perform the work. Those reclassifications which result in a position being moved to a higher salary grade will be considered promotions. A job reevaluation may also result in the position's title being changed (with no change to salary grade) or in no change to the position's classification. Requests for reclassification will generally be considered during the annual salary review cycle and any salary adjustment resulting from the reclassification will be effective January 1.

A request for reclassification may be initiated by the supervisor or by the employee through the supervisor and must be supported by substantial evidence that there has been a **significant** and **sustained** change in the degree of independence with which an individual works, the level of judgment the individual must exercise, the degree of difficulty of the tasks performed, or the individual's supervisory responsibilities. A change in the number of tasks associated with a job or the number of individuals supervised does not alone provide sufficient justification for reclassifying a position.

Reclassification Procedures for Administrative and Computer Services Staff: The employee will complete a Job Description Questionnaire form, which may be obtained from the personnel office. The supervisor will review the employee's responses and complete the supervisory section before forwarding the completed questionnaire and any other substantiating data, along with a written request for reclassification, to the director of personnel.

The personnel office will compare the questionnaire to existing job descriptions and other job classification data to determine the appropriate classification for the position. If appropriate, the director of personnel will recommend a new job title, classification, and salary grade to the senior vice president. The employee will be notified of the decision through the supervisor.

Reclassification Procedures for Research Staff: When a researcher has demonstrated consistently over a period of time work at a higher level of independence and ability than expected of others at the same grade level, the center director may recommend a promotion. The center director must submit a Request for Promotion form (available from the personnel office) or a written memorandum noting specific examples of performance which demonstrate a higher level of work than expected for the current grade level. A current resume and samples of the individual's most recent written work should accompany the memo.

Requests for promotion are generally considered during the annual salary review cycle. The director of personnel will review the recommendation for completeness and consistency with the most recent performance appraisal and forward it to the salary review committee for a decision. The employee will be notified of the decision through the supervisor.

Raymond J. Struyk

3

Ensuring Good Advice: Quality Control[1]

Perceptions about the high quality of a think tank's work are critical for maintaining the credibility of the organization's reports and recommendations, and perhaps for its very survival. Because many clients of policy research organizations are not in a position to judge the quality of a particular product independently, a strong reputation is fundamental to attracting work.

Therefore, most third-stage private, independent public policy research organizations—think tanks—in the West pay scrupulous attention to quality control. Hiring and retaining highly capable staff members is the best method of ensuring high-quality work.[2] But even if recruitment is successful, some oversight is mandatory.

A peer review process is a critical element in the overall quality control regime, and virtually all third-stage think tanks with more than a handful of staff have such a process in place.[3] The standards used in a peer review process—explicit or implicit—are a good proxy for quality: The analysis should be factually correct, logically consistent, methodologically sound, grounded in current and historical literature, objective, and written in a way that will be useful to the primary audience. At some think tanks, such as the Urban Institute, the reviewer is held jointly responsible with the author for significant problems discovered after a report is disseminated. In a few think tanks, such as

Abt Associates, the names of reviewers appear on the title page along with that of the author.[4]

This chapter provides concrete advice on how to organize the peer review process appropriate for first- and second-stage think tanks. I begin with an outline of the elements of a standard peer review system in third-stage think tanks. Next I overview a survey done of think tanks in the Eastern Europe–CIS region regarding their actual peer review practices and draw conclusions about the adequacy of the coverage and procedures. In the final section I provide recommendations on what developing think tanks should be doing for quality control.

THE PEER REVIEW PROCESS

The following describes a model peer review process, most elements of which are present at third-stage think tanks in the United States and presumably at think tanks in other countries as well.

The peer review process is formal in the sense that it is mandatory and that there is a written policy statement concerning it. The statement indicates

- The range of products subject to review;
- The person responsible for designating reviewers for different products;
- The criteria to be used in the reviews—usually, high-quality methods of analysis, conclusions based on the analysis, clear and effective presentation, and ensuring that the product corresponds to what was required under a contract or grant agreement;
- The form in which comments are to be provided (e.g., written, oral, in a particular format);
- The process for resolving possible disputes between the reviewer and the author(s); and
- The extent of the responsibility of the reviewer for any problems later identified with the product.

Typically there is a form for each product that records the name of the reviewer and that the reviewer signs to accept responsibility for the review.

In reality, many institutions have peer review programs that differ from that just outlined. Many are simply less formal: Team leaders are held accountable for having products reviewed, and no explicit records are kept. Another difference is that organizations may in effect exempt products by the most senior staff from the process. Some think tanks may use in-house review seminars in place of product reviews as the method of exercising quality control. Such seminars can be very valuable for guiding the project, but they may not safeguard the quality of the final product.

CURRENT PRACTICES OF SECOND-STAGE THINK TANKS

The Sample

The information presented below was obtained from a survey sent to 15 think tanks, 10 of which responded, in Eastern Europe and the Commonwealth of Independent States. The think tanks targeted for the survey were generally organizations with at least 10 full-time and part-time analysts. All have been in operation for at least five years. The author visited all but one of the think tanks included in the final sample. While the sample is fairly broad in its geographic coverage, neither the initial nor the final sample should be considered to be a statistically representative sample.

Table 3-1 lists the names and locations of the think tanks that responded. The 10 think tanks are from eight countries. The table also gives two indicators of the group's size as of 2000—the number of full- and part-time research/policy staff, and the number of reports completed that year. In this and other tables the think tanks are arrayed from large to small, to facilitate the identification of differences in practices associated with size. Six of the larger organizations produced 30 or more reports in 2000, while none of the other four think tanks produced more than 14 reports. Two of the think tanks—CPSCA and CREI—are quite small, with two and zero full-time research staff, respectively.

A questionnaire was e-mailed to a principal at each organization, along with a letter explaining the purpose of the survey and requesting that he or she participate in the project by completing and returning the questionnaire. The questionnaire covered the topics discussed above. Wherever possible, precoded responses were given as an option to make completion of the form easier and to foster comparability. The contents of the questionnaire were based on the practices at the Urban Institute and other third-stage think tanks with which the author is familiar.

**Table 3-1 Participating Organizations: Staff and Report Volume
              in 2000**

Organization (name/abbreviation)	Location	Number of Full-Time Research Staff	Number of Part-Time Research Staff	Number of Reports Produced per Year
Gdansk Institute for Market Economy (Gdansk)	Poland	35	7	60
Institute for Urban Economics (IUE)	Russia	38	5	80
International Center for Policy Studies (ICPS)	Ukraine	25	10	30
Center for the Study of Democracy (CSD)	Bulgaria	23	30	40
Institute for Market Economy (IME)	Bulgaria	9	25	32
Metropolitan Research Institute (MRI)	Hungary	10	2	10
Social Research Institute (TARKI)	Hungary	8	25	80
Viitorul Foundation (Viitorul)	Moldova	14	12	2
Center for Policy Studies and Comparative Analysis (CPSCA)	Romania	2	8	14
Crakow Real Estate Institute (CREI)	Poland	—	2	10

— = not available

Current Practices

The review of the current practices of the respondent think tanks is
divided into three areas: process, coverage, and responsibility.

The Review Process

The principal elements in the peer review process include the presence
of a formal policy, the appointment and payment of a reviewer, the
preparation of written comments, and the existence of methods for
resolving conflicts between a reviewer and an author. A final question is
whether in-house seminars are used as an element in the review process.

Nine of the 10 think tanks included here have a policy that research
products should be peer-reviewed (table 3-2). The exception is
Hungary's MRI, which indicated that the need for a review procedure is
recognized, but that the organization does not have the capacity to
introduce one.

Interestingly, only the largest four of the nine think tanks with a review policy have a written policy statement governing the review process. While the absence of written guidelines does not necessarily make the review process less reliable, it does leave the door open for different interpretations of what is required, particularly within larger organizations. Where there are no written guidelines, senior management should pay close attention to the process.

A written review is mandated by seven of the nine think tanks that require a peer review. Only two of the smaller think tanks do not have this policy. The obvious advantage of the written review is that there is less chance of misunderstanding and the comments are formally on record.

There is significant variation among respondents in who is responsible for appointing the reviewer. For example, in four cases the team leader or an individual researcher makes the choice. Senior management generally seems to be overseeing the process, however. For example, at

Table 3-2 Elements of the Peer Review Policy

Organization	Is There a Formal Review Policy?[5]	Is There a Written Statement of Review Prepared?	Is a Written Review Prepared?	Who Appoints the Reviewer?	Are Outside Reviewers Ever Used?	Are the Reviewers Paid?[6]	If Dispute, Who Adjudicates
Gdansk	Yes	Yes	Yes	Project leader	Often	No	Author[a]
IUE	Yes	Yes	Yes	Division director	No	Yes	Management
ICPS	Yes	Yes	Yes	Management	Always	Yes	Management
CSD	Yes	Yes	Yes	President	No	No	Research director
IME	Yes	No	Yes	Team member[b]	Sometimes	Yes	Management
MRI	No	No	NA	NA	NA	N/A	NA
TARKI	Yes	No	Yes	Project leader	Sometimes	Yes	Research director
Viitorul	Yes	No	Yes	Team leader	Often	No	—
CPSCA	Yes	No	No	Executive director	No[c]	No	Discussion
CREI	Yes	No	No	Management	No[c]	No	Author has final word

NA = not applicable
— = not available
a. Management must still approve the publication.
b. Choice must be approved by management.
c. Required for English-language reports.

IME, where an individual researcher nominates the reviewer, the nomination is subject to approval by management. In most cases, management appears to be aware of the reviewer being selected, even if management does not explicitly approve each choice.

There is considerable variation in the use of outside versus internal reviewers and in payments for reviews. ICPS has a policy of using external reviewers for nearly all projects, and it pays for the reviews. But IUE, CSD, CPSCA, and CREI rely on internal reviews exclusively; among these, only IUE has an account to which reviewers can charge their time. The other think tanks are between these poles, with outside reviewers employed for particularly important projects or when there is no one on staff who has the necessary expertise.

The underlying theme in the responses concerning settlement of disputes between reviewers and authors is that it is seldom necessary for a third party to become involved. The author and the reviewer typically discuss the comments and come to an agreement about the changes that should be made. As the respondent for TARKI put it, "We do not want to assess, but rather to improve." In the rare instances when there is disagreement on a principal point, the research director or other senior management participates in the resolution. At IUE, the issue is discussed at the weekly meeting of team leaders chaired by the institute's president.

In principle, in-house seminars can also be an integral part of the quality control process. Such seminars can provide additional points during a research project for managers to make critical comments beyond the end-of-project peer review. Seminars may actually take the place of a peer review. Among the ten think tanks that responded, six hold in-house seminars on ongoing projects (table 3-3, last two columns). Of these, five use the seminars in addition to peer reviews. One, MRI, uses seminars as its only review vehicle. Only at ICPS are in-house presentations a rule. At IUE, for example, for about half of all projects researchers present findings at a seminar attended by project staff, department directors, and the management team. At ICPS, the seminars are generally given around the midterm of the project, and outside analysts are invited to participate. At both organizations, and at TARKI as well, more than one presentation may be made for the most important projects.

Coverage

Table 3-3 lists seven types of products that could be subject to review. The list is expansive in its coverage and includes some types of that often are not subject to review even in third-stage think tanks, such as papers being submitted by staff to scientific journals and articles for the popular press.

Reports to clients, the practice for the most important category in terms of a think tank's reputation, are covered in the first column of the table. Most respondents indicated that their answer for this category also applied to the organization's own publications—a class of product not separately asked about in the questionnaire. Seven of the nine think tanks with a policy of reviewing products subject all the documents in this category to review, with some small exceptions. The other two, CSD and Viitorul, indicated that some of these products are not subject to

Table 3-3 Types of Products Subject to Review, and Exceptions to Review Requirements

	Type of Product						
Organi-zation	Reports to Clients[a]	Conference Presentations	Papers to Scientific Journals	Books to be Published	Articles for Popular Press	Documents for Press Conferences	Documents for Conferences
Gdansk	Yes, Ex.1	Sometimes	No	Yes	Sometimes	Almost never	Almost never
IUE	Yes, Ex.2	Yes	Yes	Yes	Yes	Yes, Ex.3	Yes, Ex.3
ICPS	Yes	Yes	No	No	Yes	Yes	Yes
CSD	Sometimes	Sometimes	Yes	Yes	Sometimes	Sometimes	Sometimes
IME	Yes	Yes	No	No	No	No	Yes
MRI	NA	NA	NA	NA	NA	NA	NA
TARKI	Yes	No	No	No	Sometimes	Sometimes	Sometimes
Viitorul	Sometimes	Sometimes	—	Yes	—	Sometimes	Sometimes
CPSCA	Yes	Yes, Ex.4	Yes, Ex.4	NA	Yes, Ex.4	Yes, Ex.4	Yes, Ex.4
CREI	Yes, Ex.4	Sometimes	Sometimes	Yes, Ex.4	Sometimes	Yes, Ex.4	Yes, Ex.4

NA = not applicable

— = not available

Note: Codes for exceptions are (1) small projects, working papers; (2) projects executed by multiple divisions with reports reviewed by two or more managers; (3) standard materials and previously reviewed papers; and (4) papers by team leader unless they request a review.

a. Generally includes the institute's in-house publications as well.

review but did not elaborate. In short, coverage in this category is strong, far stronger than for any other product.

Books intended for publication are often targeted for peer review. Five of the eight think tanks with staff preparing books require such reviews. The others believe that the publisher will impose quality control.

Few respondent think tanks routinely review papers being submitted to scientific journals (three of nine—IUE, CSD, and CPSCA) or articles for the popular press (three of nine—IUE, ICPS, and CPSCA). The respondents are somewhat more vigilant about reviewing conference presentations (four of nine) and documents to be distributed at conferences (five of nine). Perhaps surprisingly, only four of nine think tanks have a clear policy of reviewing materials to be distributed at press conferences; three more review documents for some press conferences; and the other two never or almost never subject such documents to reviews.

Responsibility

Some think tank managers believe that making the reviewer, as well as the author, responsible for the final product provides a strong additional incentive to the reviewer to do a careful, thorough job. It is useful to distinguish between two aspects of the communication of responsibility to the reviewer for the final product. One is the formal assignment of shared responsibility for the quality of the final product (assuming that the reviewer's comments are fully reflected in the final version of the product). The other is informal and concerns the way responsibility is impressed upon the reviewer. In other words, are there external signals to the reviewer that he or she has some responsibility for the quality of the final product—signals in addition to being formally told of such a responsibility?

The questionnaire asked directly whether it was the think tank's policy to hold the reviewer responsible with the author for the quality of the final product. Only four of the nine think tanks that have a policy to peer review products answered affirmatively (table 3-4).

With respect to signals or indicators of the reviewer's responsibilities, respondents were asked whether the think tank used a form that records the specifics of the review assignment, the title of the document, the author, and the identity of the reviewer, and whether the reviewer signed the form. Three organizations—IUE, IME, and Viitorul—use a standard form and ask the reviewer to sign it. They are also among the four organizations that hold the reviewer jointly responsible with the author for the quality of the final product (table 3-4).

Summary

Quality control is generally taken seriously by the think tanks studied, as indicated by the fact that nine of the ten included in the analysis have a policy of peer review for certain documents. The review process is widely understood to be the improvement of the product, not just the delivery of a critique. Seven of the nine think tanks with a policy for peer review require reviewers to prepare written comments on the documents they read. Four of the largest think tanks in the sample have a written policy statement in place.

Nevertheless, some organizations in the sample could clearly do better. One obvious suggestion for the think tank that does not have a

Table 3-4 Responsibility and the Role of Seminars

Organization	Form Used?[a]	Form Signed?[b]	Joint Responsibility?[c]	Seminars Used As Review Forum?	Complement or Substitute for Peer Review?
Gdansk	No	No	No	Occasionally	Complement
IUE	Yes	Yes	Yes	Most	Complement
ICPS	No	No	No	Always	Complement
CSD	No	No	No	No	NA
IME	Yes	Yes	No	No	NA
MRI	NA	NA	NA	Occasionally	Substitute
TARKI	No	No	Yes	Yes	Complement
Viitorul	Yes	Yes	Yes	No	NA
CPSCA	No	No	No	No	NA
CREI	No	No	Yes	Occasionally	Complement

NA = not applicable

a. Question asked: Does the institute have a form that indicates that a paper was reviewed and by whom?

b. Question asked: Does the reviewer sign it [the form] indicating that he/she has completed the review?

c. Question asked: Authors, of course, have primary responsibility for the contents of their reports. With respect to the reviewer, does the institute also hold the reviewer responsible if a poor-quality product is delivered to a client or published?

review policy in place is to adopt the necessary policy and procedures. In addition, the two think tanks that are not obtaining written comments should do so, since such comments create a record of the reviewer's criticisms which management can use to make a final decision on whether to release a document.

Seven of the nine think tanks with a peer review policy require that all reports to clients and their own publications be subject to a review. These are the critical class of products generated by think tanks. The other two organizations require peer reviews for some of these documents. For other types of products—for example, conference presentations and handouts at conferences, articles for the popular press, books being published—review practices are much more variable. Overall, the incidence of these reviews is about half of that for reports to clients.

These think tanks have concentrated peer reviews on client reports and on their publications. This is certainly understandable, given the importance of these products for a think tank's reputation. But their reputations can also be damaged by poor presentations at conferences, inaccurate materials distributed to the press, poorly written newspaper and magazine articles, and misleading books authored by their staff. Many of the think tanks seem to be relying on others (e.g., publishers and the media) to exercise quality control for some of these products. This may be a mistake: No one has a stronger incentive to ensure the strong quality of its output than the think tank itself.

A REALISTIC PROGRAM

There is no question that proper quality control is critical. But each public policy research institute should determine the resources that it can and should devote to quality control. Factors to consider in deciding on an institutional review policy include the following:

- The competency and experience of the staff—the more seasoned the staff and the greater their skills, the lower the need for detailed monitoring;
- The mix of staff in terms of experience and skills—the more variation, the greater the need for explicit monitoring;
- The expected sophistication of a particular product and its anticipated distribution and visibility; and

- The extent of the organization's experience with each analyst and with various products; for example, management may have read several reports of a new senior analyst and have confidence in his or her writing skills but know nothing about this person's abilities as a public speaker or author of press releases.

Consider the example of a very small think tank, composed of three or four senior staffers who have worked together for years with a record for producing high-quality work. The think tank could have a policy of comparatively little peer review. But even among such a small group, one team member might be a weak public presenter and need to rehearse presentations for critical review. Person-specific policies are difficult to implement because of staff sensitivities, so a general policy of reviewing presentations could be in order in this case. But even here two arguments might be made for adopting a more comprehensive policy now. First, adopting this policy implicitly assumes that the composition of the staff will not change. If, however, there is a nontrivial chance that staff will be added or replaced over the next couple of years, then this partial review policy could be a mistake. If staff change is foreseeable, then a more comprehensive review policy will be necessary. Second, even very senior people produce a poor product occasionally, usually when they are overcommitted. A comprehensive review policy guards against such problems. One highly visible quality problem can weaken a think tank for years.

Clearly, larger and more diverse think tanks have a greater need for comprehensive peer review, and a general policy is practically always the preferred solution.

A peer review process has two principal components—the process itself and its coverage (i.e., which products and which analysts are subject to review). Recommendations on both scores are provided below.

The Process

Of the various components of the review process outlined at the beginning of the chapter, the four elements listed in text box 3-1 are particularly important: The system should be governed by a written statement; reviews should be written; a standard form should be used to record the key information about the review and should be signed by the

Box 3-1 Key Points in the Recommended Review Process

1. The review policy should be formalized in a written statement that covers all aspects of the process, including description of which products are subject to review. (A serviceable policy statement is included in the appendix to this chapter.) A written statement clarifies what is required and eliminates misunderstandings about the process.
2. Reviews should be written. This reduces communication problems between the reviewer and the author, provides a clear record that management can consult in assessing a product, and provides an enduring record of the review.
3. There should be a standard review form. The form should record the identity of the product, the author, and the reviewer. It should also include at least a summary of the reviewer's comments. The form should be signed by the reviewer to reinforce the reviewer's responsibility. (An example is included in the appendix.)
4. The reviewer should be jointly accountable with the author. The reviewer and the author should share responsibility for the quality of the final product, assuming that the reviewer's comments are duly taken into account. This should be stated in the review policy and on the standard form, so that it is very clear to the reviewer and to the author.

reviewer; and the reviewer should be held explicitly responsible with the author for the final product.

Coverage

Which products and which staff members are subject to review may be the most contentious issue in the peer review process; recommendations appear in table 3-5. Overall, the author recommends broad coverage—nearly all products except journal articles and books being published externally should be reviewed. The rationale for this position is clear: The cost of peer reviews is modest compared with that of the damage to a think tank's reputation from publishing erroneous or otherwise flawed analyses or recommendations. *All staff* should be subject to the peer review process.

A think tank's reputation is its principal asset. One of management's foremost tasks is to safeguard it.

Table 3-5 Recommended Coverage of the Review Process

General Review Status	Type of Product	Comments
Very high priority	Reports to clients Institute publications	Very few exceptions— examples of exceptions might be report drafts going to clients and working papers
High priority	Conference presentations	Should be subject to "dry-run" reviews for all but the most experienced presenters.
	Conference handouts Articles for the popular press Press releases and documents for press conferences	Subject to review unless underlying research has already been reviewed. Still, products that will have high visibility should be reviewed.
Lower priority	Articles submitted to scientific journals Books for publication by an outside press	May want to review the submissions of less senior staff to help them establish their reputations for good work

NOTES

(Complete references can be found in the Reference Section at the end of this book.)

1. Dessislava Petkov provided valuable comments on the draft of this chapter.

2. See chapter 2 for a discussion of good practices for staff motivation and retention at think tanks.

3. Some think tanks also consult their clients about their performance; in some instances, a think tank's principal sponsor will invest in a comprehensive assessment of the organization's contribution. A survey of ten leading think tanks (eight in the United States and two in Europe) in the early 1990s reported that six had had an external evaluation in the past decade and three others had undertaken substantial, intense self-evaluations. Only two of the nine evaluations involved a survey of the institutions' clients, and these evaluations were viewed as highly productive (Struyk 1993, 51–52).

4. There is little literature on the practices of think tanks in Western countries. Kingsley (1993) gives some guidance on how think tanks in general organize the product review process.

5. Question asked: Does your organization have a policy that reports and/or other documents should be reviewed by someone not working on that specific project before the reports/documents are sent to a client or submitted for publication?

6. Inside reviewers may charge time to a project or an overhead account; external reviewers are paid.

7. Question asked: If the reviewer and the author(s) disagree about some of the comments, what is the process for reconciling the differences in opinion?

Quality Control Policy of the Institute for Urban Economics (Moscow)

INSTITUTE FOR URBAN ECONOMICS

Approved Regulations   President of the Institute
for Urban Economics
05/30/00

N. B. Kosareva

On Outgoing Documents and
Publications Quality Control

General

These Regulations establish the procedures for exercising control over the documents
and publications produced by IUE personnel and intended for external dissemination.

Procedures of Control

Heads of research departments (jointly with the authors) shall bear responsibility for
all outgoing products of the unit and shall ensure compliance of the products with the
requirements of these Regulations.

Publications intended for external dissemination shall be subject to mandatory
internal review.

Control over compliance with the time schedule set forth in these Regulations shall
be assigned to Director of the Information and Publications Center.

Organization of the Reviewing Process

The reviewer for each particular outgoing product will be appointed at weekly IUE
joint meetings of department heads and management in accordance with proposals
made by the head of the department producing this product.

The need for general discussion of the reviewed product shall depend on the
importance of the product under review and shall be assessed at the IUE weekly meetings simultaneously with the appointment of a reviewer and in accordance with the
proposal made by the head of the department producing this product.

The reviewer shall be notified about the task to issue a review at least one week
prior to the date when the material is to be submitted for review.

Author of the material shall provide it for review at least two weeks prior to the
final date for the submission of the material. Responsibility for the completeness of the
material and the availability of proper references and attachments shall be borne by
the author of the material. The material submitted for review shall be signed by the
author.

The author shall submit the material for review with a cover letter attached
(*Annex 1*).

The reviewer shall review the material within one week in accordance with the requirements set forth in Section IV of these Regulations and return it to the author together with a review and the cover letter.

The product subject to general discussion shall be offered for discussion to the attendees of the IUE weekly meeting immediately upon issuance of the review.

The author of the material shall introduce all changes recommended by the reviewer and participants of the general discussion within one week. The final draft of the corrected material shall be approved by the reviewer.

Department heads shall approve the final draft of the material and submit it to the Information and Publications Center with the original copy of the review and a cover letter attached. A copy of the review shall be kept in the department to which the author of the material belongs.

Reviews

A review represents an opinion on the material, including its analysis, characterization, and evaluation.

Requirements that the report should meet:

- Objective and opinions based on established principles.
- Evaluation based on high-quality standards and conclusive opinions.
- Proper substantiation provided for all conclusions and recommendations.
- Reliability of every source data, references, and examples.
- Correspondence with the assignment as specified in agreement/contract/grant under which the material is produced.

Requirements for preparation of the review:

- The review shall be written on a separate sheet of paper.
- The review shall be signed by the reviewer with indication of the date of the review.
- The length of the review shall be at least 1 page but not more than 3 pages printed on A4 sheets with 1.5 spacing in 12th font with an exception made for products of more than 150 pages—then the review can be more than 3 pages.

Settlement of Disputes

In the event that author of the material disagrees with the opinion of the reviewer, the decision to accept or reject recommended changes shall be taken at IUE weekly meeting.

The most important issues shall be placed for the consideration of the IUE President or IUE Executive Director, who is entitled to make the decision independently or call a meeting with the participation of all interested parties.

Exhibit 3-1 Cover Letter

Product Title	
Author	
Reviewer	
Structural Unit Director	
Date of Submission for Review Scheduled Actual	
Date when the reviewed product is returned to the author Scheduled Actual	
Reviewer's conclusions	• Product can be published as it is • Product shall be slightly amended before publishing • Product shall be substantially amended before publishing • Product shall be redone
Comments (if any)	
Signatures: Author Structural Unit Director Reviewer	_____ _____ _____

Raymond J. Struyk

4

Renewing the Work Program: Creating Innovation

Think tanks, like other organizations, need to renew their agendas from time to time for at least three reasons. First, they may have to shift the direction of their research in order to ensure that their work remains relevant to their nation's evolving policy agenda. Second, staff retention and morale can depend on key members having the chance to change the focus of their research and policy analysis. Third, and perhaps most fundamentally, in order to raise funds, organizations must offer to work on subjects for which there is a demand for new information and analysis—they must follow the market.

The process for creating and adopting innovations in a work program is often called *strategic planning.* In its most developed form, strategic planning yields a formal written product; developing the plan involves considering the relevance of the organization's mission statement in light of its current situation and systematically analyzing new work programs for the think tank. Such significant new directions for an organization's agenda are *innovations.* Importantly, the most successful think tanks make such planning a continuous process; each year or so, there may be a series of events for taking stock and assessing new options—new research topics, alternative clients, and different activities (e.g., offering new training programs, or starting a for-profit subsidiary to conduct household interviews). The atmosphere at these think tanks encourages staff to consider innovations.

In other words, strategic planning should not be undertaken only when a think tank faces severe financial problems. While some pressure for change can be helpful, the best decisionmaking is seldom done in a crisis environment. Nor should investment of an institution's scarce discretionary resources be based primarily on the president's intuition about the presence of a market for a new line of endeavor. Careful preparatory analysis is essential to increasing the odds of an innovation's success.

Preparation of a formal strategic plan can certainly be useful. Nevertheless, this chapter concentrates on the process of identifying and assessing new opportunities for a think tank. The reason for this focus is that the requirement of preparing a formal plan can create a high entry cost to innovation. Better to spend the limited available resources on generating and assessing ideas for new products the think tank might offer, new clients for some types of analysis or evaluation, or new audiences for its policy findings.[1]

This chapter addresses the task of fostering, developing, and assessing innovations at think tanks. But it is important to acknowledge that striking out in a new direction can be a wrenching experience for an organization. For this reason, the first section of the chapter discusses the kinds of challenges as well as the rewards that introducing new, radically different activities can engender. The second section reviews innovations adopted by four think tanks in Eastern Europe and Russia—how they were identified, assessed, and launched, and what problems were encountered in the process. The final section presents lessons distilled from the literature on encouraging innovations in for-profit and nonprofit organizations.[2]

CHALLENGES AND REWARDS

Think tanks can undertake a variety of innovations, several of which are described in the next section. To simplify the present discussion, this chapter focuses on a specific change: providing consulting services in addition to conducting foundation-supported research and policy analysis. In principle, private public-policy research institutes in the former Soviet bloc could have any of four groups of clients: national government agencies, local governments, the donors, and businesses. Contracts with the donors and with national government agencies often support the type of work think tanks prefer doing: policy development, including empirical background studies; program evaluation; implementation of pilot projects; and training of officials in implementation of a new program or design shifts in an existing program. Work with local governments tends to be more hands-on. While policy issues still figure in the mix of assignments, the emphasis is on addressing concrete problems to improve the efficiency with which services are delivered, taxes are raised, budgeting done, or funds are secured to finance capital investments. Work for business can be extremely diverse. For example, banks contract for macroeconomic forecasts, staff training, design of new loan products, loan servicing procedures to support new loan products, and assessments of potential new markets.

Challenges and rewards associated with such diversification are listed below, and each is discussed briefly later in the chapter.

Challenges to think tanks from consulting or other commercial activity include the following:

- Agenda-setting and lack of focus;
- Restricted use of data and publications;
- Perceived lack of independence;
- Conflict of cultures within the think tank;
- Restive clients or sponsors; and
- Management challenges.

Possible rewards include the following:

- Broader base of experience for policy development;
- Improved efficiency;
- Support for overhead functions; and
- Improved visibility and marketing possibilities.

Challenges

Agenda-Setting and Lack of Focus

Consultants, almost by definition, are responding to the perceived needs of their clients. Very often the consultant is not familiar with a client's needs or operations before being contacted. Because clients are setting their own agendas, the greater the share of a firm's work based on consulting, the more reactive the firm will be overall and the weaker its ability to set its own agenda.

In the United States, for example, major think tanks that receive a substantial share of their income from U.S. government contracts, such the Manpower Development Research Corporation and the Urban

Institute, maintain control over a significant portion of their agenda by obtaining funds from foundations to pursue topics that may not be on the federal agenda at the moment. The difficulty this model presents for think tanks in many other parts of the world is that the volume of funds from foundations may not be sufficient to permit a critical level of self-determined projects.[3]

Restricted Use of Data and Publications

In consulting for businesses and, increasingly, in work for a number of the donors as well, there are sharp restrictions on consultants' rights to use data assembled or reports produced during the consultancy for any purpose besides those of direct interest to the client. Such restrictions correspondingly limit the work of consulting think tanks in the policy process.[4]

Perceived Lack of Independence

The appearance of a think tank's lack of independence from the influence of regular consulting clients is a definite problem for think tanks that take on such work. Even when the right to publish materials based on work done under contract is present, there is still some question of whether the think tank consultant is engaging in some self-censorship to ensure continuing good relations with the client.[5] Credibility can only be achieved by a consistent record of taking policy positions that are squarely based on the research. Inevitably, sometimes such positions will be contrary to those of the sponsors.

Conflict of Cultures within the Think Tank[6]

Staff at think tanks who are dedicated to the public purposes for which the think tank was created could be seriously disturbed if the institution were to decide to take on for-profit work. Charges of incompatibility of objectives, operational styles, and "corporate behavior" are likely to be raised.

Restive Clients or Sponsors

An institute's traditional sponsors may not agree with the arguments for a think tank taking on more traditional consulting work. At an extreme they could withdraw their support.[7]

Management Challenges

While think tank directors must have good management instincts to run a successful firm, their instincts alone are frequently insufficient to guide the enterprise when the scale of operations expands significantly, particularly when the number of projects under way simultaneously and the number of separate sponsors rise. In short, establishing a consulting practice often requires further development of management and financial systems, and the size of the task can easily be underestimated.

Rewards

The foregoing list is a formidable recitation of the difficulties to think tanks from taking on consulting assignments. These problems, however, are balanced significantly by certain benefits from doing such work—gains that go beyond simply increased revenues.

Broader Base of Experience for Policy Development

Many consultancies require researchers to delve more deeply into the operational details of public programs or a firm's operations than they would have occasion to do in their regular research. For example, to advise a bank about its prospects in investing heavily in retail banking operations, researchers would likely have to conduct consumer surveys about the current services the consumers use and their preferences for improvements. Detailed analysis of the current market and the extent of competitiveness would be another critical element of the work. This is highly specific analysis. But the experience gained would be invaluable, even if as only general background, in working with the Ministry of Finance or the Central Bank on policies governing retail banking.

Improved Efficiency

Some think tanks work predominantly for a restricted set of clients in the foundation world. Foundations tend to favor work on the cutting edge of policy development, work where some risk of low return is present. Moreover, for at least some of these projects the work schedule is not very intense. The contrast with the work regime involved in consulting for businesses is stark. First, services are typically provided to businesses on short, very intense schedules. An opportunity or problem has been defined, and the business wants to act quickly to address it. Schedules for work for government agencies and the donors can be nearly anywhere between those for foundations and business. Another difference between work for foundations and other clients concerns the difference between work done under grants and contracts. Contracts are more specific about products, deadlines, and reporting. In addition, competition is generally keener for these contracts, because for-profit as well as nonprofit entities compete. So think tanks that work under contract to government agencies, businesses, and the donors are exposed to a different and in some ways more demanding work regime than those working exclusively for foundations. Several think tank directors interviewed in the earlier think tank study made this point about consulting work, and they saw the result on the efficiency of their overall operations as positive (Struyk 1999).

Support for Overhead Functions

From a financial perspective, consulting contracts are usually viewed positively because they keep the professional staff occupied on reasonably interesting projects. But there is a second important financial dimension. By raising the overall revenue base of the firm, consulting income reduces the firm's overhead rates. For example, the operation of the library, an overhead item, is now amortized over a larger revenue base, driving down the cost of library services associated with each hour of staff time. True, the existence of more projects is likely to result in more books being ordered, but for many overhead items the increases are less than proportional. Thus, over a reasonable range of expansion, a greater volume of work results in lower overhead costs per hour of professional labor, provided that the array of overhead services remains constant.[8]

Improved Visibility and Marketing Possibilities

By expanding the range of clients with whom and the topics on which the think tank works, the consultancies should lead to greater exposure of the organization's capabilities to new market segments.

INNOVATIONS IN PRACTICE

This section discusses the innovations adopted by four think tanks in Eastern Europe and Russia that were identified as being particularly entrepreneurial in developing new lines of work, including commercial activities similar to those of consulting firms or in tapping the business community for donations by offering seminars or other products of direct interest to this community. The included institutions are the Center for the Study of Democracy (Sofia), the Institute for Urban Economics (Moscow), the Center for Democracy and Free Enterprise (Prague), and the Center for Social and Economic Research (Warsaw).

The firms included were identified through the interviews with think tank leaders for the earlier study and through consultations with people knowledgeable about think tanks in the region. It is worth emphasizing that those who nominated think tanks consistently cited the same institutions, and the list was short—suggesting that such entrepreneurialism is far from common. In total, only four institutes beyond the four included were recommended. Three did not agree to participate in the project, and the author was unable to visit the fourth.[9] No claim is made that this group is a representative sample of any sort.

The information presented below is based on semi-structured interviews of institute leadership by the author in 1998 and 1999 and a review of annual reports, web sites, and other materials.

Overview of Initiatives

How many and what types of initiatives did these think tanks undertake? Why did they do it? How important are such initiatives to the institutions? Table 4-1 and box 4-1 provide summary information; box 4-1 gives a short description of each initiative.[10]

Of the four study firms, three are clearly in the second stage of development, meaning that they have more than five full-time researchers, have stable funding, and are well established in their markets. The other, the Center for Democracy and Free Enterprise (CDFE), is nearly there. The three second-stage organizations are all large by regional standards.

Each of the firms included cited one or two initiatives that had progressed far enough along to be reported upon. Initiatives are wide-ranging and include setting up a market survey operation, a credit rating agency,

Table 4-1 Number, Timing, and Importance of Initiatives

Item	CSD	IUE	CDFE	CASE
Timing				
Year institute founded	1989	1995	1991	1991
Year institute began seriously thinking about diversification	1994	1996	1996	1992
Motivation				
Reduce dependence on primary funding source	No	Yes	Yes	Yes
Necessary to engage in new type of work	Yes	Yes	No	Yes
Number of initiatives				
a. number allied to principal activity	1	2	1	2
b. number quite separate	1	0	0	2
Importance of all initiatives to revenue of the main company	30%	10%	20 to –30%	40 to 55%
Size				
Number of professional staff (full-time equivalent)	28	36	6[a]	40

CSD = Center for the Study of Democracy
IUE = Institute for Urban Economics
CDFE = Center for Democracy and Free Enterprise
CASE = Center for Social and Economic Research
a. Excludes parliamentary interns.

customized corporate training programs, and an in-house consulting center for working in other transition countries.

Most initiatives had been undertaken after the think tank had been in operation for two or three years, but there are exceptions to this rule. One is the radio station established by the Center for the Study of Democracy (CSD); founding the station was one of the center's first activities, and was meant to break the government's monopoly on local news broadcasts by rebroadcasting Voice of America (VOA) programs. Over the years the programming format has changed in line with evolving consumer preferences. Another example is the Center for Social and Economic Research (CASE), which began providing advice to other transition countries very early in its life, when a foundation invited one

Box 4-1 Summary of Initiatives

Firm	Initiative Title and Summary
CSD	*Radio station.* Began in April 1991, rebroadcasting Voice of America (VOA) programs. Received early U.S. government and other support for equipment and otherwise establishing the station. Once the transition began, the station tried a strong news format but soon discovered that this was not appealing. In response to lost market share, in 1993 the station shifted to a music format with news briefs, and expanded to three stations. Under this format, the station is profitable.
	Marketing surveys. Although CSD's first survey was conducted in 1990, Vitosha Research (VR), which conducts marketing surveys and analysis for commercial clients, was not created until 1994. VR has a number of international clients and specializes in more demanding survey research tasks.
IUE	*Credit rating agency.* IUE created the first Russian credit agency in 1997; initially the activity focused on rating bonds issued by municipalities and subjects of the Federation. In summer 1998 it was spun off as a wholly owned subsidiary (E-A Ratings Service) and signed a strategic affiliation agreement with Standard and Poor's. In 2001, S&P purchased a 70 percent interest in E-A Ratings.
	Municipal economic development. Established in fall 1997, a team within IUE provides consultancy services to middle-size cities in the creation of their economic development plans.
CDFE	*Corporate training.* The program provides development and management of customized education programs for senior staff of banks and enterprises.
CASE	*Technical assistance to transition countries.* The program was initiated in 1992, when a foundation invited CASE staff to provide technical assistance to Russia on its evolving macroeconomic policy. Further requests from donor organizations followed and activity expanded. In 1994–95, CASE became more active in seeking support for such work.
	Corporate sponsors. CASE recruited "corporate patrons" from among Poland's 70 largest and most respected corporations and banks. Patrons make a fixed contribution and receive CASE's publications, invitations to open seminars, and invitations to occasional "patrons only" events.

of CASE's senior staff to work with Russian reformers on macro-economic policies.

The Institute for Urban Economics (IUE) was also a fast starter because it believed that it could survive only if it aggressively diversified its activities and client base from the initial project—a large housing and real estate reform project supported by the U.S. Agency for International Development (USAID).

Motivation for the initiatives varied. CDFE was facing very tough times financially and diversified out of financial necessity. CASE's "corporate sponsors" initiative was also a straightforward attempt to diversify funding sources. On the other hand, CSD set up its marketing research operation primarily because it offered the chance to become engaged in new topic areas. Similarly, CASE's technical assistance to transition economies resulted from its desire to share its staff expertise. IUE was motivated by wanting both to reduce dependency on its primary sponsor and to enter new fields.

One key element in determining the nature of the initiative is the institution's initial activity base. CSD built its marketing survey operation on its existing survey capacity, and IUE created its credit rating agency for local government bonds around a team already doing related municipal-finance projects. Similarly, CDFE was able to exploit its established reputation for conducting training projects in preparing its custom training packages for corporate clients. CASE's international consulting operation built squarely on the group's work on similar topics in Poland.

In short, the firms generally built on the positive reputation they had established for related activities and exploited the capabilities of existing staff in selecting an initiative. Building on strength is a common business strategy. However, the modest capital available to underwrite the start-up costs of an initiative also prevented firms from launching an initiative further afield from their core activities.

Identifying and Launching Initiatives

The most common pattern for the launch of an initiative was for the basic idea to come from the president of the organization or from a staff member (table 4-2). The idea was then discussed among the staff and a few people outside of the organization and usually with the board of trustees. If it was agreed upon as feasible, then the new line of work would be marketed by word of mouth and participation in seminars,

Table 4-2 Origin, Development, and Rating of Each Initiative

Firm and Initiative	Source of Idea	Type of Analysis Undertaken[a]	Promotion Effort[b] (Yes/No)	Annual Number of Orders	Financial Success (Yes/No)
CSD: radio station	USG rep.; CSD president	2	No	NA	Yes
CSD: marketing surveys	Staff	2,4	No	25 to 30	Yes
IUE: credit rating	Staff	1,3,4	y2	3 to 5[c]	Yes
IUE: municipal economic development	Staff	1	y2	2	Too early to tell
CDFE: corporate training	CDFE president	1	No	varies	Yes
CASE: tech assist to transition economy	Staff	1	y1	5 to 6 countries 3 to 4 sponsors[d]	Yes
CASE: corporate sponsors	Staff	1	y2	8 sponsors	Yes

a. 1 = staff discussion; 2 = sought outside advice from knowledgeable people (volunteers); 3 = paid for outside expert advice; 4 = prepared professional-standard business plan

b. y1 = Promotion consisted of actively seeking opportunities to make presentations at seminars and conferences; preparation and distribution of reports; and mentioning of the activity on the organization's web site.

y2 = Formal marketing activities undertaken beyond those listed in y1, such as holding a press conference, organizing seminars, or publication and distribution of special promotional brochures. Also, in rare cases, pilot projects were carried out to provide a "product" to demonstrate (e.g., IUE's economic development team worked on a nonfee basis with a mid-size Russian city to develop an economic development strategy that the institute could then show to other cities).

c. A single "order" can involve ratings for a number of cities (e.g., a multilateral donor requesting information on debt-carrying capacity of several cities).

d. A sponsor sometimes supports work in more than one country.

where this specific expertise could be demonstrated and promotional material distributed. In short, these have been low-tech, often rather informal processes. Instinct has played at least as large a role as analysis in making the decision to proceed.

Preparation of a formal business plan to test the feasibility of an initiative was relatively rare, with plans being prepared for only two initiatives—CSD's marketing survey initiative and IUE's credit rating facility. IUE was the only group surveyed that contracted for assistance in analyzing its initiative. It hired an international management consulting firm to help prepare the business plan. IUE believes this was a good investment because the strong business plan was instrumental in inducing Standard and Poor's (S&P) to sign a strategic affiliation agreement with the credit rating agency less than a year after the agency began operations.

Similarly, formal promotional efforts beyond seminar participation to launch a new initiative were exceptional. IUE has been more aggressive than most think tanks in explicitly marketing an initiative. For its credit rating initiative, for example, it sponsored presentations by the key researcher at numerous seminars within Russia, gave the activity prominence on its home page, produced a slick three-fold marketing brochure and distributed it widely at conferences, and sponsored a session at a major international conference in London on credit ratings in the Commonwealth of Independent States. The affiliation with Standard and Poor's was announced at a splashy press conference in a five-star Moscow hotel. CASE launched its "corporate patrons" program with a customized sophisticated mailing to 70 of the largest corporations and banks in Poland, with telephone follow-up to recruit patrons.

Common, if modest, promotional efforts included devoting space in the institute's newsletter and on the institute's web site to the initiative, where these vehicles were available. Since most projects result in reports, these, too, were available to show to new potential clients.[11]

Of those interviewed, only CASE cited an example of an initiative that has not worked to date. CASE attempted to obtain contracts from the Polish government for carrying out research and policy analysis; while government offices use the Center's work, they have resisted paying for it. This initiative was handled very informally. Equally informal attempts by other think tanks to recruit new clients may have gone unreported in the interviews because they were so informal.

Rewards and Challenges

How did the pluses and minuses of introducing innovations balance for these think tanks? Table 4-3 provides an overview using the same factors listed above.

Rewards

Financially, the revenues generated by the initiatives have generally been moderately important, representing 10 to 30 percent of total revenues (table 4-1). But CASE's assistance to transition economies has been uniquely successful, with revenues from this activity accounting for 33 to 50 percent of total revenues in the two years before the interview.

The directors of the think tanks rated the initiatives as financially successful. This is, however, a fairly imprecise term. While each of the initiatives is generating significant revenue, as seen above, the rating of financial success is *not* based on revenues net of start-up costs. For many initiatives these costs were quite modest, so the needed adjustment would be small. But in a few cases, such as IUE's substantial promotional efforts and paid assistance in business-plan development, the rating of financial success could be affected. Unfortunately, these think tanks do not keep records in a way that permits all the relevant costs to be readily identified.

Table 4-3 Summary of Responses on Challenges and Rewards

Reward/Challenge	Number of Firms Citing Reward/Challenge
Rewards	
Broader base of experience for policy development	3
Improved efficiency	2
Support for overhead functions	0
Improved visibility and marketing possibilities	4
Challenges	
Agenda-setting and lack of focus	0
Restricted use of data and publications	0
Perceived lack of independence	0
Conflict of cultures within the think tank	0
Restive clients or sponsors	0
Management challenges	2

Some respondents emphasized that the form in which the funds were received made them especially valuable. Both CDFE and CSD reported that the use of profits from corporate training and the radio station, respectively, had no restrictions and could be used very flexibly. For example, they could serve as matching funds for foundation grants or used for computer purchases or other institution-building tasks. On the other hand, if the activity increases total operations but leaves profits unchanged, then funds in the overhead accounts increase—but these are all dedicated to specific purposes.

All four think tanks believe that their initiatives improved their reputation and/or visibility with certain local communities, especially the business community. IUE's credit ratings made the young institute visible to financial circles. CASE's corporate patrons program helped establish a firmer relationship with the business community. CDFE's customized training courses were more important in giving the Center access to other projects than for reputation per se. Finally, CSD sees its market survey work for major multinational firms as a recognition of its capabilities—recognition that they can use to woo future clients.

Three of the sample think tanks also saw various aspects of their initiatives as broadening their experience base for policy development. Working in these new areas expanded the perspective of the researchers involved, and in some instances informed other policy analyses. IUE's ratings of municipal bonds gave analysts new insights into the actual financial condition of local governments and the structure of intergovernmental fiscal relations.

Interestingly, certain unanticipated benefits were cited as an important part of the overall success of the new ventures. First, CSD thought that its market survey operation helped the group retain staff, by giving analysts a change from the typical research and writing assignments. CASE also thought that the change of pace provided by foreign travel and somewhat different assignments made the center a generally more attractive place to work for some staff members.

IUE and CASE cited a second unexpected benefit: The new activities generated important staff training. For IUE, the training in the credit rating initiative came from the classroom training provided by Standard and Poor's and by the IUE staff working directly with the S&P staff on benchmarking and other tasks. The leadership at CASE stated that young staff were challenged by working largely on their own in other countries of the region, helping them mature quickly as researchers and policy analysts.

The training and adjustments to management (described below) can be considered to indicate improved efficiency of operations.

None of the think tanks spoke about the benefits of expanded overhead revenues, although this may have been covered in point on financial success.

Challenges

Think tank leaders reported remarkably little in the way of problems accompanying the new, more commercially oriented initiatives. The interview included explicit questions about the half-dozen different types of problems the institution might have encountered (listed above), so the respondents were thoroughly prompted to recall problems.

Neither IUE nor CDFE could identify any problems. The IUE director said she thought that this was due in part to the orientation of the organization, which from the beginning had worked on multiple demonstration projects that involved close relationships with local government officials and banks. CDFE stated that the financial pressures were so severe that the staff understood that the organization had to change direction if it was to survive.

CSD reported no philosophical problems with the staff, the board of trustees, or foundation clients. Rather, the problem was in changing employees' task orientation; staff shied away from doing the necessary marketing. At CASE, the only problems encountered were managerial. There was a certain conflict between the demands of short-term consulting jobs in other transition countries and keeping the larger home-based projects on schedule: The major projects fell behind as staff dashed off on short-term assignments. This conflict was finally resolved by expanding the size of the permanent and associate staff. Both of these difficulties can be classified as management challenges.

It is important to note that none of the four institutions reported problems with dilution of the focus of their work, perceived independence in the policy process, or cultural conflicts within the organization. This happy record may result from the fact that the new lines of work are all closely aligned with each institution's main activities and that these are young organizations whose identities are not yet carved in stone and hence are still able to be quite flexible in creating or responding to opportunities.

Concluding Observations

These four case studies clearly illustrate that it is possible for think tanks to go beyond the traditional funding sources to sustain and expand their operations. Indeed, they almost make it look easy. As related in the interviews, the identification and analysis of potential opportunities was not overly demanding—nor was the set of actions needed to launch the activity. All four think tanks reported remarkably few problems with management, institutional identification, or staff morale from adding the new, more commercially oriented activities—probably in part because they are young, flexible, and dynamic organizations. All four are also searching for more opportunities to expand into new types of work areas.

Can other think tanks count on such a smooth experience? Probably not. There are two important factors that must be taken into account in assessing think tanks' ability to emulate these examples. First, all four of the think tanks included in this analysis were careful to build on existing strengths—the innovations were in areas where their existing competence and reputation gave them a running start. Working in an area close to an existing competence increased their ability to judge the potential demand for a new service. It also minimized start-up costs, as staff could continue to work on the traditional tasks while the demand for the think tank's new services increased. For an innovation further from the core competence, one or two new experts would have been hired, they have charged most of their time to program development (overhead).

Second, these four groups are all entrepreneurial institutions whose leaders have good market instincts, can realistically assess possibilities, and have demonstrated the willingness to take the initiative when opportunity appeared. This characteristic is not very common. Also, in some cases these institutions have a culture and a system in place to encourage staff to think creatively and to propose ideas beyond the current work program. It is these qualities that caused the organizations to be consistently recommended as innovative organizations.

ENCOURAGING INNOVATION

The business community is characterized by a constant struggle to produce new products and services for clients. Interestingly, in recent years similar pressure has been placed on the U.S. nonprofit sector, forcing nongovernmental organizations (NGOs) to rethink the services they provide and how they provide them, including the incorporation of more fee-generating activities.[12] This is an era of increasing competition both among NGOs for support from foundations and between NGOs and for-profit firms for the role of delivery agents for social services for local governments. Nonprofits are finding it necessary to think and organize themselves more like businesses (Letts et al. 1999; Light 1998).

A principal challenge these NGOs—and think tanks—face is to develop an environment and practice of innovation. Students of innovation in nonprofit organizations in the United States say unequivocally that most guidance available to nonprofits focuses on how single acts of innovation were created and implemented, not on creating an environment that fosters innovations again and again (Letts et al. 1999, 73; Light 1998, 7). Indeed, Letts et al. state categorically that there are no good concepts for nonprofits for program development (1999, 74). At the same time, experts in the field are calling for "the relentless pursuit of opportunity" (Kitzi 2001, 44).

The following presentation has two parts. The first addresses key factors in a think tank's working environment that are conducive to generating innovations, including specific leadership attributes that promote innovation. The second provides tips on key points for identifying, assessing, and piloting promising innovations. In this discussion, the accent is on principles rather than on development of a "strategic plan." Focusing on a formal document may discourage think tanks from considering how they innovate; for those who do proceed, it could detract from the degree of creativity about the innovations themselves when the focus is on developing a formal report.[13] Indeed, the literature on the development of strategic plans by U.S. nonprofits indicates that such plans are often developed in response to the requirements of a major funder or at a time of organizational crisis; the needs of clients seldom receive much weight (Stone et al. 1999). Both sections of the following discussion are based on the literature about fostering a process of innovation at for-profit and nonprofit organizations.

Creating a Conducive Environment

There are half a dozen actions a think tank can take to create conditions conducive to staff thinking about new directions for the organization.[14]

A flat, informal organization is the most effective. Those studying innovation have observed that the more layers between staff and senior management, the more likely it is that management will not learn about many good ideas. The corresponding lesson is to keep the organization "thin," (i.e., with few layers). In the same vein, the greater the extent to which responsibility is pushed downward in an organization, the more likely it is that lower-level staff will have access to and a working relationship with management and believe themselves important to the entity's success. In larger think tanks, if responsibility is concentrated on the team leader, rather than on a combination of the team leader and the subordinate project leaders, the project leaders are likely to have less contact with management and be less comfortable advancing ideas. A concomitant point is that greater informality in an organization increases the odds that a staffer will directly approach management with innovative ideas.

The reality is that most think tanks are small enough that they do not have multiple layers of managers separating a project leader from the director of the organization. But even a single layer, if not properly managed, can create a barrier to good ideas flowing upward. A positive sign, at least for the Eastern Europe–CIS region, is the generally informal nature of the relationships among the staff at all levels (see chapter 2).

Staff diversity is helpful. Put simply, the decision process will typically be stronger when people with different backgrounds and views are involved: What may appear to be a good idea to a group with academic backgrounds may strike someone from the business community or a local government background as much less sound. If a think tank has a homogeneous staff, then inviting trusted advisors with other perspectives to discuss possible innovations is certainly worthwhile.

Internal turbulence can stimulate change. Sometimes a jolt is necessary to induce staff to think creatively; without it they tend to focus on what they have been doing and on marginal changes to this agenda. Internal turbulence, in the form of the departure of a key staff member or a bleak funding outlook, can push staff to think beyond their normal boundaries. Of course, the key question is how much turbulence is too much. Beyond a certain point, shocks and uncertainty can make the staff literally dysfunctional. A telltale sign of too much disruption is staff huddled in groups talking about their possible futures rather than doing their regular jobs.

Low internal barriers help staff exchange ideas. Think tanks with as few as 10 full-time researchers are likely to have separate units for addressing different policy topics. Managerially this certainly makes sense. But if these units become isolated islands, the organization can lose the ideas that result from the interaction of teams working on different subjects and for different clients. One technique used by a number of think tanks is to have seminars devoted to ongoing projects that are attended by staff from all groups. This informs everyone about the substance of the projects and provides a base for further interactions. Another technique is to hold joint regular meetings of senior managers and team leaders to exchange notes on projects and institutional questions.

Internal resources are needed to pursue possible innovations. If staff know that there are funds available to support the development of an innovative concept, they are much more likely to advance it for discussion.[15] There are two distinct elements involved here. First, the funds must actually exist. Many think tanks fund initial work on an innovation from a pool composed of fee income (essentially profit) and funds from overhead, through a line item designated for "institutional development" or similar purposes. Second, the staff has to know that funds actually are used to develop or pilot-test innovations. Think tanks can make this clear by actually financing the development of an innovation from time to time. Even in a large organization composed of 50 staff members, most will know the source of the funds financing the new activity.

Innovation as an ongoing process. Staff will understand that proposing new projects and alternative directions for the organization is encouraged if there are clear indicators to this effect. If the think tank has an annual retreat of senior staff to consider current operations and the future of the organization—including possible innovations in the work program—and inputs are widely solicited for the retreat, then staff will be encouraged to be creative and expansive in their thinking. But it would be wrong for management to signal that ideas are welcome only at specific points. Opportunities seldom wait. Other "markers" to indicate that staff can contribute to the store of fresh ideas are certainly possible, especially if management supports some of those offered. This ongoing process is in sharp contrast with the one-big-initiative model, in which a significant change of direction is adopted once and then the organization goes back to business as usual.

The annex to this chapter describes how one think tank, the Institute for Urban Economics, works to establish a climate that fosters innovation.

Leadership is key. Paul Light makes the following statement about the importance of leadership for innovation:

> Leaders play a central role at virtually every stage of the innovation process, from initiation to implementation, particularly in deploying the resources that carry innovation forward. Leadership is so important that some scholars see it as the sole factor in success. (1998, 19)

Four leadership attributes seem to be particularly important for innovation. It is worth emphasizing that the leadership role for innovation does not have to be lodged in the leader of the think tank; it could be assigned to someone else who has the necessary skills, if that person is fully supported by the leader.

Vision. Leaders have to be able to imagine different roles for their organization if they are to help innovation succeed. The leader of a tightly focussed policy research organization might see it as a training and educational institution as well, or, as in the case of the Center for the Study of Democracy, as having a for-profit market survey arm. Leaders should also be able to imagine attracting different types of talent to the organization as a means of accomplishing new objectives. Vision may involve defining new roles, but it also suggests being able to decide how to move the organization to these new roles, at least in general terms.

Flexible temperament. One can readily imagine the key personal attributes in this area: being intellectually curious, having flexible interests and operating style, being open to staff, being supportive of those assigned responsibility, being action-oriented, and having the patience to see experiments through. Some degree of entrepreneurialism also is essential.

Communication skills. A motivated staff is informed about and understands what is happening in an organization. Good leaders communicate regularly with the staff, either directly or through subordinates who are clearly charged with informing their coworkers about developments within the think tank. It is especially important for staff to know what innovations are being pursued and how the innovations fit into plans for the long-run development of the organization. This both encourages employees to think of additional innovations and reassures them about the think tank's future.

Innovation skills. Leaders must be able to nurture an idea through the innovation process—from idea through a critical examination phase and pilot testing—knowing how much to invest, how fast to go, how to be fair in judging critiques, and how to help shape adjustments to the initial idea. The leader must also be willing to take prudent risks. These skills require intellectual acumen, team spirit, patience, and a fine sense of judgment and entrepreneurialism.

This is a formidable list of attributes, and not all think tank leaders have all of them. The list is nevertheless a useful guide for leaders, who can use it to make sure that there are members of the key decisionmaking team who together have all of the attributes and can execute the essential functions, such as communicating well with the staff.

The Process of Innovation

The process can be divided into three phases: the call for ideas, assessment, and piloting the strongest candidates. These are unlikely to be clean, discrete phases, and there will probably be overlap both for phases of a single innovation and between successive innovations. One can imagine, for example, that the piloting of one innovation will still be under way when a new idea is already under discussion.[16]

Call for Ideas

First, staff must understand that the welcome mat is out for ideas. If a retreat for team leaders and management is planned, team leaders should solicit and discuss ideas from their groups. They should understand that the retreat will be more productive if people arrive with well-articulated ideas, but first musings should also be on the agenda.

It is essential for the think tank's director to provide some early guidance for the type of ideas being sought. If the topic of the retreat is to identify significantly new directions for the organization that have a good prospect of external support, then it is not appropriate to present research topics only marginally different from those already being addressed. This point is made more generally in box 4-2, which is oriented to for-profit

Box 4-2 Alternative Business Orientations

Production Orientation

Focuses on	What we can produce
De-emphasizes	Meeting customer needs

Sales Orientation

Focuses on	Promoting what we already do
De-emphasizes	Meeting customer needs through product innovation

Market Orientation

Focuses on	Meeting customer needs—including customers for newly identified services
Requires	1. Detailed understanding of customer needs
	2. Precise definition of target markets
Results in	1. Business functions oriented toward serving customers
	2. Above-average long-run orders for work

Source: Bacon and Butler (1998), figure 11.

firms but is nonetheless applicable to think tanks: Staff should adopt a market orientation, rather than the production or sales orientations. Only by envisioning the needs of their clients and sponsors (or "effective demand," in the economist's language) will think tanks' staff succeed in defining viable innovations.

Staff can be encouraged to think about innovations in several different areas. Drawing on a list presented in Dees (2001b, 163–64), the topics listed in box 4-3 could be flagged as areas to consider.

Those advancing innovative ideas should be asked to give initial consideration to five questions in testing their thinking:

- What is the need (functional requirement) and the target market (analytic studies, consulting services, on-site technical assistance, training, software)? How large is the potential market?
- What is the basis for the competitive opening—is there an unmet need that no one has previously identified or is in a position to address?

Box 4-3 Types of Innovative Opportunities

1. *Creating a new or improved product or service*—one with which users are not yet familiar or one with aspects that are new to clients.

Example: An organization with a real estate practice could consider producing a text for use in trade association or university courses.

2. *Introducing a new or improved strategy or method of operating*—one that has been not been used by the organization adopting it.

Example: A think tank that has worked with municipalities in a range of areas could offer bundled services that would be both more strategic in their perspective and more effective for a municipality, and that would involve some savings to the client compared with multiple single-focus initiatives.

3. *Reaching a new market, serving an unmet need*—making a product, service, or program available to a group that did not otherwise have access to it.

Example: An organization could provide credit ratings on municipal bonds where none had existed before.

4. *Framing new terms of engagement*—changing the terms on which the organization relates to clients, consumers, funders, and/or employees.

Example: Think tanks that have worked with national or local governments on preparing reform legislation and implementing pilot projects under funding from the donor community could begin offering similar services on a fee basis as donor support is withdrawn.

5. *Developing new funding structures*—exploring different options for reducing or covering the costs of producing or delivering a product or service.

Example: A think tank with a large training component for local NGOs or local governments could reduce the number of sites where training is offered by trying to teach larger groups with smaller faculties at fewer locations.

Source: Based on Dees (2001a, 163–64).

- What is the basis for the think tank's competitive advantage: superior product, lower cost, better outreach and marketing capabilities compared with other providers, greater potential for continuous product innovations (e.g., being able to provide cutting-edge technical assistance to local governments in a particular sector by transferring best practices among them)?
- Does the organization have the expertise to pursue this opportunity? If not, is it likely that the expertise can be acquired at a reasonable cost?
- Does the organization have the capacity to support the initiative (e.g., classroom space, the computer hardware and software for the creation of a sophisticated web site)?

Think tanks face a particular challenge in analyzing the potential demand for services: The client for the services is often not the entity providing funding for them. For example, a bilateral donor may fund technical assistance to local governments who are the direct client for the services. In such cases, think tanks must try to identify programs that will better serve the interests of both the clients and the funder. In some cases, a think tank can advance ideas to a donor based on market research with beneficiaries for new projects. But it is critical that the source of effective demand be clearly identified when innovations are being assessed.

Finally, guidelines that encourage bold thinking about new areas of activity should make it clear that new directions should build on the organization's existing strengths. Recall that this was the pattern for the innovations reviewed earlier in this chapter. Building on success is desirable because the think tank can take full advantage of its reputation in entering the new area; marketing will be more efficient, as some of the key actors and potential clients will be known already; and start-up costs will be lower than they otherwise would be, as existing resources can be directed to the new activity.

Assessing Alternatives

Bacon and Butler (1998, 60) name three attributes of a desirable opportunity (innovation) for a firm:

- An unmet customer need of significant value to a current or potential customer exists;

- The firm can provide the needed services and make a suitable profit doing so; and
- The work advances the firm toward both its tactical and strategic goals and objectives.

A think tank must assess each idea against these attributes.

The assessment process is critical to achieving the desired outcome. As Dees points out, "Successful innovation is as much a matter of execution as it is of having new ideas" (2001b, 161). The review process must be deliberate. Of course, some ideas advanced will be clearly inappropriate and can be turned aside without further ado. For the ideas surviving the initial screening, the review process must be rigorous (after all, the think tank's scarce resources for innovation should be invested in the best ideas). It should also be viewed as objective and fair by the staff; otherwise staff will be discouraged from contributing to the process in the future.[17]

For think tanks, the final attribute is perhaps the most important: The new work must be consistent with its mission and objectives. The organization must remain true to itself. An earlier section discussed the challenges of taking on activities sharply different from those of the past, but it also pointed out that it is easy to overestimate the turbulence that new activities will produce in a think tank.

The greatest emphasis must clearly be placed on assessing the market for the innovation. A formal business plan can be produced, and it may help map out expected costs and revenues.[18] But determining the probable market is the key task. Staff at think tanks typically have little experience in assessing markets. Put simply, for the kind of services that think tanks offer, they need to canvass potential clients, such as[19]

- Major donor organizations, in the case of technical studies and technical assistance projects;
- Local governments for technical assistance with certain policy and management reforms and training events;
- National governments for policy analysis and possibly program evaluations; and
- Trade associations and their members (banks, municipalities, hospitals) for training courses and possibly technical assistance.

Besides speaking directly with clients, staff can get ideas about potential demand from other sources, such as presentations at conferences and the direction of change set by the national government (e.g., more responsibilities being assigned to local governments could mean an expanded market in technical assistance and training to these entities). Moreover, monitoring what the competition is doing can often stimulate thinking in new directions. Determining the extent of the market is time-consuming, demanding work, but think tanks shy away from it at their own peril.

The team assembled to assess proposed innovations must use the five points listed above to examine for any proposals that pass the initial screening. In conducting this assessment, it is important to proceed briskly; spending too much time collecting data can lead to "analysis paralysis," a particular danger for research organizations (Kitzi 2001, 51). The team should also consider whether there is a particular window of opportunity for an innovation: How important is timing to success? Is demand likely to be one-off or continuing?

Piloting Promising Innovations

A think tank will typically decide to pursue one or perhaps two innovations in a year, reflecting the presence of two kinds of constraints: limited financial resources for discretionary spending and limited capacity to launch and manage the initiatives.

Determine Resource Requirements

Once the think tank's leadership has decided to implement an innovation, plans are usually made to pilot the innovation by developing the new offering and testing the market. At this stage, a draft budget should be prepared. The budget will include costs for a range of expenses:

- Developing the new product, such as a training course or the expertise that can be applied in the new area. This may entail hiring a new expert and making a one- or two-year commitment to the person.
- Carrying out one or more applications in the new work areas in order to develop greater expertise and to establish a track record to use in further marketing. A think tank may need to find cooperating clients and carry out a trial application of the new service (e.g., working with a bank to develop its mortgage lending program or assisting a municipality to develop its economic development plan, or offering a training program for NGOs). Alternatively, it may

need to finance the writing and publication of the initial issues of a
new magazine aimed at a broad policy audience. In each of these
cases, the initial experience may need to be subsidized.

- Developing and executing a carefully conceived marketing program
  that is tightly targeted on the specific client group. This could
  include producing print materials, such as brochures, but might also
  involve allowing staff to participate in conferences where the new
  offering could be announced. The marketing campaign would be
  timed to follow the development stage and, where appropriate, the
  pilot stage so that this experience could be used as a qualification.

At this point it is critical to define the total resources that can be
devoted to piloting the innovation and the timing of their availability:
How much will be available each month for the first six months and
quarterly thereafter during the trial period? Some iteration between the
draft budget for the pilot and the funds available may be necessary.

Three ideas for minimizing the cash outlays are listed below:

- *Phase in the implementation, funding only one or two stages at a
  time.* Allocate cash on a stage-by-stage basis as the milestones are
  reached.
- *Convert fixed costs into variable costs.* Instead of hiring the new
  experts needed for the program, try to engage them as part-time
  consultants during the early phases. An organization establishing an
  extensive training program could rent space for classes as needed
  instead of acquiring a larger office and classroom space.
- *Look for excess capacity and underutilized resources.* Can staff from
  an area where work is light be reassigned to help develop the innovation? Can the public relations specialist work on the marketing
  campaign instead of hiring outside resources?[20]

The think tank needs to be clear about what noncash resources will be
needed for the launch. Often these will include enlisting political support or sponsorship for the innovation. General sponsorship might
come from the think tank's board of trustees, but further support may
be needed. Questions to consider include the following:

- Who is being designated to contact the head of the relevant trade
  association, the relevant minister, or the head of the World Bank's
  representative office?

- What are the chances that those making the contacts will succeed in arranging the meeting and in obtaining support? What is the fall-back position if there is a refusal?
- Specific activities may also need sponsorship: Who can approach the mayor to solicit his city's participation in an economic development pilot project?

Think again. Even after the general plan for implementation is developed, there are a number of further preparatory steps that can increase the odds of success. The major tasks remaining include the following.[21]

Define performance targets for the testing period—usually one to two years. Setting targets forces everyone to be explicit about their expectations for the innovation. These goals should be set out in terms that are as concrete as possible. Obviously, the expectations should be determined in light of the resources being devoted to launching the innovation.[22]

Create a calendar of activities necessary for achieving the goals. This is the monthly "to do" list. Again, being explicit about the schedule for each component, the relation among components, and who is responsible for each can save resources and frustration during the pilot phase.

Write down the assumptions behind the definition of the pilot's success and identify the most crucial ones. For example, the most crucial assumption in an innovative technical assistance program designed to foster economic development in municipalities might be the rate at which the municipalities contract for this service *after the new approach has been demonstrated in two cities.* What if the assumed rate is too optimistic? How large a margin of error can be tolerated without the innovation being a failure? If more realistic assumptions render the margin of error too thin, the decision to go forward may need to be reconsidered.

Design the venture with explicit milestones that reflect the points at which the most crucial assumptions will be tested. The milestones should cover the development stages for the product or service and should track the interest, orders, and cash generated by the innovation at various points in time.

Include "permission to fail" in the plan. Although a think tank should be able to monitor the degree of success of an innovation, it must also be prepared to admit that there is not a demand for the new product or service when this is the case—and to do so in a timely way. It is important for the staff to know that advancing an innovation that ultimately fails is not necessarily a demerit on the person's standing within the organization.[23] If the innovation were assessed in the thorough manner outlined above, then the failure, like a success, would have a "thousand fathers." Senior management ultimately makes the decision and bears the responsibility, but there is little gain in assigning blame.

It is profitable, however, to try to understand which assumptions were wrong and how the review process failed. The answer may be that there was only limited useful information available on the point. But it may be that the organization did not conduct enough market research—an area that could be improved in the future.

In addition, it is also important to try to assess whether the critical condition that led to the failure of the innovation is likely to change in the near future or could be changed with a different promotional approach. While the odds are generally against this, there may be reason to allocate modest additional investment to keep the innovation alive or to make a different promotional campaign.

SUMMARY

Think tanks can be successful innovators, and the four case studies presented here suggest a range of possibilities. Many others also come to mind—writing textbooks for trade associations, partnering with trade associations to offer training programs, or adding a new area of expertise to a research program. We have also seen that innovative think tanks—those that consistently have innovations to consider—are few and far between, just as innovative firms and NGOs are rare in the for-profit and nonprofit worlds. A think tank's ability to innovate results from an environment that encourages staff to think broadly and creatively and from the presence of leadership that organizes and inspires a process for capturing the ideas and vetting them in an open and objective fashion.

It is critical that the organization have some discretionary funds to support implementation of the most promising innovations. The piloting of an innovation should be structured with great care. Indeed, an objective observer might say that the preparation for some of the case study innovations was not sufficiently thorough. The fact that they nonetheless succeeded is a tribute to the strength of the unmet need for the new service. But most innovations are not so robust.

In the end, the process of innovation may be essential for the survival of most think tanks; they must adjust to the changing policy agenda and shifting needs of their various client groups. Think tanks will adjust with greater agility if they consciously foster innovations through an orderly process containing the elements outlined herein.

NOTES

(Complete references can be found in the Reference Section at the end of this book.)

1. Two new guides to managing innovation in nonprofit organizations make the same decision (i.e., they do not cover how to prepare a strategic plan): Light (1998) and Dees, Emerson, and Economy (2001). See Bryson (1995) and Covello and Hazelgren (1995) on the preparation of a strategic plan.

2. The text concentrates on innovations to a think tank's work program and sponsors. There are two other forms of innovation that deserve mention: restructuring the organization to achieve significant improvements in productivity, and mergers of currently independent think tanks.

One hears little about major internal reorganizations designed to drive down costs and make a think tank more efficient and competitive. The lack of information likely results from the fact that such changes are wholly internal events. Nevertheless, one can imagine the kinds of changes that could be made. For example, a think tank that had organized its work along thematic lines (e.g., health policy, local government finance, social assistance) may decide that this is inefficient because each thematic group is involved in technical assistance projects, evaluations, and econometric analyses. The groups are too small to permit each to possess true expertise in each technical competency. The result is that some work is being poorly done by nonexperts, some staff are not fully employed, and some staff are frustrated because they are not working on their preferred assignments. Reorganizing by type of expertise (technical assistance, econometric analysis, evaluation) combined with much smaller thematic teams could address these problems.

The root cause for most mergers is financial pressure to cut costs, gain market share, and offer a broader array of capability to sponsors. This pressure has been especially acute in Eastern Europe in the past few years as donor support for the economic and political transition in the region has fallen very sharply and think tanks that had relied upon donor funding are forced to retrench and consider fundamental adjustments. There are two forms of adjustment among the several possible (LaPiana 1997) that seem particularly relevant. One is back-office consolidation, under which the costs of core administration functions are shared among think tanks while each think tank maintains its own identity. Examples of these functions are accounting, copying, public relations, secretarial services, and, in some cases, even research assistants.

More common is the merger of near-equals or the effective acquisition of one think tank by another. There is a growing literature on these processes for nonprofit organizations generally that gives pointers on what leaders of a think tank might expect in such a process. A common theme is that few of the mergers are carefully analyzed from a business perspective as part of the preparation. The greatest problem in achieving agreement to merge is the relative status of the two organizations—and their leaders—after the merger. Where mergers are hurried, post-merger staff morale problems are common. Finally, key ingredients for success are deemed to be good leadership and honest, open communication between an organization's leadership and the staff. For more on these points, see, for example, LaPiana (1997), McMurtry, Netting, and Kettner (1991), Singer and Yankey (1991), and Wernet and Jones (1992).

3. Bruckner (1996) has commented on the tendency for think tanks in the region to begin chasing contracts to survive and the problems this has engendered.

4. In the West, think tanks deal with this problem in two ways. First, they work hard at negotiating publication and use-of-data clauses in their contracts so that their rights in these areas are preserved. Sometimes this involves giving the client exclusive use of the data for a period of time—often three to six months. In other cases the clients secure the right to receive an advance copy of any publication dealing with the project with the right to comment on it within a specified period, but they cannot block publication. Second, think tanks simply refuse to accept contracts from some classes of customers. In the United States, one of the requirements for think tanks to maintain their nonprofit tax status is that all the work done by such organizations be broadly for the public good—proprietary research and consulting is inconsistent with this requirement.

5. Think tanks in the United States and Europe employ a variety of methods to handle this delicate task. These include, at a minimum, notification of clients about the policy position the think tank is taking on a particular issue and an advance copy of articles being submitted for publication in either a popular or scientific outlet. A more generous approach is the offer of a briefing to the client in advance of a press conference or release or testimony before the legislature. In either case, such actions keep the client from being caught unawares or unprepared to respond to the think tank's statements. These are notices and opportunities for discussion; they are not an offer by the think tank to alter its conclusions. These steps help maintain good relations with the clients, but they do nothing to reassure others of the objectivity of the think tank's recommendations.

6. This and the next two problems are discussed in Davies (1996, 33–44).

7. See, for example, Tschirbart (1996) on how to manage such transactions effectively.

8. The firm can elect to take advantage of this "dividend" in two general ways: Overhead rates can be reduced, making the firm more price-competitive for acquiring additional work; or new overhead services can be added. For example, as the firm expands it can hire a public relations officer without undermining its competitive position.

9. My sense is that in at least two of these cases the heads of the think tanks did not want to give away what they viewed as their commercial secrets.

10. Note that not all actions cited as entrepreneurial by the respondents have been included. Some had begun too recently to be of interest, and others were simply a somewhat different approach to marketing to prior clients.

11. CDFE was not anxious to advertise its special corporate training activities, because some viewed the training as not fully consistent with its primary mission, so it used none of these tools.

12. See, for example, Bullen et al. (1997), Burlingame and Ilchman (1996), Davis (1997), and Maxwell (1996).

13. Wheeler and Hunger (2000) provide a comprehensive treatment of strategic plans.

14. Of the sources consulted, this discussion draws the most on Light (1998, chapters 1 and 4).

15. Letts et al. (1999, 73), among others, stress this point.

16. This section draws generally on Bacon and Butler (1998) and Kitzi (2001).

17. Light (1998, 50) also makes this point for nonprofit organizations.

18. On the preparation of business plans, see, for example, Covello and Hazelgren (1995).

19. Majeska (2001) gives a good review on analyzing customer requirements.

20. Dees (2001a) has additional ideas in this direction.

21. This discussion draws substantially on Dees (2001a).

22. The importance of concrete goals is also emphasized by Bacon and Butler (1998, 66).

23. Light (1998, 145) lists several ways that "permission to fail" can be transmitted to the staff, including a lively "New Orleans" funeral for an innovation that died, an awards program for the year's most impossible dream, or even forgiveness coupons and permission slips from the executive director.

Raymond J. Struyk 5

Creating Team Leaders

Team leaders—think tanks' middle managers for research—are second in importance only to the think tanks' presidents. Team leaders, who are called many things in different think tanks—center directors, department heads, division managers—direct groups of researchers ranging from two or three analysts to more than 20 people. In large departments, project directors report to team leaders.[1] As soon as an organization has an analytic staff of as few as 10 persons, teams are usually formed and team leaders are designated—sometimes formally, sometimes informally.[2] Team leaders are mainly responsible for carrying out projects, but other duties include keeping staff productively employed, maintaining a positive work environment, ensuring the high quality of the reports, being active in the policy process, and acquiring new business.

The role of the team leader can be described as having four general elements: To set objectives, manage, and coordinate the team so that it does its best work; to provide resources to the team; to link the team to the rest of the organization; and to be a contributing team member.[3]

Ideally, team leaders at think tanks will possess a formidable array of attributes. They should:

- have solid research and policy skills in order to direct staff and be a leader in the policy development process;
- have the strong interpersonal and leadership skills essential in getting the most out of the team;
- be good project managers; that is, know what volume of resources is needed to carry out a project and how to schedule and organize these resources effectively;

- have strong organizational skills to keep the team fully and productively employed, meet deadlines, and maintain product quality;
- be effective in marketing the team's skills to existing clients; and
- be innovative in assessing the needs of existing and new clients and
  identifying new policy issues and activities for the group to pursue.

It is not surprising that few team leaders excel in all of these areas.
What is surprising is that almost no think tanks have programs for training or mentoring team leaders to ensure that they will be effective. In a
typical situation, a good researcher who seems to be reasonably well
organized, sufficiently affable, and has some taste for marketing is promoted into the team leader position. From that point on it is learning by
doing, with some support from the president or research director if the
new team leader is observed to be struggling. Most team leaders are
eventually able to perform their jobs to a reasonable standard, but a significant share perform marginally—too well to be reassigned and too
poorly to satisfy the needs of their staff and the think tank.

Think tanks can improve the effectiveness of these essential managers
by explicitly working with would-be or new team leaders on a series of
tasks for which they will be responsible. This chapter presents steps that
senior management can take to develop the highly effective team leaders
they need, based on practices in private industry and observations of
successful team leaders.

This chapter differs from the others in that there are no examples of
the current practices of think tanks, even third-stage organizations.
There is essentially nothing to talk about because think tanks have yet to
confront the topic.

The presentation has been organized into two sections. The first briefly
discusses the qualities that senior management should look for in a team
leader and how management can help team leaders do their jobs better.
The second part addresses a series of tasks that team leaders have to carry
out, giving pointers on performing the jobs effectively and efficiently.

RESPONSIBILITIES OF SENIOR MANAGEMENT

The leadership of a think tank is responsible for recruiting team leaders.
In some cases this is easy because there is an obvious candidate already
on staff, usually in the group he or she will direct. But often it is necessary to recruit from outside of the organization. In all cases the candi-

dates should be rigorously judged against a set of explicit criteria. Once the selection is made, there are several actions senior management can take to increase the odds of the new team leader succeeding.

Selecting a Team Leader

The requirements for succeeding as a team leader are demanding. Useful criteria for assessing candidates are listed in table 5-1. These are the generally accepted set of qualifications and cover all the key attributes noted above. The table also shows the relative weights assigned to the various attributes. The values assigned are more subjective than the criteria themselves, and will be explained below. However, the essential point is that senior management should assign weights to this or a similar set of qualifications so that they can agree among themselves in assessing candidates.

The highest weight has been assigned to the substantive knowledge and policy acumen of team leader. Above all, the team leader must be a true expert in the topic for which he or she is leading the team. Without this expertise, the team is likely to do work that is not cutting edge, and will be forced to do too much learning on the job. Thorough knowledge is essential for providing intellectual leadership to the rest of the team.

Table 5-1 Weights Assigned to Desirable Attributes of Team Leaders

Weight Assigned	Attribute
26	*Substantive knowledge*—is extremely familiar with topic area, has years of experience, and has strong understanding of policy
20	*Interpersonal skills*—is a natural leader and mentor; will be a productive participant in management meetings
16	*Initiative and vision*—seeks out opportunities; thinks of ways to strengthen staff; is good at anticipating changes policy priorities and client needs
14	*Well-organized*—plans ahead, keeps close track of and meets commitments and deadlines
12	*Analytic skills*—has command of more sophisticated econometric and other techniques[4]
12	*Growth potential*—is intellectually creative and flexible; appears to have strong management skills
100	Total points

But substantive knowledge is not enough. The candidate must also have proven skills in the relevant policy arena. Anyone who has worked with researchers knows only too well that many researchers have great difficulty making strong connections between their analysis and specific policy questions. Only a minority of researchers develop into strong policy analysts. Hence, the need for the policy skills to be clear already—both in written products and in the candidate's dealings in the policy arena, in other words, in advancing ideas skillfully with government officials, NGOs, and legislators. If possible, the candidate should be someone who is already recognized in the policy community as an expert. Even if the candidate is not yet at such a level, his or her views on policy issues in should be cogent, well founded, and compelling. Policy writings and public presentations offer a good idea of what to expect.

The second greatest weight is assigned to interpersonal skills. This may seem strange in a profession where individual qualities such as technical facility and the ability to make effective presentations are so highly valued. Nevertheless, the justification is clear: A team leader with poor interpersonal skills can reduce the team's productivity and may even destroy a team by causing good people to leave. I know both second- and third-stage think tanks where this has happened within a team before the president decided that there was simply no alternative to reassigning or dismissing a technically competent, policy-effective team leader who made life miserable for subordinates. But a team leader who works well with people can inspire a team to greater productivity and creativity than one might have thought possible.

How can management gather information on the interpersonal skills of candidates for a team leader position? If the candidate is already on the think tank's staff, there should be ample opportunity to make the assessment. Signs of potential problems include the staffer being a loner (i.e., preferring not to work on team projects or not volunteering to help others); being constantly critical, especially if the criticism is done without a clearly constructive purpose; or trying to avoid responsibility for the quality of products or for making presentations.

Outside candidates are harder to judge. There are ways, however, to gather information besides the candidate's interviews with the top people at your think tank. Some possibilities include:

- Ask staff or other experts in the particular field—who are known by staff at your think tank and who have been at conferences and policy working sessions with the candidate—about the candidate's style: Was it cooperative and constructive, competitive, or even destructive?

- Check with people who have worked with the candidate about the candidate's working style and relations with co-workers. It is often difficult to make inquiries of workers where the candidate is currently employed, but experience in earlier positions is also relevant. The best opportunity is if someone within the hiring organization can ask a personal friend at another institution where the candidate has worked.

- Have the candidate interview with two or three people who will be on his or her team. Sometimes candidates will be quite aggressive in these meetings, and other times they send a clear signal of their own superiority. In either case, this is a worrisome sign. Get candid feedback from your staff.

- Invite the candidate to give a seminar on a topic in his or her area of expertise.

The next three attributes listed in the table have been given somewhat smaller weights, but these are nevertheless very important factors to consider. It might seem strange that analytic skills are in this group with smaller weights. But this analysis assumes that all candidates have graduate degrees, equivalent to a Ph.D. from a U.S. university, in one of the social sciences.[5] There may be a large variance in candidates' econometric and other statistical competence, but many think tanks recognize that candidates can be assisted by those with highly specialized statistical skills. The Urban Institute, for example, has an in-house consulting econometrician who can either provide advice on an econometric problem or conduct the needed analysis. Many think tanks can assign staff with the necessary skills to a team for a particular project or bring in a consultant. In short, it is easy to overestimate the technical requirements of the team leader. Although the leader must have an appreciation of which techniques are generally appropriate to address different problems, he or she need not be a specialist.

The discussion thus far has concentrated on the candidate's demonstrated qualities. But the potential for growth is often as important as the record to date, especially for younger candidates for the team leader position. What can one look for as signs of this potential? This is subjective and tricky to judge in practice. Table 5-2 lists standards for judging

Table 5-2 Standards for Judging Potential

Substantial Leadership Potential	Limited Leadership Potential
• Exhibits broad and deep range of operating, technical, and professional skills • Exhibits sound managerial skills • Demonstrates leadership skills consistent with the team leader position • Regularly works at developing new skills and abilities • Aspires to higher-level challenges and opportunities • Demonstrates high interest and energy in the institute's work • Is oriented to the success of the whole institute, not just this team	• On balance, exhibits operating, technical, and professional skills that are acceptable for current level • Demonstrates little effort to build new skills but keeps current skills sharp • Aspires to stay with the institute, but does not demonstrate much interest in assuming larger challenges • Is motivated to do what is needed in the current job • Understands the current job • Is focussed primarily on technical success

Source: Based on Charan, Drotter, and Noel (2001, exhibit 10.1).

potential compiled for for-profit firms (Charan, Drotter, and Noel 2001). The left-hand column lists attributes for persons with substantial potential, while the right-hand column lists those for a person who is likely to develop only to a limited degree in his or her current position.

These standards should give managers a good idea of a candidate's potential. Clearly, it will be easier to apply them to internal candidates than to external candidates. For internal candidates the results of past performance assessments and discussions with their raters are important inputs.[6] But even candidates outside the organization can be asked a series of questions about their interest in management, as well as about their skills. Candidates might be asked, for example, how they would handle certain tasks, such as planning the work of the team, thinking about new directions for the team's work, or delegating responsibility for certain jobs.

In the end, the decision about who to name as a team leader depends on both the demonstrated skills (as defined in table 5-1) and the candidate's potential for growth and development. In comparing alternative candidates it is useful for two or three leaders at the institute to carry out an explicit rating of each candidate, using the same set of factors. The group should then discuss their ratings and explore the reasons for differences. While nothing eliminates the risk of making a poor choice, such group reviews have proven effective.

Supporting the Team Leader[7]

Making the transition from being a productive policy analyst to being a team manager entails a sharp change in thinking. Most people want to continue doing the things they are good at and that they enjoy. But the new team leader must learn to reallocate his or her time—shifting it away from research and toward management tasks. This is often very difficult for first-time managers, who are being asked to devote less energy to the very work that has made them successful to date. They must also learn to delegate responsibility, rather than trying to do too much themselves. Table 5-3 outlines more systematically the range of changes in the skills, time allocation, and work values inherent in moving from being an individual contributor to being a team leader.

Given the major changes involved in becoming the new team leader, support from the think tank's leadership is important. Timely help with taking up the new duties can save an enormous amount of frustration on all sides. This section briefly outlines how senior managers can facilitate the transition to the team leader position.

Define the Job Carefully

A typical real-life scenario is for a staff member to be a policy analyst one day and a team leader the next. The think tank's president may meet with the team to make the announcement and outline the team's work program and prospects for the coming months. But the new team leader will have little in the way of a detailed understanding of the new responsibilities—the specific tasks he or she must carry out. Many think tanks do not have a written job description; where such descriptions exist, they tend to be quite general. The new team leader is expected to know what to do from having watched other team leaders in the past.

The president or second-in-command can help the new team leader by providing a written job description and a supplementary list of concrete tasks that are the team leader's responsibilities. The task list should specify how often each task needs to be done. Such tasks might include preparation of quarterly projections of staff coverage under existing and

Table 5-3 Work Program Changes Inherent in Moving from Team Member to Team Leader

Team Member	Team Leader
Skills	
• Tech ical or professional proficiency • Team play • Relationship-building for personal benefits, personal results* • Using company tools, processes, and procedures	• Planning—projects, budget, team • Job design • Selection of team members • Delegation • Performance monitoring • Coaching and feedback • Rewards and motivation • Communication and climate setting • Relationship building up and down and with clients for team's benefit • Business acquisition
Time Allocation	
• Daily discipline • Meet personal due dates for projects—usually short-term management over time	• Annual and monthly planning— budgets, projects • Make time available for subordinates— both at team leader's own request and theirs • Set priorities for team • Communication time with other parts of organization and clients
Work Values	
• Getting results through personal proficiency • Producing high-quality professional work • Accept the institution's values	• Getting results through others • Success of team members • Managerial work and disciplines • Success of unit • Self as manager • Visible integrity

* Items to be sharply reduced when person becomes manager.
Source: Table 2.1 in Charan, Drotter, and Noel (2001).

expected grants and contracts, monthly activity reports due to certain clients, quality control for reports produced, and monthly travel schedules for members of the team.

Beyond this, the senior management should be clear about the expectations for the team. Marketing and revenue generation by the team is certainly one topic. A useful context for the revenue target is the monthly billings required to maintain the team at its present size. Another topic could be the president's ideas about the future direction of the team's work—which will directly affect the team leader's marketing and hiring activities.

Being clear about the tasks for which the team leader is responsible has at least two advantages. First, it keeps the new team leader from constantly being surprised by new requirements. Such unexpected additional duties can be particularly disruptive if the team leader carefully allocates his or her time. Second, such clarity gives the president and the team leader a common understanding about a core set of activities for which the team leader is responsible, establishing one basis for monitoring the team leader's performance.

How to Help

Senior management needs to monitor the team leader's performance carefully during the first six to twelve months and to provide regular feedback and coaching to help make the team leader make the transition.

Monitoring Performance

Management can use an array of documents to monitor the team's activity: time sheets to check the allocation of time charged by the team and the team leader; staff coverage projections; project-associated travel records; and peer reviews of the team's products. In addition, discussions with the team leader can be used to determine how the team leader is using team staff (changes in specialization, travel patterns) and whether he or she is marketing the team's and the organization's services in an effective way. Equally important is feedback from team members on working relations, the atmosphere within the team, the team's productivity, and their reactions to the team leader's style. Obtaining client feedback is also key.

What kinds of problems may be encountered? They fall into two groups: those indicated by the outputs of the team and those more directly associated with the team leader's style. Examples of these are listed in table 5-4. These two types of problems differ sharply in the ease with which they are identified and addressed.

Problems with the team's results are clear red flags—the think tank's very integrity is at stake. Such problems require immediate attention. In

Table 5-4 Examples of Problems Team Leaders Can Experience

Problems with the Team's Results
- Projects are not completed on time and/or within budget
- Quality control problems
- Poor forward planning means that team members are under- or over-employed
- Marketing results are weak

Unproductive Behaviors from the Team Leader
- Unfairly capitalizes on his or her personal authority to abuse people.
- Overvalues his or her capabilities, has trouble accepting other's views, comes across as arrogant.
- Distrusts others, micromanages, delegates poorly.
- Operates alone and communicates strategies poorly.
- Is enthusiastic one day and indifferent the next.
- Is eager to please and unwilling to challenge authority to support team members.
- Is unwilling to try new things to keep up with changing trends.
- Obsesses about details, is carried away with rules and procedures, and is inflexible.
- Appears to support decisions and then does what he or she wants afterward. Disregards requests with no explanation.

Source: Some of the examples in the lower panel are from Dotlich and Cairo (1999, 96).

principle, management should identify most of the problems easily, with the possible exception of those with quality control: If all of the peer reviewers are drawn from within the team and the team leader does not take an active interest in this process, then the research product problems could go unnoticed for some time—until a client complains or an outside analyst criticizes a report. With the exception of the marketing problem, this set of problems can be handled in fairly straightforward ways, mainly by improving the organization of the work. Senior management can give pointers on how to do this and perhaps suggest the team leader enlist a team member to help keep track of schedules for accomplishing various tasks.

Unproductive behaviors, on the other hand, are more difficult to identify and to address. They may be harder for management to discover because they could be confined within the team. Once identified, such problems may resist easy correction, because they often have to do with the team leader's basic attitudes and personality attributes rather than insufficient vigilance or energy in carrying out the basic research management functions.

Charan, Drotter, and Noel (2001) suggest several ways for senior management to gain insights into the success of the new team leader's transition from being a "contributor " to being a manager and leader. Three techniques in particular look promising for the situation at hand.

- *Understand how the team leader is allocating his or her time.* The allocation of time offers a good window on understanding the value the team leader places on different activities. There should be significant time devoted to planning, discussions with individual staff members and the team as a whole, and marketing. Compared with team members, team leaders should spend less time should on direct research and report writing.
- *Listen carefully to how managers evaluate subordinates.* Excessive negative comments on staff members or fixation on a single performance dimension are both reason for concerns.
- *Look at plans that team leaders develop (in written or verbal form) from a values standpoint.* Plans often tell where the manager is placing his or her greatest value. It may be that too much of the team's time is being devoted to research and analysis—the topics of greatest interest to the team leader—and too little to marketing and coaching of team members. The quality of the plan is also important. A muddled plan signals poor thinking or a low value on planning in general, both cause for concern.

Once a significant problem is identified, how can senior management help?

Start with the Boss, Not the Team Leader

When a problem is detected, senior management should first examine its own actions with respect to the team to be certain that it is not contributing to the problem. For example, have senior managers

- micro-managed the team leader, sending the signal that they are handling scheduling and planning and that the leader has little space to try innovations in running the team?
- done a poor job of communicating expectations for the team or shifts in the direction of the think tank?

- provided inadequate resources to the team and hence undermined its ability to complete projects on time?
- bypassed the team leader to give assignments to individual team members, thereby undermining the leader's authority and reducing the resources available to carry out the research and analysis?

Self-awareness on the part of the senior managers will prevent them from unintentionally undercutting and discouraging the team leader, and may prevent conflict between them and the team leader.

Coaching

Almost inevitably, the new team leader will make mistakes. Proper monitoring permits identifying missteps before they lead to serious problems. There is no substitute for one-on-one coaching from the new team leader's boss. "Coaching is personal help given to develop skills and improve a person's way of working. It is a highly practical activity concerned with today's task, not a future job " (Leigh and Maynard 1995, 141). The literature on coaching outlines a general process for a coach (e.g., one of the think tank's top people) to work with a "client " (the team leader) once a problem is evident. This process has been organized into four steps, and appears in the appendix to this chapter so it can serve as a general resource on coaching.

The old saw that leaders are made, not born, sums up the discussion presented here. Most think tank directors have learned this lesson over time. Developing an efficient, reliable team leader usually requires a significant up-front investment in the kind of activities outlined above. Although expensive, such investment typically carries a high rate of return.

TEAM LEADER TASKS

This section provides pointers to team managers on executing some of their tasks. The tasks have been divided into three groups: planning and controlling staff utilization, project execution, and staff productivity.

Planning for and Controlling Staff Use

For a typical research or technical assistance project executed by think tanks, the great majority of costs are for staff inputs. Leaving aside overhead costs, which are mostly loaded on the hourly wage of staff executing the projects, staff costs often exceed 70 percent of total costs. It follows that controlling staff inputs is the key for keeping projects within budget. Similarly, making certain that work is available for team members in the months ahead is the most important element in ensuring that the team can continue to work at its current level. This section briefly reviews ways for team leaders to track staff utilization during project execution and to assess future team coverage.

Tracking Utilization

The first step to controlling time charges to a project is for the team leader to prepare a careful plan for executing the project that budgets specific time allocations for each person who is to work on the project. Equally important, a task the person is to do and the amount of time available must be clearly communicated to each staff member. Thereafter, control is a matter of monitoring staff time charges and comparing them with progress with the work on the task.

As simple as this sounds, projects at many think tanks, including third-stage institutions, regularly get into trouble because of poor monitoring of staff time. The result can be large cost overruns that are damaging, sometimes severely, to the think tank's financial health.

Monitoring time charges is more effective than tracking total expenditures, although both are important. Total expenditures are harder to track because there is generally a time lag between when costs are incurred and when they are posted by the accountants and the cost reports generated. Time charges, on the other hand, can be recorded as soon as time sheets are submitted.

If managers do not track time expenditures against budgets, staff who find themselves unable to fulfill their assignment in the allocated time—or perhaps have no other project to which to charge time—may simply continue to charge time to a project. (This assumes that the staffer is aware that he or she is exceeding the budgeted time allocation, which is certainly not always the case.) Because of such lapses, team leaders and senior managers should have a system for routinely monitoring staff time charges by project.

Tables 5-5 and 5-6 illustrate the time management system at the Institute for Urban Economics. Each table is an excerpt from a larger monthly report. The report illustrated in table 5-5 is organized by project

Table 5-5 Control Table for Staff Time Charges: Project Based*

Employee	Project	Total Hours Spent	Hours Spent Last Month	Hours in the Budget	Balance
Gasyak, Vladimir	10468-702-04	4	4	346	342
Gofman, Dima	10468-702-04	448	32	778	330
Khamova, Lena	10468-702-04	145	7	346	201
Molchanov, Andrei	10468-702-04	88	0	259	171
Puzanov, Sasha	10468-702-04	60	0	86	26
Rumiantsev, Igor	10468-702-04	366	32	518	152
Sedova, Lena	10468-702-04	89	4	173	84
Tolstova, Ira	10468-702-04	11	0	173	162
Zadonsky, Georgy	10468-702-04	596	24	1123	527
Total	**10468-702-04**	**1,807**	**103**	**3,802**	**1,995**
Anopochkin, Volodia	50039-000-00	76	10	90	14
Belozerskaya, Lena	50039-000-00	56	2	192	136
Elagina, Elena	50039-000-00	456	88	2079	1623
Golenkova, Galina	50039-000-00	4	2	96	92
Levina, Liza	50039-000-00	16	4	96	80
Makhova, Lena	50039-000-00	30	15	96	66
Tolstova, Ira	50039-000-00	18	10	48	30
Yashanin, Victor	50039-000-00	20	5	96	76
Zykova, Tatiana	50039-000-00	48	8	192	144
Total	**50039-000-00**	**724**	**144**	**2,985**	**2,261**

*Table excerpt from the Institute for Urban Economics, for August 2000.

number (column 3), and shows the hours charged for everyone who has charged time to the project. The project-based report is for team leaders and management to use in assessing time utilization for a particular project. The report excerpted in table 5-6, on the other hand, is organized by staff member, showing the time charged to each project to which a staff member is budgeted to charge time or has otherwise charged time. The final line for each staff member shows the totals for all projects to which this person can charge time. It is intended to help staff keep track of their time, and the finance office uses it to do a final control of time charges at the end of the month. In principle, every hour charged by a staff member should be shown in the amount of time budgeted for that person appearing in this report.

Table 5-6 Control Table for Staff Time Charges: Staff-Based*

Employee	Project	Total Hours Spent	Hours Spent Last Month	Hours in the Budget	Balance
Khakhalin, Andrei	10468-501-00	48	0	86	38
	10468-503-00	176	28	346	170
	10468-505-01	732	40	950	218
	10468-703-04	40	8	69	29
	10468-802-04	64	32	69	5
	10468-807-04	223	16	864	641
	20279-000-00	40	16	40	0
	50029-000-00	209	16	208	−1
	OVH-019-10	16	8	16	0
	OVH-019-23	8	4	8	0
Total		**1,556**	**168**	**2,656**	**1,100**
Kutakova, Tatiana	10468-300-00	242	22	259	17
	10468-300-01	1304	96	1382	78
	10468-704-04	48	24	173	125
	20019-000-00	4	4	4	0
	20069-000-00	136	16	136	0
	20279-000-00	24	0	40	16
	OVH-018-30	8	4	12	4
	OVH-019-01	8	2	4	−4
Total		**1,774**	**168**	**2,010**	**236**

*Table excerpt from the Institute for Urban Economics, for August 2000.

Look at the reports more carefully. Both reports are for use in August 2000. The budget column shows the number of hours allocated to a staff member to charge to a project. Normally, this would come from the budget prepared to determine the cost of executing the project. The column labeled "New Total" shows the number of hours used through April. The column labeled Balance shows the hours remaining for the staff member to use. So, in table 5-6, the first row for Andrei Khakhalin shows that he was initially allocated 86 hours for project 10478-501-00, has used 48 hours through July, and has 38 hours remaining to charge to the project. If the team leader changes the allocation of time among staff working on the project, he or she informs the staff person responsible for maintaining these records.

The system is straightforward and eliminates uncertainty. It is updated monthly on the basis of the previous month's time sheets. It is certainly not necessary for a think tank to have computer-prepared reports such as those shown, but team leaders do need to keep some form of records to avoid overrunning project budgets.

Forward Planning

Planning for future staff use is just as important as controlling staff utilization on current projects. Neglecting this kind of planning can result in several kinds of problems.

Insufficient Attention to Marketing

Where there are looming shortfalls in staff coverage, the team should be especially active in generating new projects. If the team leader is not aware of the impending fall-off in work, a serious coverage problem is likely to ensue, possibly requiring some staff to be put on part-time work or even let go.

Overbooking

At the opposite extreme, the team leader may accept too many assignments. While this is a happier situation than coverage problems, it generates its own strains. Most obvious is the pressure on staff to work exceptionally hard to meet all of the contract or grant requirements. There are significant possibilities of drops in quality under such stressful work conditions.

Selective Overbooking

In some cases, one or two key team members are overcommitted. It will usually be possible to substitute other staff for the key people to some degree, but there are definite limits. Consistent overbooking of key staff may force them to look for work in a less stressful environment.

Senior management would be unhappy to learn that a team leader had encountered any of these situations through negligent planning. Some think tanks use an explicit projection process to help team leaders do their forward planning. Table 5-7 shows a composite form based used those

Table 5-7 Example of Forward Planning Staff Chart

Staff person name: Richard Jones
Department: Local government
For the period from: April 1, 2001 to July 1, 2001
Completed by: Andrei Suchkov

Project Name	Project Number	Month 1	2	3	Total Days
Ongoing projects					
Legislation on nonprofits	00127-00	10	8	2	20
Loc Gov housing TA	00136-00	9	9	9	27
Subtotal		19	17	11	47
Projected projects					
TA to NGO service deliver		—	8	8	16
Proposal preparation		3	5	—	8
Asst to MinFinance	OV	2	—	—	2
Subtotal		5	13	8	26
Totals					
Actual/projected work		24	30	19	73
Work days in month		21	19	20	60

used by several think tanks. The form is completed for each staff member for the next three months. The top part of the form shows coverage on projects currently being executed. The lower portion is for prospective projects, usually those for which proposals are outstanding. Based on past experience with the client or on discussions with the client about this particular proposal, the team leader may be able to assign a probability to various grants or contracts being won and adjust the projected coverage accordingly.[8] Summing the staff person's coverage over the current and expected projects provides the team leader with a realistic assessment of the coverage situation for each staff member for the next three months.

Table 5-7 shows that the staff member, Richard Jones, has very good coverage for the first three months, beginning in April 2001. Indeed, for the first two months Mr. Jones is overcommitted. His workload is particularly acute in May, when he will have 11 more days committed than work days, should the team in fact win the contact to provide technical assistance to NGO service deliverers. The team leader should use this information to consider who else on the team could work on one of Mr. Jones's projects, should all commitments remain in force. The team leader might also consider trying to get the client's permission to delay some of the deliverables.

Who should complete this form? Experience shows that individual staff members often lack realistic information on proposed projects. Frequently they are not involved in preparing the proposal nor in discussions about the likelihood of winning. So they are not in a good position to complete the lower part of the form. This usually leads to inflated estimates of coverage. It is generally easier for the team leader to complete the forms for all team members. Projections should be done at least every calendar quarter. In a particularly dynamic environment, where new proposals are being regularly submitted and the results of others are being announced, more frequent updating is necessary for the team leader to have a realistic view of the situation.

Project Execution

The five tasks essential to project execution are listed in table 5-8. The cycle begins with defining the policy objective—which may or may not be well-articulated in the research or technical assistance contract—and the corresponding communications strategy (i.e., identifying the primary policy client and how best to deliver the results effectively to this person or group). Of these five tasks, this section focuses on the third—project scheduling—the task with which a new team leader probably has the least experience.

Scheduling the project is the organization in time of resource inputs into the project. Scheduling staff input is critical: The team leader seeks both to not waste resources by having researchers be underemployed during some periods and to insure against delays that arise because too few staff are available to work on the project at critical points. In addition, major events, such as surveys, seminars, and report submission dates, must be scheduled.

Elaborate project management regimes, now mostly computerized, are used in the construction industry, for example, to schedule subcontractors, labor, and the arrival of materials on the job site. These systems are far more elaborate than is needed for nearly all research, evaluation, and technical assistance projects. But preparing simple charts and corresponding milestones is very useful for guiding projects.

Table 5-8 Five Steps of Project Execution

1. **Define the policy objectives and the corresponding communications strategy.**
   Prepare a clear statement of the policy question(s) being addressed, identify the persons or organizations with the greatest interest in the issue and who are therefore those most willing to be the "champion for change," and define a communications strategy for reaching them. Compare this to the explicit requirements of the contract or grant, and reconcile differences as needed.

2. **Define the analytic approach.**
   In a research project, this includes explicitly stating the relevant hypotheses, determining the source of data for testing the hypotheses, and defining the analysis to be done. For a technical assistance project, tasks include working with the client to define the reforms needed to accomplish the objective; identifying needed legal changes, if any; choosing the approach to execution—training and/or pilot projects; and assessing results.

3. **Project scheduling.**
   Outline the time line for the project and the corresponding milestones. Determine who will be working on the project at what points. Schedule travel, training events, seminars, and all reports.

4. **Quality control.**
   Schedule start-up, mid-term, or end-of-project seminars as needed. Identify a peer reviewer and allow time in the schedule for the review.

5. **Communication of the results.**
   Transmit results both to the client and to the primary policy audience (if these are different and if the contract permits disclosure of results to someone other than the client).

Charts 5-1 and 5-2 give an example of simple charts. They were prepared by the Urban Institute for a training project in Poland. The project called for the contractor to prepare case studies to be used in the training; organize all aspects of the training, including hiring and briefing qualified local trainers; and deliver the training in multiple sites in two principal phases, with follow-up training to the main training in each phase. The project was on a compressed seven-month time frame, requiring a comparatively large contingent of trainers.

Chart 5-1 shows the timing of the execution of each of the 12 tasks (top panel) and the schedule of report completion and submission (lower panel). Chart 5-2 then shows the corresponding staff inputs. In this fairly simple project, the trainers and managers are engaged full-time when they are working on the project. So the scheduling is simple

Chart 5-1 Activity Schedule

	Months from Project Inception						
A. Field Investigation and Study Items	*1st*	*2nd*	*3rd*	*4th*	*5th*	*6th*	*7th*
Activity (Work)							
Task 1. Project Start-Up	▓	▓					
Task 2. Needs Assessment/ Final Work Program	▓	▓					
Task 3. Selection of Training Participants	▓	▓					
Task 4. Venue Selection	▓	▓					
Task 5. Training Material Preparation	▓	▓					
Task 6. Team Training		█					
Task 7. Case Study Preparation	▓	▓	▓	▓			
Task 8. Phase 1 Training			█	█			
Task 9. Phase 2 Training					█		█
Task 10. Training Follow-Up			▓	▓	▓	▓	▓
Task 11. Study Tour						█	
Task 12. Training Evaluation			▓	▓	▓	▓	▓
B. Report Completion and Submission							
1. Needs Assessment/Final Work Program (Task 2)		X					
2. Workshop Evaluation Form (Tasks 8 and 9)		X					
3. Phase 1 and Draft Phase 2 Training Materials (Tasks 8 and 9)		X					
4. Phase 2 Training Materials (Final) (Task 9)				X			

Chart 5-1 Activity Schedule (*Continued*)

	Months from Project Inception						
	1st	2nd	3rd	4th	5th	6th	7th
5. Case Studies (Task 7)	X	X	X	X			
6. List of Study Tour Participants (Task 11)					X		
7. Evaluation Report (Task 12)							X

■■■ Indicates full-time activity
▨▨▨ Indicates part-time activity

relative to the situation where staff are working part-time over an extended period. When staff are scheduled to work on a part-time basis over multiple weeks, team leaders should conduct more detailed planning with each staff member as their time is needed.

Simple charts of this type easy to construct and update. They are an invaluable tool for team leaders in organizing their teams' work, especially when multiple projects are being executed simultaneously.

Maximizing Team Productivity

New team leaders face a number of concerns. The promotion is certainly welcome but it comes with challenges, especially for someone promoted internally. Often the biggest worry is how to handle the people who were previously the team leader's peers or friends. How they will respond to the new leader as an authority figure is an open question and depends critically on the team leader's conduct.[9] The challenge is to exert authority while enhancing the self-esteem of each member of the team.

Teamwork has two dimensions: task and social. The task element concerns the work the team is to do: to gather and analyze data, prepare reports, prepare and deliver seminars, or, in the case of technical assistance projects work with local officials or NGOs, implement pioneering projects. The social dimension concerns how team members feel toward each other and their membership in the team (Rees 1999). The team leader must be equally concerned with both dimensions. If the social dimension is neglected the team's productivity in executing its tasks may be impaired, perhaps severely.

Chart 5-2 Time Schedule for Professional Personnel

Name	Position	Reports Due/ Activities	Months (in the Form of a Bar Chart) 1–7	Number of Days
K. Alison	Trainer	Training		37
M. Borkowska	Trainer; Environmental/ Economics	Training		85
T. Driscoll	Trainer; Water	Training		35
D. Edwards	Trainer	Training		35
A. Eymontt	Trainer; Environmental	Training		85
B. Ferrone	Trainer; Roads/ Schools	Training		35
G. Frelick	Trainer	Training		45
A. Grzybek	Trainer; Economics/ Energy	Training		85
A. Law	Trainer; Procurement	Training		35
M. Lebkowski	Trainer; Finance	Training		85
R. Marcola	Trainer; Finance	Training		85
B. Markiel	Trainer; Environmental	Training		85
R. Milaszewski	Trainer; Water/ Economics	Training		85
G. Mikeska	Trainer; Project Manager	Training, Mgmt.		79
A. Muzalewski	Trainer; Economics/ Waste	Training		85

Chart 5-2 Time Schedule for Professional Personnel (*Continued*)

Name	Position	Reports Due/ Activities	Months (in the Form of a Bar Chart)							Number of Days
			1	2	3	4	5	6	7	
A. Pecikiewicz	Trainer; Project Manager	Training, Mgmt.	▓	▓	▓	▓	▓	▓		140
J. Pigey	Trainer	Training		█			█			35
F. Rosensweig	Trainer	Training, Mgmt.	█							27
B. Ruszkowska	Trainer; Environmental	Training		▓	▓	▓	▓			85
D. Wallgren	Trainer; Solid Waste	Training		█			█			35
T. Wojcicki	Trainer; Finance/Roads	Training		▓	▓	▓	▓			85

█ Indicates international trainers
▓ Indicates local trainers
Full-time: Pecikiewicz and Rozwadowska (all others are part-time)
Reports Due: End of project
Activities Duration: 7 months

This section first discusses the current context for being a team leader—the changing relation among bosses and workers that is occurring around the world. Thereafter, the section addresses how team leaders can handle four specific issues that are key to their overall performance.

Changing Workplace, Changing Leadership Styles

Many organizations have evolved from places where staff were generally told what to do to places where employees are involved in figuring out and deciding how best to accomplish key tasks. The change is especially noticeable in the knowledge industries, where well-educated workers are demanding an alternative to the authoritarian leadership style common in the West until 15 or 20 years ago. Nevertheless, in Eastern Europe, the Commonwealth of Independent States, most of Africa, and much of Asia, authoritarian leadership styles are often found.

Table 5-9 Characteristics of Alternative Leadership Styles

Controlling Style	Facilitating Style
• Tells • Sells • Directs • Decides • Solves problems • Sets goals • Uses authority to get things done	• Listens • Asks questions • Directs group process • Coaches • Teaches • Builds consensus • Shares in goal-setting • Shares in decisionmaking • Empowers others to get things done

Source: Rees (1999, 55).

Table 5-9 highlights the differences between the traditional leadership style and the more facilitating role being adopted by progressive organizations. There is a striking contrast between the controlling style, in which strong direction and problem solving by the leader are central, and the more open, consultative, and thoughtful process, in which responsibility is more widely shared.

The reason firms have pushed managers to change their style is straightforward: More inclusive and consultative styles result in greater staff productivity and longer staff retention. Workers in such organizations contribute more by making suggestions on how to do things, are happier in their work, and are more willing to accept additional responsibility and to work longer and harder.[10]

But the basic tasks of a manager have not changed: They remain the four listed at the beginning of the chapter. It should also be stressed that a facilitating manager does not give up the ultimate responsibility for making decisions. In other words, compared with a traditional leader, a facilitating team leader consults more with team members, allowing them to provide information and interpretations; but the team leader still reserves the right to make the final decision.

Developing a team that is substantially "self-managing" can be challenging. In countries and organizations where a facilitating style is novel, team leaders may find it hard to solicit the kind of input and cooperation they are seeking and that is needed for this management style to be truly effective. The best advice is to take it a step at a time. Leaders can encourage participation by asking for opinions and ideas and by being good listeners; more responsibility can be assigned downward. Over time, what seems a new style will become routine and staff are likely to participate more fully.

Experience suggest that there are several signs the team leader can look for to confirm that the leadership style outlined above (and discussed further below) is working, that a positive team spirit is emerging.[11] Three have particular application to the research and analysis teams and teams implementing technical assistance projects at think tanks.

- *Supportive relationships.* Staff help each other in various ways. This includes sharing information and other resources as well as directly assisting in completion of a task, such as volunteering to read a draft report.
- *Personal investment.* Team members "take ownership" of the team's work. They feel directly responsible for the quality of the work and are willing to go beyond the routine work effort to achieve the team's goals.
- *Permissive encouragement.* Team members generally react positively to new ideas advanced by their peers on how to do the work or proposals for new areas of work. It is "yes" rather than a "no" culture; jealousy over who has the ideas tends to be minimized.

A team exhibiting these characteristics will be effective in its work and rewarding to the team members as a place to work.

Goal Setting

Experts on team management stress the importance of teams having articulated goals that transcend the completion of project-specific tasks.[12] The goals usually provide a unifying theme for the project-based work and help orient the day-to-day work of the team, and can be very important in generating the kind of team cohesiveness described above. Cleverly set goals can provide a greater meaning to successfully executing individual projects, as staff see completion of each project as building something more important. In short, goals make more concrete the general vision that guides a team's work, and can even inspire a team's efforts. A vision is the grand picture, what the team aspires to. Goals are steps to achieving the vision.

An example will illustrate these ideas. In the late 1990s, the guiding vision of the International Activity Center at the Urban Institute was for the group to be the most effective provider of technical assistance and policy advice on issues of local governance, finance and social assistance to transitional economies.

In developing a strategy to realize this vision, the Center understood that it had to accomplish several tasks which it set as goals. One such goal was to develop the capacity to win contracts to work with national and local governments in transition economies on key issues, including improving intergovernmental fiscal relations, strengthening the capacity of local governments as fiscal managers and designers and deliverers of services to their citizens, and improving the transparency of government operations and the responsiveness of local governments to their citizens.

It was clear, however, to realize this goal another goal had also to be achieved: The group had to develop working partnerships with local think tanks with whom to compete on projects and execute projects under contract. The partnership of the Urban Institute and a local think tank would be efficient because of the combined local and international expertise, and it would be competitive because of the blending of the cost structures of the two organizations. But in addition, partnering is good in itself, because it increases the capacity of local institutions to work with local governments in the future.

To achieve this goal, the Institute worked to establish and maintain the Transition Policy Network of think tanks in Eastern Europe and the Commonwealth of Independent States. In 2001, the Network consisted of nine think tanks in the region—one in each of nine countries—plus the Urban Institute.[13]

To be useful on a practical level, these goals had to be made operational. Progress on the first goal was measured by the share of contracts for working with local governments for which the team had competed that the team had won. For the second goal, targets were set for establishing partnerships in a specific number of countries over a two year period.

In this example, a vision and goals give an overlying structure to everyday activities. The leaders of most think tanks do have implicit visions and goals, but it is important for the staff to share them. Moreover, the institution-level goals are often not sufficient to motivate or guide individual teams. For this reason, it is important for team leaders to work with their teams to define goals from time to time. By making it a cooperative exercise, leaders make it more likely that team members will understand the goals, buy into them, and be more dedicated to achieving them. The more specifically the goals are defined, the better.

In practice, not many team leaders at think tanks explicitly define goals. Team leaders will communicate their implicit vision and goals in various ways, but often with a significant degree of ambiguity. It is far better to make the effort to be clear and to motivate a team by making the goal-setting a participatory event.

Guiding Team Meetings

Gatherings of a team can be opportunities for improving productivity, sharing information, increasing knowledge, and strengthening coordination and teamwork. In short, team meetings constitute an important management tool. In reality, most team leaders meet too infrequently with their teams; when meetings are held, they are frequently unproductive. Indeed, the lack of productivity probably explains the infrequency of the meetings.

Rees (1999, 126-27) describes four prototypical types of meetings.

- *"Tell 'Em, Sell 'Em" Style.* At such meetings the leader comes prepared to inform team members of decisions already made. To be certain, there are explanations and discussion, but the purposes are to inform and to solicit support.
- *Information-Dissemination Style.* The team leader uses the meeting to inform everyone of what is happening in the department and in the larger organization. There may be reports, prepared in advance or spontaneous, from team members. Often, issues of all sorts can be raised at such sessions, but they are seldom discussed in much depth or resolved.
- *Participative, "Free-For-All" Style.* These loosely run events give participants plenty of time to contribute and discuss topics tabled. However, little progress is made on resolving issues or making decisions, because the team leader does not have the skill to guide the discussion to closure or does not want to. Frustration is common among those seeking clear direction. A prime cause for the lack of closure is the absence of a clear agenda for the meeting. This kind of meeting provides active interaction, but to no particular end.
- *Focused, Participative Style.* The meeting is focused, since its objectives are decided upon at the start of the event. While participation is encouraged, the team leader keeps the discussion focused on

resolving the issues on the agenda. The meeting may wander off on to other topics from time to time, but the team leader is able to bring it back to the agenda and concentrate on reaching the objectives. At the same time, it is essential for the team leader to draw people out and get their opinions in order to generate support for the conclusions reached. Sufficient time must be allowed for thorough discussion.

Clearly, the final model is the one that team leaders should strive to deliver. Possibly the single most important factor driving the success of a team meeting is having a thoughtfully developed agenda. The discipline of preparing an agenda will make the team leader check that the meeting is really needed and to consider who should attend it. The agenda should be written, even if it is fairly skeletal, and it should be shaped as a series of action items to the extent possible. Use of action verbs—*plan, develop, decide, determine, identify, recommend, list, prioritize, solve, generate*—to describe agenda items conveys a sense of purpose in addressing each item.

The actual conduct of the meeting is important. After presenting the agenda, the team leader should ask for other agenda items and, as appropriate, add them or not. The leader may suggest, for example, that a proposed item is likely to require more time to discuss than will be available at this meeting and that a separate meeting at a later date should be devoted to this topic.

As stressed in a previous section, the team leader must draw out contributions from the staff, both because staff members often have valuable views on the topic being consider and because consulting the staff will make them more motivated to implement the result. The team leader needs to be a good listener, ask follow-up questions, promote discussion among the team, summarize or rephrase arguments, and guide the discussion to closure at the right time.

Reporting and information-sharing are important elements in many meetings. The challenge is to focus the contributions from team members so as to be maximally useful to the team as a whole. The team leader should make clear that reports on project activity should not merely convey information (e.g., "We have done this kind of analysis and the results are . . ."). Rather, presenters should be challenged to concentrate on the lessons from the analysis that are most likely to be useful to other team members. What are the general points?

Consider two options for presenting findings from field work. Take, for example, a team that focuses on providing technical assistance to local governments. Two analysts working with a municipality find that the administration with whom they are working has decided to bid out contracts for the delivery of certain social services instead of having municipal agencies be the single (monopolistic) delivery agency. Clearly, this would be a major development about which the whole team should be informed. It is an innovation that the team may want to consider promoting with other cities. Phrased in this way, the topic is of strong interest to the team. Had the work been described as a series of meetings with various officials on the general topic of delivering social services, with the innovation glossed over, it would not have been the least bit engaging.

At the end of the meeting, the team leader should review the conclusions reached. This is essential. But it is equally important to follow up this statement of findings with a short written statement of conclusions— a page is sufficient. The written statement reinforces the message from the meeting, creates a clear record of the decisions made, and informs those not at the meeting of the major results. A series of bullet points, which would take only minutes to prepare, is all that is necessary. Unfortunately, few team leaders or senior managers follow this practice, often leading to confusion about exactly what was decided at previous meetings.

People Issues

Leaders can get the best from a team when the team is positively motivated by its mission and objectives and is pulling together. Achieving and maintaining this happy state is no accident. Table 5-10 lists a series of steps that a team leader can take to demonstrate the value of each person's contribution to the team. Putting the rules on this list into action will go a long way to minimizing personnel problems within the team.

Nevertheless, team leaders must be vigilant in watching for morale problems among team members. Common personnel problems (real or perceived) that can undermine a team's cohesion and productivity include

- Grievances between team members;
- Feelings of powerlessness;
- Insufficient information-sharing;

**Table 5-10 How Team Leaders Can Show that They Value Each Person
in a Team**

Provide members a worthwhile role by
- Giving people meaningful tasks
- Confirming that what they do really matters
- Delegating fully

Recognize members' efforts by
- Showing appreciation when people try hard
- Regularly thanking people for their contributions
- Acknowledging people's successes

Listen to members carefully by
- Giving full attention through active listening
- Using responses that show the leader has listened
- Encouraging people to say what they think

Show members respect by
- Treating each person as important
- Accepting that each person has a point of view
- Not impugning a person's motives

Discover how people are feeling by
- Seeking a personal response
- Asking for their instinctive reactions
- Paying attention to emotions

Express concern about their welfare by
- Showing that the leader cares if people have problems
- Offering help in difficult times
- Asking how they are getting on

Ensure employees' work is valued by others by
- Telling others what the person has done
- Offering public praise and recognition

Source: Based on Leigh and Maynard (1995, 121).

- Dissatisfaction with the allocation of work;
- Competitive behavior;
- Anger at decisions;
- Failure to receive support;
- Frustration about some past incident; or
- Resentment at a lack of appreciation or recognition.

In many instances these problems will be amply evident to a team leader. Obviously, the problem must be discussed with the person(s) involved and a solution found. Where appropriate, the kind of coaching described earlier can be employed.

In some cases, the reason for a drop in team productivity will be more difficult to identify. Long-time team members may simply be bored. Keeping the job interesting is a constant challenge for leaders. One way is to assign staff new jobs, perhaps cross-training people within the team on the various team tasks. While there may be some initial staff resistance to this because of basic fear of the unknown, the results are often highly positive, giving individual team members renewed interest in their work and the team leader greater flexibility in staffing projects. Similarly, staff can be given tasks that may at first seem beyond their competence, but with proper mentoring can be executed competently. Again, the staffer's self-confidence and job satisfaction will be enhanced.

The team leader should be alert to possibilities and try them out as the opportunity permits. A common failing at many think tanks is to underestimate the level of responsibility that comparatively junior staff can carry. Senior researchers tend to think of junior staff as the people who do the data analysis or literature reviews, when in fact they can often also do other tasks, such as certain kinds of field work, with the aid of some mentoring. Such work can include conducting elite interviews, leading focus groups, and organizing and analyzing the qualitative information obtained from the interviews and focus groups.

Even with these efforts, there will occasionally be staff members who are deeply unhappy in their work. In many cases the problems have little to do with their job per se. Common problems are medical disorders (or side effects from medicines taken to treat the disorder), a lack of confidence, stress or emotional problems, or family difficulties. When the team leader understands that the problem is deeper than he or she can address, the leader should quickly alert senior management and the personnel officer, if there is one. The organization will want to help the employee return to his or her former role at the think tank. How long and how much assistance is possible will depend on the conditions at the think tank (e.g., whether there is someone else who can take over the responsibilities of the staffer for some time) and, perhaps, the quality of the medical insurance available to the staffer. The way the team leader is perceived to deal with this problem—the degree to which he or she is humane and compassionate—will have a strong impact on team morale more generally.

SUMMARY

Team leaders occupy a pivotal position at think tanks: They are the first-line managers who carry the day-to-day responsibility for project execution, planning, and marketing; and it is their job to ensure the productivity of their team. Given that this is the case, it is surprising that the development and mentoring of team leaders receives so little attention from experts on think tanks.

The senior management of most think tanks need to awaken to the fact that the productivity of the whole organization depends on the effectiveness of the team leaders. Ensuring that team leaders are successful in their jobs begins with very careful selection of those to fill these positions. After the hiring or promotion, senior managers should mentor and coach the newcomers.

Team leaders in organizations with an "authority figure" management style have an especially challenging job. Experience shows that teams are better led and more productive under a more participatory and consultative style of leadership. The inclusion of team members in setting the direction of the team must be genuine. Team leaders need to listen attentively, be open to differing opinions, and, where appropriate, reshape their position according to the input received.

Goal setting is important for motivating teams and giving them a broad sense of direction. Establishing goals can be particularly effective if done with the team through a participatory process.

Well-conducted team meetings are another useful management tool. If these meetings are guided by an objectives-oriented agenda and embody a participatory style, they are particularly efficient for sharing information and arriving at decisions.

Team leaders can take advantage of a number of aids in managing their teams. Some of these were outlined above, such as techniques for scheduling inputs on large projects and controlling staff utilization and project costs. Equally important with these project management tasks, however, are the "people tasks": being attentive to the personal dynamics within the team and working as needed with those who need coaching or mentoring. A team leader with a participatory management style and who pays attention to his team members is likely to boost the productivity of his group above the expectations of senior managers used to working with a more authoritarian model.

A Guide to Successful Coaching

The process of coaching a staff member can be broken into four steps. The following example illustrates these steps for a team leader who is having difficulty.[14]

1. Determine what needs to happen to improve the quality of the analysis the team is producing or to increase the responsibilities allocated by the team leader to the staff. Clearly, the team leader's view of the causes for the problem should be understood. A leader may not be planning the use of the staff's time well because he or she believes it absolutely essential to devote most of his or her time to writing reports, because of the large work load and the poor writing ability of several team members. Or the leader may believe that senior managers are causing the problem. These explanations should be fully considered. But the coach must not permit the team leader to deny a problem when it exists. The team leader could, for example, try to minimize the problem, saying that it is temporary and will pass soon; deny an important piece of information that is obvious to others; or being willing to make only small changes when larger ones are necessary. These denials of the reality of the situation must be overcome through persistence and persuasion. Self-awareness on the part of team leader is essential to addressing the problem.

In developing an action plan for remedying the problem, consider the following three questions:[15]

- Are the needed changes only for the team leader, or are other involved—support staff, such as the financial manager; one of the senior managers; or certain staff members?
- Is the team leader likely to resist the actions being contemplated? It is important to distinguish between resistance arising from the team leader's perception that there is insufficient time to work on the changes, because he or she is overwhelmed with work, and resistance stemming from a view that the proposed change is incorrect. In the former case, additional staff resources can be allocated in the short term to ease the pressure. If there is a clear conflict in views, however, a combination of persuasion and consistent pressure is necessary.
- What are the benefits to the team leader? The coach should work hard at defining the gains, both immediate and longer-term, to the team leader from addressing a problem.

Mentoring is often a key ingredient for improvement, and the coach must be ready to provide this kind of support. Consider, for example, the case where the team leader is experiencing difficulties marketing. The coach could conduct a couple of visits to potential clients with the team leader to demonstrate his or her approach to such a visit—what materials are used, how the coach solicits more information about the situation confronting the client, how the problem that the think tank is offering to address is described, and how the coach presents the organization's qualifications. As another example, take the case of the team leader who has difficulty organizing the work of the team. The coach could simply make it a regular duty to attend team meetings at which the team's work program for the next two to four weeks is discussed, and could then provide feedback to the team leader and monitor changes.

2. Discuss what results are expected from the team leader. The coach needs to be clear about what changes are expected. Examples could include quarterly staff utilization plans that are fully accurate (not sloppily completed as in the past); having team leader personally review all peer-reviewed reports and be satisfied that a thorough review was completed before reports are released; or having at least three marketing contacts made monthly, either to offer existing types of research, analysis, or technical assistance to new clients or to offer new products to existing clients.

More difficult is setting goals where behavioral problems are involved. Staff morale is hard to measure, but the team leader could agree to define and organize two events each month for the next three months designed improve team spirit. Or, where insufficient delegation of authority is a problem, the team leader could agree that two specified research projects would have written responsibility for tasks given to staff, with clear standards by which the leader will monitor performance.

Whatever the problem being addressed, make clear the time period of the contract. One month or two is often the right period for product problems but six months or more may be needed to address substantial behavioral problems.

3. Collect information and provide feedback. Monitoring change typically takes significant time and effort, and many coaches do it poorly. Depending on the problem area, the coach may need to monitor the team's products, the scheduling prepared by the team leader, the tasks the team leader is allocating, how meetings are organized and conducted, and the team leader's interaction with the team. Conversations with team members are often necessary to get the full picture, even when the coach attends team meetings, since the team leader might be on his or her best behavior then.

Equally important to obtaining information on the progress in addressing a problem is communicating this information to the team leader. Avoiding telling the team leader that progress is limited or nonexistent will only exacerbate the problem. As Dotlich and Cairo say, "Coaching almost always requires fact-based confrontation delivered in a provocative but caring manner" (1999, 42). Some useful guidelines on providing feedback are listed here:[16]

- Make feedback simple and memorable
- Choose a moment when the person is receptive
- Offer negative opinions in private
- Where progress has been made, note and praise it
- Be specific; use concrete examples
- Avoid personal comments ("A child can do better than this . . .")
- Check that the person has really understood the points you are making.

4. Recontract and go forward.[17] If the problem has been successfully resolved, then the tips in this section are not needed. But often problems are not resolved after the initial round of diagnosis, plan-and-contract, and implementation. Where the problem persists, then the process just outlined may have to be repeated—but with some possible variations.

- Review the goals and, if necessary, reset them. Be sure that the goal is properly defined in terms of the business outcome senior management wants.
- Explore different ways to accomplish the goal. The approach tried in the first period may not have been well suited to the combination of the problem and the specific team leader.
- Renew the contract between the coach and team leader, including the time period for it.

This process may have to be repeated two or three times. For each round, the coach needs to be creative in thinking of new options for helping the team leader improve. At the same time, the coach should clarify and reinforce the organization's requirement that changes be achieved. Obviously, if improvement is not forthcoming in a reasonable time despite coaching and mentoring, the team leader will have to be replaced.

NOTES

(Complete references can be found in the Reference Section at the end of this book.)

1. To be clear, the team leader positions discussed here are permanent management positions. In contrast, many companies today form teams to address a specific task and disband it when the task is accomplished.

2. There is one type of think tank that does not follow this model. This is an organization composed of senior scholars who work substantially alone on research projects, sometimes aided by a research assistant. These scholars may be grouped into divisions or centers, but this a merely an administrative convenience. Examples of think tanks following this model are the Brookings Institution and the Carnegie Endowment for International Peace.

3. Based on Rees (2001, 86).

4. Assumes that all candidates have equivalent of a Ph.D. from a U.S. university or sufficient analytic experience to be the functional equivalent in economics or other social science.

5. In the European system, this is what is often called a "candidate degree" (i.e., having completed all the requirements for the doctorate except the very demanding doctoral dissertation).

6. See chapter 2 for a discussion of the assessment process.

7. This section draws generally on Dotlich and Cairo (1999); Charan, Drotter, and Noel (2001); and Conger and Benjamin (1999).

8. For example, a proposal may include 30 days of a researcher's time. The team leader estimates the probability of success in competing for the work at 0.6. So the expected number of days of coverage could be assessed as 18 (30 * 0.6).

9. To paraphrase Leigh and Maynard (1995, 156), leadership style is "how the leader relates to people and influences her team."

10. Leigh and Maynard (1995); Rees (1999); Conger and Benjamin (1999).

11. Leigh and Maynard (1995, 105ff).

12. Rees (1999); Leigh and Maynard (1995).

13. Information on the network can be found at http://www.urban.org/tpn.

14. This description draws on a more elaborate eight-step process detailed in Dotlich and Cairo (1999).

15. Based on Dotlich and Cario (1999, 63).

16. Based on Leigh and Maynard (1995, 133).

17 This section draws on Dotlich and Cairo (1999, 42-43).

Raymond J. Struyk[1]

6

Getting the Most from Your Board

The key managerial actors in think tanks are the board of trustees or board of directors, the president, a management council if one exists, and the research team leaders. A board of trustees or directors has the potential to be an extraordinarily valuable asset to a private public-policy research institution. Unfortunately, this promise is seldom met. Such failures can result from such factors as ill-defined roles for the boards, mismatch between its talents and the assignments it receives, and the president's failure to work creatively with the board to get the most from members' participation in institutional affairs.

In addition, board productivity can be impaired if the responsibilities for principal managerial decisions are misallocated among the board, the senior executive, and the management council. Key decisions include setting the institution's agenda, setting staff compensation, and determining how to structure the institution's research operations. In many countries the formal distribution of responsibilities is heavily conditioned by laws that mandate particular organizational structures for nonprofit organizations. But even in these situations, boards are often free to provide advice on a range of issues informally thus improving organizational effectiveness.

This chapter discusses the structure and potential contributions of boards of trustees or directors (hereafter referred to simply as boards). The presentation is addressed to the president or executive director (hereafter, the president) of think tanks, and outlines methods a president can use to work most effectively with and benefit the most from the institution's board. The president's principal objective in such dealings

153

should be to have the board spend its time advising on key issues in the think tank's development.

The discussion begins with the definition of a board and alternative governance-management models used by think tanks. Then the major tasks all boards should execute are outlined and the reasons why many boards waste time and energy during their meetings are explored. The next section covers ways to focus the board's work and balance the distribution of responsibilities between the board and the president. After that operational issues concerning the form and content of board meetings are addressed. The penultimate section discusses the important business of recruiting new members for the board and the neglected task of orienting new board members to their tasks. The chapter closes with some ideas for assessing a board's effectiveness.

Much of the presentation concerns the interactions of presidents and the boards of comparatively mature organizations—that is, those 10 or more years old that have been a "second-stage" think tank for several years and have low turnover rates for the president and board. The organization's maturity and stability are critical because they bear fundamentally bearing on how much authority a board will feel it can confidently delegate to the president. The more mature and stable an institution, the more the board can concentrate on "big picture" questions and leave management to the president.

The contents of these guidelines come from three sources: the author's experience as a board member,[2] interviews with senior leaders of 10 "third-stage" think tanks,[3] a review of recent books on enhancing board productivity.[4]

FIRST PRINCIPLES

The supreme authority for think tanks is either a board of trustees or a board of directors—exact terms depend on the law and practice of each country. (Here board means the governing board, the body with the ultimate corporate responsibility.) The duties of the board are clearly stated in the national law governing the formation of nonprofit organizations.[5] At their heart, these duties can be reduced to two: maintaining accountability and safeguarding the public's trust. Responsibility for accountability means ensuring that the organization's resources are properly spent—not wasted excessively expensive offices, travel, and salaries or lost through graft. Think tanks must also maintain the public trust. In most countries, all nonprofits, are accorded certain legal advantages, especially tax advantages, compared with for-profit entities. In exchange, think tanks are expected to contribute to the public good. For instance, think tanks should do work that improves decisionmaking and educates the public on the principal policy issues of the day. The board's task is to ensure the think tank works toward these goals.

Organizational Options

Many think tanks have two kinds of boards: a management board or committee, and a board of directors or trustees. The management board should have day-to-day responsibilities for operational issues. Directors or trustees, on the other hand, get more involved in strategy and has the ultimate fiduciary responsibility. This is the standard model.

However, there are variations. In some countries, the founders of the organization constitute the equivalent of a board. In such cases, think tanks sometimes form an advisory board of thoughtful and prestigious individuals who provide the kind of guidance that a board typically gives. Advisory boards do not have fiduciary responsibility, however, so generally they will not be concerned with the institution's audit and related questions. The balance of the discussion assumes that the standard model is followed.

Dimensions of the Board's Role[6]

Three aspects of the board's role can be distinguished: legal, functional, and symbolic. The laws that govern the creation of think tanks mandate boards to supervise compliance with certain requirements. Some (e.g., the board meets at least once a year) are fairly routine, but two requirements are more fundamental: The board is responsible for the organization's fiscal integrity and for ensuring that the organization stay true to its mission (i.e., the purpose for which it was created).

Functional responsibilities of the board vary greatly from think tank to think tank. Indeed, as discussed below, the greatest problem for boards is that their primary tasks are not clearly defined. A typical list of responsibilities includes ensuring that the organization is realizing its mission effectively, hiring the president, evaluating the president's performance, understanding the organization's financial performance, and assisting with fundraising. But many boards find themselves ensnared in operational details, including having to determine what telephone or computing system to purchase, or how to establish salary ranges for different positions—tasks best left to management. Often attention to such details comes at the expense of time to give advice and determining the institution's main directions.

The symbolic dimension of the board's work is critical. Board members lend the think tank prestige by associating with it and become part of its public image. The list of names on the organization's letterhead and in its printed materials tells a story about the organization's values and strength.

Board members have a significant advantage over the president and other staff in representing the organization, by carrying an organization's message and expanding its circle of influence. Board members are perceived as having little to gain from promulgating a think tank's good name and, hence, have *prima facie* credibility. Board members can play this ambassadorial role to advance policy positions or raising funds. A key task for the institution's president is to figure out how to motivate board members to take on these active roles.

COMMON BOARD PROBLEMS

Books on creating effective boards are replete with examples of ineffectiveness, wasted time, and lost opportunities. The author's conversations with think tank presidents about the utility of their institution's boards have also exposed some frustration with presidents' inability to get more from boards which are made up of creative, dynamic, and successful individuals.

Certain common practices of the board and the structure of board meetings can drain its effectiveness. Carver (1997, 9–10) gives some good examples:

- *Time spent on the trivial.* Items of trivial scope or importance receive disproportionate attention.
- *Short-term bias.* The board concentrates on day-to-day items that could be handled by the staff rather than those issues that may have much greater consequences for the organization.
- *Reactive stance.* Boards respond to staff initiatives and information rather than assert leadership (e.g., indicating topics for the meeting's agenda).

- *Reviewing, rehashing, redoing.* Boards spend too much time reviewing what staff has already done, this should be a management function.
- *Leaky accountability.* Board members "go around" the president to assign tasks to staff members, making it hard to hold the president responsible for results.
- *Diffuse authority.* The specific responsibilities of the president and board are often not well defined, frustrating accountability.

Because the president drafts the agenda for board meetings and decides how much background material to provide to members, he or she has the potential to make the board much more effective. But how to move a board in this direction?

FOCUSING THE BOARD

Consultants who work with boards to increase their effectiveness universally decry the kinds of problems just listed as a clear waste of board members' expertise and experience. Consultants look for ways to promote the idea of focusing the board's energy and intellectual resources on the key tasks of the organization and on long-term planning. In other words, the board of a think tank should concentrate on how well the organization is fulfilling its primary missions of conducting high-quality policy research, influencing policy, and informing policy debates. As to long-run planning, the critical issues are the country's emerging policy agenda and potential sources of support for the institute's work. The board's advice should deal primarily with these matters. Of course, not all board members are equally qualified to proffer advice on these topics, and the president must guide discussions skillfully to get the most from the board.

The president and the board should agree on the board's responsibility for providing management advice. As needed, the board can request information and intervene in management issues. Requests for more information are likely to arise from open discussion of principal issues, which will be addressed later. But this should be the exception rather than the rule.

To move a board in this direction, the starting point is to craft a clear statement of the organization's mission. Exhibit 6-1 gives an example of such a statement. It is quite general, so once the board accepts it a set of indicators to measure the think tank's performance would have to be added. For example, indicators related to the "conduct of policy research

Exhibit 6-1 Example of a Board of Directors' Mission Statement for a Think Tank

The Institute for Policy Studies will focus its activities so as to

- Conduct policy research, program evaluations, and pilot projects at a high professional standard, with the objective of contributing the results of this work to the development of public policy.
- Effectively communicate the results of this work to policymakers and other interested parties, including nongovernmental organizations, political parties, and the public, in ways designed to influence the development of policy positively.
- Conduct seminars, workshops, and courses to contribute to the professional development of public officials, teachers, and researchers and analysts in the area of public policy design, implementation, and training.

at a high professional standard" could include placing a certain number of articles by staff in refereed journals and a certain number of their books published by respected presses.

Convincing the board that its primary task is to work on the big-picture issues of the think tank's central missions is only half of battle. The other half is establishing a clear understanding between the president and the board about their respective management responsibilities. The following is an illustrative list of management topics that often siphon attention from more important issues, and should not be a major focus of presidents or boards (Carver 1997, 75–76).

- *Personnel:* making decisions about job design, hiring, firing, promotion, discipline.
- *Compensation:* dealing with issues involving salary ranges, grades, adjustments, incentives, benefits (the exception is the president's salary, which the board should determine).
- *Supply:* making decisions about purchasing, bidding authorization, storage, inventories, salvage.
- *Accounting:* addressing questions of forecasting, budgeting, depositories, controls, investments, retrenchment.
- *Facilities:* determining space allocation and requirements, rentals, upkeep, refurbishment.

- *Risk management:* dealing with insurance, exposures, protective maintenance, and disclaimers.
- *Reporting:* ensuring grant reports, tax reporting, law and regulation compliance.
- *Communications:* developing policies affecting telephone systems, meetings, postings, mail distribution.
- *Management methods:* dealing with goal-setting, staffing patterns, team definitions, feedback loops, planning techniques, control methods, participation levels.

Clearly, if a board wades into many of these areas, it will spend most of its time immersed—if not drowning—in details. Still, as noted, the board of a young organization will need to pay more attention to these managerial issues than will the board of a more mature organization with proven systems in place. Similarly, the longer a board and its president have worked together, the less time the board needs to spend on such items.

Regardless of how much responsibility the board delegates to the president and his or her management team for such tasks, the responsibilities delegated to the president need to stated explicitly, for two reasons. The intent of a codified Executive Limitations is twofold. First, the Limitations prohibit staff practices that the board regards as unethical or too risky. Second, in organizations where full trust has not been established between the president and the board, such Limitations give the president additional guidance on how to execute certain management duties. The board and president both need to understand who is responsible for what. The board is responsible for periodically checking that management is complying with the rules set forth in the Executive Limitations.

Exhibit 6-2 provides an example of two key statements regulating the relations between the board and the president. The "Delegation to the President" outlines the president's powers and responsibilities, and the "Communication and Support to the Board" informs the president of his obligations to the board.

The "Delegation to the President" ties the delegation of responsibilities to the board-approved mission statement and the Executive Limitations. The statement makes it clear that Executive Limitations can be changed to shift the allocation of responsibilities between the board and the president. It protects the president from unreasonable requests for information

Exhibit 6-2 Examples of a "Delegation to the President" and a "Communication and Support for the Board" Statement Issued by a Board[7]

Delegation to the President

All board authority delegated to the staff is delegated through the president, so all authority and accountability of staff—as far as the board is concerned—is considered to be the authority and accountability of the president.

As long as the president uses any reasonable interpretation of the board-approved mission statement for the organization and Executive Limitations policies, the president is authorized to establish all further policies, make all decisions, take all actions, establish all practices, and develop all activities.

- The board may change its mission statement and Executive Limitations policies, thereby shifting the boundary between the board's and the president's domains. By doing so, the board changes the latitude given to the president. So long as any particular delegation is in place, the board will respect and support the president's choices.
- Only decisions of the board acting as a body are binding on the president.
- Decisions or instructions of individual board members, officers, or committees are not binding on the president, except in rare circumstances when the board has specifically authorized such exercise of authority.
- In the case of board members or committees requesting information or assistance without board authorization, the president can refuse such requests that require—in the president's judgement—a material amount of staff time or funds or are disruptive.

Communication and Support to the Board

With respect to providing information and counsel to the board, the president may not permit the board to be uninformed. Accordingly, he or she may not

- Neglect to submit monitoring information required by the board in a timely, accurate, and understandable fashion.
- Let the board be unaware of relevant trends, anticipated negative media coverage, and material external and internal changes, particularly changes in assumptions on which previous board policies were based.
- Fail to advise the board if, in the president's opinion, the board is not in compliance with its own policies.
- Fail to marshal for the board as many staff and external points of view, issues, and options as needed for making fully informed board choices.
- Fail to meet with the board as a whole except when (a) fulfilling individual requests for information or (b) responding to officers or committees duly charged by the board.
- Fail to report an actual or anticipated noncompliance with any policy of the board in a timely manner.

from individual board members. It also makes it clear that the president need only follow decisions of the whole board, not those of individual members or even committees. The statement is crystal clear on the president's operational authority.

The statement on "Communication and Support to the Board" requires the president to provide certain information to the board. This includes the information needed to assess the think tank's progress toward its primary goals and information on any circumstantial changes that could affect the organization's reputation or financial health.

These two statements establish the general rules, but they need to be supported by guidance from the board on the parameters of the president's vested authority. Exhibit 6-3 gives examples of such statements for financial, asset, and staff management. For example, the president has authority to commit the organization to contracts and grants up to $50,000. Beyond this limit, the president must seek board approval.[9] Similarly, the president has wide authority vis-a-vis the personnel area, but decisions on compensation and promotion must be objective and defensible.

The critical point is that the statements of Executive Limitations define the operating domain of the president versus those retained by the board. There is no reason for the board to enter the president's sphere, especially at the expense of its bigger-picture responsibilities. The board's task is to periodically satisfy itself that the rules it has set forth are being followed. (In the financial and asset protection areas, the annual audit would probably provide most of the necessary information.) Naturally, the president can seek the board's advice on matters squarely within his or her jurisdiction and many presidents routinely do so. As long as such interchanges are infrequent and informal, such interchanges can build support and confidence.

Adoption of a clearly articulated mission statement with corresponding indicators of accomplishment and Executive Limitations helps focus the board's work on strategic issues. Playing to their strengths this way makes board membership a satisfying experience.

THE BOARD MEETING

Obviously, a think tank's president must prepare carefully for each meeting of the board. Two critical tasks must be conducted before the meeting itself: setting the agenda and distributing materials for the meeting to board members.

Exhibit 6-3 Examples of Executive Limitations Issued by a Board to the President[8]

Finance Management

With respect to operating in a sound and prudent fiscal manner, the president may not jeopardize the long-term financial strength of the institute. Accordingly, he or she may not

- Cause the institute to incur indebtedness other than short-term loans for routine expenses.
- Use advances from the cash reserve fund other than for ordinary operating expenses.
- Use restricted contributions for any purpose other than that required by the contribution.
- Settle payroll and debts in other than a timely manner
- Allow expenditures to deviate materially from board-stated priorities.
- Allow the cash reserve fund to fall below 6 percent of operating expenses.
- Sign contract or grant agreements with a value exceeding $50,000 without the explicit approval of the board.

Asset Protection

The president shall not allow assets to be unprotected, inadequately maintained, or unnecessarily risked. Accordingly, the president shall not

- Fail to insure against theft and casualty losses to at least 80 percent of replacement value and against liability losses of board members, staff, or the organization itself in an amount greater than the average for similar organizations.
- Allow uninsured personnel to handle funds.
- Subject plant and equipment to improper wear and tear or insufficient maintenance.
- Unnecessarily expose the organization to claims of liability.
- Make any purchase or commit the organization to any expenditure of greater than $25,000. Make any purchase (a) wherein normally prudent protection has not been given against conflict of interest; (b) over $1,500 without having obtained comparative prices and quality.
- Fail to protect intellectual property, information, and files from loss or significant damage or unauthorized duplication.
- Receive, process, or disburse funds under controls that are insufficient to meet board-appointed auditor standards.
- Invest or hold operating capital in insecure investments.

(continued)

Exhibit 6-3 Examples of Executive Limitations Issued by a Board to the President[8] (*Continued*)

Staff Treatment

The president may not cause or allow conditions that are inhumane, unfair, or undignified. Accordingly, he or she may not

- Discriminate among employees in payment, assignments, or promotion except for reasons that are clearly job-related and have to do with individual performance or qualifications.
- Fail to take reasonable steps to protect staff from unsafe or unhealthy conditions.
- Withhold from staff a due-process grievance procedure, which should be able to be used without bias.
- Fail to acquaint staff with their rights under this policy.

Setting the Agenda

The agenda should drive the board meeting, so the items on it should be thoughtfully considered. A few pointers about formulating the agenda:

- The president usually drafts the agenda. But it should be given to the chairman of the board to review before it is distributed to the rest of the board.
- Discussion at the meeting should be reserved for important points. Confine points to those that concern the organization's principal tasks—both reporting on accomplishments and considering future activities—and those dealing with the organization's financial soundness.
- Whenever possible, information on management matters should be provided to the board in the materials sent out before the meeting instead of placing the items on the agenda. A board member can raise questions about these "information items," but they should be clearly relegated to a secondary position.
- The agenda should indicate what action the president wants from the board on each item—be it information, advice, or a decision.
- Dinner meetings the night before board meetings can create the dynamic the board needs to do its job. Informal social occasions are

reportedly popular with board members, most likely because they permit networking.[10]

Exhibit 6-4 presents an example of a typical agenda for a meeting of a think tank's board of trustees. The first of the three main sections is the report of the Executive Committee. At this meeting, the initial section includes discussion of the annual audit report, a topic that must be considered by the full board as well as by the Committee. The Committee will also report on any administrative issues on which the president has sought guidance or a decision.

The second section is devoted to the president's report on the institution's performance in key areas. The information provided should cover at least the indicators of performance agreed upon earlier with the board. The president should also use this opportunity to inform the board about important developments that may affect the organization's financial well-being or influence on policy-making—the so-called "environmental scan." For example, the election of a new government is often has important implications for a think tank. The think tank may have received important contracts from a ministry under the prior government, and the change could diminish the chances of obtaining future work. Equally important, the changing of the guard may increase or

Exhibit 6-4 Typical Agenda for a Meeting of a Think Tank's Board of Directors

Call to order
Approve minutes of prior meeting
Executive committee report

- Financial audit results
- Discussion of candidates for board membership
- Report on administrative matters

President's report

- State of the institution
- Issues on which advice is sought

Presentations by senior researchers

decrease the senior staff's access to key decisionmakers. Similarly, whenever a major donor or an important source of work for the organization, such as the World Bank, announces a change in its program's direction, it should be on this part of the meeting agenda. Other items might include the announcement of a government austerity program that will likely mean deep cuts in ministry budgets for research and program evaluation, or a major competitor's decision to challenge the think tank on ground where the organization had long enjoyed a clear advantage.

This information should serve as the basis for discussion about possible adjustments to the organization's plans.

The final section of the agenda allows two or three senior researchers to present timely or important projects to the board. Normally, these are crisp—no more than 15 minutes—and well-rehearsed presentations that inform the board of the organization's ongoing work.[11] A good rule of thumb is to allow as much time for discussion by the board as for the presentation itself; board members are senior people used to commanding attention and expressing their views. The president should select the presentation topics partly to capture the board's interest and partly to give board members information they can use in discussions with policymakers.

Materials Distributed before the Meeting

Any materials that management sends to the board should be designed to make the upcoming meeting efficient and productive. Before each meeting, the board should receive background information on substantive agenda issues and information on procedural matters of legal or administrative importance.[12] The materials should be carefully selected and concise. Sending out too much or poorly prepared materials will defeat the purpose of providing information in advance, because busy board members will not read them.[13] Formats and presentations should be kept simple and inviting.

Exhibit 6-5 is the table of contents for the materials sent to members of the Urban Institute's board of trustees before its spring 2001 meeting. No more than about half an hour would be needed to review the materials. Many of these materials are provided only for the board's information and involve topics that will not be discussed at the board meeting unless a member raises a question. These include, for example, the reports on personnel and communications and the annotated list of

Exhibit 6-5 Table of Contents for Materials Sent to Members of the Urban Institute's Board of Trustees before the May 2001 Meeting

1. Agendas for the executive committee meeting and full board meeting
2. Minutes of previous board meeting
3. Financial statements
4. Board membership report
5. Endowment report
6. Funding report
7. Expenditures report
8. Communications report [Urban Institute in the media, publications, etc.]
9. Personnel report
10. Ongoing projects and submitted proposals [annotated list]
11. Information about trustees
12. 2001–2002 meeting schedule
13. Biographies of participating staff

ongoing projects and outstanding proposals. Even though these items are not on the agenda, the board needs to have this background information. Consider the list of ongoing projects. If the board has delegated to the president the authority to decide which awards to accept, the list helps the board stay abreast of the institution's work. A board member reviewing the list might see a project on a topic that he had thought was outside of the work program as it was discussed with the board or that is being done for a client about whom the member has some concern. The list affords the member the chance to be raise a question.

Using the Board

As stated, the president has enormous discretion about what comes before the board. The president always has significantly more information than even the most well-informed board chairman. This advantage can be used positively or negatively. Think tank presidents are well-advised to treat their boards as a resource and to be quite open with them. After all, the individuals on the board were selected so they could contribute sound advice to the organization, particularly to the president. As

Robinson points out, "The key to a successful relationship between the board and the executive director is the care with which the director helps the board be a good partner. In the unique calculus of the nonprofit sector, a stronger board does not automatically come at the expense of the executive director's authority or autonomy" (2001, 113).

That said, the president should take care in selecting the topics presented to the board. As noted earlier, the president needs to be clear on each item as to whether he or she is providing information, seeking advice, or seeking a decision. It is extremely important that the board's task be made clear before discussion of any item. Which issues are presented should depend partly on the board's capabilities and limitations. Over time, the president will recognize both and be able to adjust the agenda accordingly.

At the Meeting

The most important part of the meeting—and the biggest block of time—is devoted to the institution's performance in its research and policy endeavors and its plans and strategy for the future. For boards that meet once or twice a year, this must be the main topic. For those meeting more frequently, these two items should still dominate the meeting unless a dramatic development between the semi-annual meetings calls for consultation. At least once a year, the board should evaluate the institution's performance, principally in terms of the indicators agreed upon with the president. It is the president's task to provide clear information on those indicators for the board's use.

The president's report on accomplishments, difficulties, and future prospects should be designed to elicit board members' thoughtful commentary and an exchange of views. Not all members are equally equipped to discuss the "idea industry," but all were selected because they could contribute meaningfully to the oversight of the institution. The task of the president and board chairman is to get the most out of the board.

One important question related to an institution's strategy for the future is defining projects to be undertaken over the next year or two. The experience of the 10 "third-stage" think tanks listed in chapter 1 in determining their work program offers a good starting point because they have been in the business a long time and have fine-tuned the process of setting the research agenda (Struyk 1993, 45–46). Perhaps surprisingly, the agendas of most of these institutes are defined rather informally.

Typically, the process is guided by senior management, who consult team leaders or senior researchers on the work they want to do. The president sometimes adds high-priority projects to the list. Because all these think tanks depend at least in part on external funding, the agendas are affected to varying degrees by whether the discussed research topics are likely to attract funding. The Urban Institute, the only surveyed institution that obtained the bulk of its funds from government grants and contracts, is particularly dependent on government research and evaluation interests.

Only three institutions reported taking all of their projects to boards of trustees for approval; another takes the largest projects to the board by providing board members with descriptions of proposed projects. Not surprisingly, two of the three institutions that take all projects to their boards are those least dependent on raising funds from outside sources. So the greater board oversight might be seen as a substitute for meeting a market test of relevancy and productivity. Note that the boards of all the think tanks consulted very seldom reject a particular project. As suggested above, in the United States and Europe nearly all boards take a strong interest in the general direction of a think tank's work, but intervene little in the work program.

As the previous information indicates, setting the agenda at a typical think tank is driven mainly by the demand for work on certain topics and by staff interests, not by guidance from the board. Still, the imprint of the president and other senior managers may be greater than this statement suggests. If senior management is actively implementing a process designed to foster innovation in the organization's agenda,[14] then management's influence may be significant, albeit expressed in the projects advanced by specific research teams or senior researchers.

In summary, most think tanks' decisionmaking authority for the agenda appears to be sensibly divided between the board and senior management. The board exerts important influence (and may even have final authority) on the broad direction of the institution's program.[15] With the general directions set, the president, or in some cases a management council, has the authority to make decisions on individual projects. This authority extends both to projects funded by external grants or contracts and to the institution's own resources.

A second topic that demands the board's full attention is the think tank's financial management. The board's review is usually centered around the auditor's annual report.[16] After reviewing the audit report and management letter, the board will typically be briefed by the auditor in private. If the audit has identified problems, the board should instruct the president, in writing, to make certain improvements by a stated time. Severe problems with fulfilling the board's requirements may call for draconian board responses.

Running the Meeting

Two observations about boards at work that the president should keep in mind: first, boards work on what is in front of them—no issue is too great or small; second, boards have no natural braking mechanism so they continue to act as they have in the past unless they are nudged off this track (Robinson 2001, 46). These observations should reinforce the president's central role in defining what comes before the board and the role of the president and board chairman in guiding the board's discussion to closure when the principal contributions on a topic have been made.

With respect to the actual conduct of the meeting, here are two pointers for conducting an effective meeting:

- Make sure that all members get a chance to contribute on significant issues. If some members hang back, the chair should ask for their input.
- Put everything on the table. In other words, all information and opinions should be presented at the meeting of the full board. Individual board members should not be lobbying the president outside the board meetings; important issues should not be reserved for a board committee because it is more in sympathy with the position of the president or board chairman. In the long run, openness is definitely the best policy.

A final word of advice for the president. The information provided to the board at a meeting should meet an important standard: "No surprises." No board wants to be caught unawares or embarrassed by the public disclosure of a problem or accomplishment about which the members should have known. If a significant problem threatens the think tank, one of its products is receiving adverse press, or a major award is expected, the board should know in advance. Otherwise, the members are likely to resent the president's decision to withhold the information. Such resentment can sow the seeds of larger problems. So keep the board informed of significant events—through board meetings or otherwise.

BETWEEN MEETINGS

Communication with board members between board meetings is highly desirable; members who are reminded of their membership are more likely to work to the organization's benefit. These communications need not be elaborate. Indeed, many think tanks keep in touch by sending each board member a copy of every new publication. This has a double purpose: It reminds the members of the think tank's work, and, if the publication deals with a policy topic of particular interest to a member, it can better prepare the member to participate in public debates.

In a few cases, think tanks' presidents send their boards a report on activities between board meetings. These reports are typically in the form of quarterly letters for think tank boards that meet once or twice a year. Two formats are commonly used. One is a fairly comprehensive report that may run to five or more pages—essentially a newsletter. The alternative is a shorter, more personal letter with a few highlights of activities that is signed by the president.

As indicated above, it is imperative that the president inform the board about major problems or positive developments at the organization whenever such events occur. In some cases, the president might be well-advised to seek the counsel of at least the board chairman in dealing with the change, crisis or windfall.

OPERATIONAL MATTERS

This section covers a handful of practical questions about the structure and composition of the board and the recruitment of new members.

Board Structure

The trend over the past decade is for both corporate and nonprofit boards to be smaller and to have fewer committees. More work is being done by the full board, and a smaller full board encourages more open discussion and exchange. While the number of board members varies widely, eight to ten members is viewed as effective; some boards total only five or six members, which reportedly promotes exchange among members—both during and outside the board meetings—as well as between the board and the president (Charan 1998, 40–41).

The era of nonprofits that have half a dozen committees for various purposes seems to be a thing of the past. It is now common for nonprofit boards to have a single committee, either an audit committee that concerns itself with financial management issues or an executive committee that deals with these and a wider range of questions.[17] An effective executive committee can ensure that meetings of the full board are preserved for important questions. For example, the executive committee could be charged with carefully reviewing the audit report and meeting with the auditors; the committee could then summarize the results to the full board and make any necessary recommendations concerning the directions to be given to the president.

Of course, the board will sometimes need to appoint a committee for a particular function. One of the most common temporary committees is that appointed to search for a new president of the think tank.

How Often to Meet?

The vast majority of the boards of third-stage think tanks meet twice a year. There are two reasons for meeting so infrequently. First, because participation as a board member is voluntary and unpaid and because think tanks work hard to attract distinguished persons to serve as members, only a limited time commitment can be expected. Second, over the years many of these organizations have developed well-established systems for ensuring financial control and research quality, so they require comparatively little board oversight of operations. The twice-a-year norm appears to be reasonable standard for such organizations.[18]

For younger institutions, quarterly board meetings may be advisable. The president and board chairman could consider using each meeting to focus on a different aspect of the think tank's work and operations. For example, two meetings a year could focus on the most important issue, the institution's progress toward its goals and future directions; the meeting following the completion of the audit report could concentrate on financial management; and the fourth meeting could concentrate on other management issues on which the president wants the board's input. A regular agenda item for one of these meetings should be the division of responsibility between the board and the president: Do the Executive Limitations need to be adjusted? When the necessity for comparatively intense board oversight diminishes, the shift to twice-a-year meetings is appropriate.

Recruiting New Members

The charters of most think tanks specify how long board members can serve and the process for replacing them. It is fairly standard for a member to be appointed for a three- to five-year term, with the possibility of being reappointed once or twice. Some organizations make it possible for members to serve even longer by having a separate category of members, such as "life trustees," who can serve indefinitely. But usually these members are in addition to the regularly appointed members and are generally less active than regular board members. Members are normally replaced on a staggered basis so that a core of experienced members is always available.

A reasonable argument claims that if a board is working effectively, its composition should not be disturbed. But while the board may be comfortable with its current arrangement and work well with the institution's management, failing to introduce new members on a regular basis is probably a mistake. New members may be the most likely to ask searching questions about performance or recognize the need for a change in the think tank's agenda, or even of its president. The "life trustee" option allows the board to keep the current members as well as add fresh blood.

Recruiting: What Board Members Want

Most people who serve as members of a think tank's board do so for some combination of three reasons. First, they would like to enjoy the company of their fellow board members. This can be an especially powerful draw if the institution's board is populated with prestigious individuals. Second, members want to feel that they are doing good work, that they are giving something back to their community through serving without compensation.[19] Third, board members want to be associated with an organization that does high-quality work. Highly regarded think tanks active in the public domain will have an easier job than others in attracting their most desired candidates.

Over time, boards can become more attractive to potential new members by helping the think tank achieve its primary objectives and by recruiting excellent new members for the board. Here success breeds further success. Given the board's central place in a think tank's life and the benefits that board members seek from serving on the board, it is not surprising that boards typically devote substantial energy to recruiting new members.

Whom to Recruit?

All boards seek to attract individuals with strong reputations in their respective fields. But what other qualities should these individuals bring?

To begin, there are two simple rules on whom *not* to recruit.

1. *No conflicts of interest.* A common mistake among think tanks is to ask the director or president of another think tank to serve as a board member. This is counterproductive because think tanks often compete against each other for funding and having leading roles in the same policy discussions. Board members have full access to the think tank's future development strategy. Giving such information to a potential competitor is bad business, and it places the board member in an untenable position.
2. *No cronies.* Some boards consist largely of friends of the president or of the board members. This makes for enjoyable board meetings but poor management. The presence of cronies also creates the potential for factions to form within the board, complicating the board's oversight tasks and impeding productive discourse.

Each candidate for board membership should be an experienced professional with a strong reputation for integrity, creativity, and thoughtfulness. Beyond this, at least some members should have substantial experience in public policy development, social science research and evaluation, and corporate finance. It is also important to include someone with a background in working with the media or other form of communications. Boards far too often lack such experience, so input from this perspective is absent or naive when new initiatives are discussed. If any of these skills are missing in the collective board, the board will have difficulty fulfilling all its responsibilities.

Board members should also be able to work well in groups and to be good colleagues: Boards are not the place for the *enfant terrible*. One reason why nearly all boards are responsible for nominating new members is that current members can vouch for collegiality in the candidates they nominate.

Finally, think tank leaders should at least consider asking a board candidate to make serving on the board one of his or her top three priorities among board memberships and other tasks beyond his or her regular job. Many of those best-suited to serve on a board already serve on several. Inevitably, serving on many boards reduces the attention one person can give to them collectively. So, when such a person is recruited to an additional board, expect some missed board meetings and not much attention to the institution between board meetings. For this reason, asking a potential board member for service on the board to be a priority can send a strong signal about the president's and board chairman's expectations. Better for a candidate to decline to participate than to formally be a member and contribute little.

By studying the regular positions occupied by board members at think tanks, we see that think tanks tend to adopt one of the two models, summarized in Exhibit 6-6, in recruiting board members. These models are caricatures to some degree and many hybrids exist. But the extreme cases are useful for this illustration.

In the "distinguished person" model, emphasis is on attracting prestigious individuals to enhance the institution's image. Of course, the key skills listed above must be present among the overall board. But if it is a larger board (e.g., of more than eight members), the board may include members with broad range of interests and backgrounds, such as industrialists, financiers, and businesspeople, many with no particular connection to the policymaking community. Such boards provide a wide

Exhibit 6-6 Occupations of Persons Recruited to Two Prototypical Boards of Trustees	
"Distinguished Persons" Model	**"Expert Advice" Model**
• Former ministers, state governors, senior legislators	• Former ministers, state governors, senior legislators
• Renowned social-science academics	• Members of the media
• Captains of industry and finance	• Leaders of prominent NGOs, including public interest groups and trade associations with interests aligned with those of the think tank
• Members of the media	
• Leaders of prominent NGOs, including public interest groups and trade associations	

range of perspectives and advice to the president. But the diversity of the members may work against board coherence.

In the "expert advice" model, interests of members are more tightly aligned with the research and policy interests of the think tank. These boards are often smaller, to help keep discussions focused and to take maximum advantage of each member's input. Such boards are more likely to be able to give tailored advice to the president on the think tank's strategy and operations. On the other hand, boards of this type may become too assertive in giving direction and members may represent a comparatively narrow range of backgrounds and experience. Neither model is generally superior.

Perhaps more important than the model picked are the goals set. The president and the chairman of the board must determine goals for the board. They should also understand that, if necessary, over time they can restructure the board to improve its effectiveness.

One more factor enters into the calculus of member selection: diversity. Most boards seek to maintain a diverse representation in terms of several factors, aside from members' professional backgrounds. Such diversity provides the board and president with a broad range of viewpoints. The following quotations from CEOs in a book on corporate boards illustrate this point (Schultz 2001, 128):

> Any CEO who has ten or eleven people just like him sitting around the board table will end up essentially talking to himself.
> You add water to water, you get water. It might be drinkable, but it's not joy juice.
> A group of people with the same background, the same experience, is going to come up with a predictable group of solutions to problems—not a good idea in the world we live in. Different points of view yield a wide approach to decisionmaking.

The composition of the board also sends a message to potential sponsors and clients about the organization's philosophy and values.

First among the balancing requirements is the political affiliation of members. Most think tanks strive to be known for producing objective policy recommendations, and few want to appear aligned with a political party. One way to signal non-partisanship is to include members with various political affiliations on the board. A second factor to balance is gender composition: Given the increasing prominence of women in public life, their inclusion in boards is essentially mandatory. The third is in the ethnic or regional representation of members. The specific type of balance in this case depends on local conditions. For example, boards composed exclusively members from the nation's capital can give the think tank an insular image. Where a country has a few dominant ethnic groups, representing each group through a board member is usually good policy.

Boards spend substantial time on recruiting members. They must first determine the qualifications needed, as outline above. Then various candidates are vetted within the board. Finally, a candidate is selected and approached.

Recruiting

Before approaching a candidate for board membership, the board needs to clearly define the minimum expectations for successful service on the board. How much time should it take? Does it just involve attending the board meetings, or is something expected between meetings? The board member who knows the candidate best is usually asked to make the initial contact. Robinson (2001, 126–27) provides a good list of questions the board needs to answer before a board member discusses membership with a candidate.

- What major issues is the board currently focused on?
- What talents, expertise, qualities, or characteristics is the board seeking in new members?
- How often does the board meet and for how long?
- Is everyone asked to serve on a committee? How are committee assignments made?
- What kind of fund-raising is required of board members?
- What is the relationship between the board and the executive director and between the board and other staff?
- Is an orientation program in place? Are other board education activities offered?
- Does the board have an annual retreat of any kind?
- Are there changes on the horizon that a new board member should know about?

Many recruitment conversations stress how little time will be required of the new board member. This is a mistake for two reasons. It may lead to unrealistic expectations on the part of the new member, possibly resulting in a lower level of involvement than required. More important, it diminishes the real reason for which the person is being recruited: Their talent and experience would be valuable in helping to shape the institution's work and future agenda. In short, apologizing for the inconvenience of serving usually backfires.

New Member Orientation

Orientation programs, formal or informal, are intended to make it easy for new board members to make a contribution right away. While there are formal training programs in many countries for the directors of nonprofit organizations, for two reasons these are unlikely to be well suited for the directors of most think tanks. First, most such programs are oriented to a wide range of nongovernmental organizations (NGOs), with which think tanks have little in common. Think tanks often more closely resemble for-profit consulting firms or university research centers than the typical NGO that provides human services (e.g., counseling, training, and various social services). Second, the kind of people recruited to think tank boards are unlikely to have the inclination or time to attend such training events.

A simple program organized by the chairman of the board and the think tank's president can deliver the necessary information. For orientation at many think tanks, the new board member is invited to the think tank for an extended meeting with the president and to meet key staff members. When the new member resides in another city, rules of common courtesy suggest that the president should visit the new member to provide the orientation, or at least offer to do so.

The orientation should include a summary of the organization's history, because the current activities and attitudes of an organization are often heavily conditioned by its roots and early development.[20] Additional topics to cover include

- Goals and objectives;
- The current program of work;
- Recent successes in research and the policy process;
- The organization's communications and dissemination programs;
- Recent financial history;
- Fund-raising, especially if this has been a problem and year-to-year swings in financing have been significant; the strategy for dealing with funding problems;

- Any other current or impending problems that have been discussed with the board; and
- The institution's key staff, highlighting each member's special contributions.

Each new member should be given a package of materials about the organization: Its charter and other legal documents are a must, as are current financial statements, and the strategic plan if one exists. Annual reports for the past two or three years and examples of the think tank's written products should also be included.

It is often said that board members learn best by asking questions.[21] The one-on-one meeting with the president offers significant scope for questions. But the president should also encourage any new member who wants to talk with senior staff members—both researchers and administrators—to go ahead.

No orientation is complete without a discussion of the new board member's duties and the kind of role the organization hopes that the member will play. This conversation can be led by the president or the chairman of the board. In either case, it should be guided by a statement produced by the board, ideally at the same time that the board discusses specific candidates to serve on the board. Most of the duties will be common to all members, including attendance at board meetings, active participation in the meetings, and so forth. But there may be particular tasks for some members. For example, a member with a strong financial background could be asked to take the lead in monitoring the organization's financial condition and controls, presumably mostly by reviewing the annual external audit of the institution's finances.

ASSESSING THE BOARD

There is no question about the desirability of a board assessing its work every few years. A penetrating, realistic look at the board's activities can catalyze steps to strengthen its stewardship. But it is a mistake for a board to begin such a process unless it understands the work involved and fully intends to complete it. Robinson (2001, 148–49) outlines the following elements in a self-assessment:

- The commitment of the full board to participate;
- A committee or small group with an assignment to oversee the review and manage the results;

- A clear timetable that specifies when the self-assessment questionnaire will be reviewed by the full board, distributed, and returned;
- Time set aside during a regular board meeting or for a special
  meeting to review the results;
- An action plan that addresses the weaknesses the board perceives in
  its role or structure; and
- A way to monitor whether the action plan is being realized.

There are a number of guides available to help the boards conduct a
self-assessment.[22] In the end, whether the board designs its own process
or follows someone else's guidelines, questions like those listed in
Exhibit 6-7 will need to be addressed.

Short of a full self-assessment, these questions offer a starting point for
the board chairman and the think tank's president to assess how well the
board is discharging its duties. The board and the president can map out
plans to address any obvious problems. The objective, whether or not the
whole board is involved and whether or not the changes result from consultations between the chairman and the president, is to maximize the
contributions made by the talented people serving as board members.

Exhibit 6-7 Typical Issues and Questions Addressed in a Board Self-Assessment

- *Mission:* Is the mission statement used to guide decisions? Is it current?
- *Board composition and structure:* Is the talent the organization needs
  represented on the board? Does the committee structure function?
- *Board meetings:* Do meetings focus on the right issues? Does the board
  have the information it needs to make decisions? Is there adequate time
  for discussion and debate?
- *Board/staff relations:* Does the board respect the authority of the executive director? Is the evaluation of the executive director useful to the
  board and to the director?
- *Core activities:* Does the board evaluate these activities' effectiveness?
- *Finances:* Does the board read and understand the financial reports?
- *Fund-raising:* Does the board understand the plan for resource development? Does the board understand its obligation to help raise funds?

NOTES

(Complete references can be found in the Reference Section at the end of this book.)

1. I thank Dessislava Petkov and Kathy Courrier for useful comments on an earlier draft.

2. My board experience includes being a member of the board of trustees of the nonprofit Institute for Urban Economics in Moscow (1995–present), the board of directors of the for-profit Metropolitan Research Institute in Budapest (1992–1997), and the board of directors of the for-profit E-A Ratings in Moscow (1997–2001).

3. These are listed in chapter 1.

4. These are Robinson (2001), Schultz (2001), Carver (1997), and Charan (1998).

5. It is worth noting that in many countries such laws lack a specific organizational form that would fit think tanks' activities very well.

6. This section draws on Robinson (2001, 11–12, 29–40).

7. Source for Exhibits 2 and 3: Carver (1997), Chapter 5; materials from Carter have been edited by this author.

8. Source: Carver (1997), chapter 5 as edited by this author.

9. This modest limit is appropriate for recently founded think tanks, but higher limits will be appropriate as the institution gains experience.

10. Schultz (2001), p. 205

11. Charan (1998, 117) suggests using the following three questions as a guide in preparing presentations:

   1. What are the two or three insights the board should get from this presentation?
   2. What are the two or three issues on which the presenter might benefit from the board's insight?
   3. What are the two or three points about which the presenter believes the board should be fully informed?

12. Charan (1998), p.116.

13. Schultz (2001), Chapter 9.

14. See the chapter "Renewing the Work Program: Creating Innovation."

15. Even in this sphere, however, it is extremely unusual for individual board members or the board as a whole to press an initiative on senior management against its wishes. The board's power lies more in discouraging a new initiative about which it has reservations than in creating one.

16. In the absence of an audit, the board or a committee will have to review the financial statements with great care, and should appoint a committee to check to ensure that basic controls are in place and are being used.

17. Alternatively, some boards appoint a treasurer who is assigned primary responsibility for financial oversight. A good treasurer can be effective in investigating the reasons for anomalies in the financial reports. On the other hand, with responsibility assigned to a treasurer, other board members often believe they are relieved of responsibilities in this area. Moreover, treasurers are not all as diligent in the performance of their duties as is necessary, but the board has little way of knowing whether this is the case. For these reasons, keeping responsibility with the board, either through a committee or as the whole, is desirable (Robinson 2001, 78–80).

18. Where the think tank has a board of management and a separate advisory board, it may be sufficient for the advisory board to meet annually and to focus on the accomplishments of the institution or the future direction of the program.

19. These two reasons are noted in Robinson (2001, 22).

20. This paragraph draws on Robinson (2001, 76–77).

21. See, for example, Charan (1998, 85–88).

22. See, for example, Slesinger (1995) and Holland and Blackmon (2000).

Raymond J. Struyk 7

Teams or Stars? Options for Structuring the Research Staff

The effective and efficient organization of a think tank's research and analytic work is one of senior management's most important tasks. But the way in which researchers are organized to execute projects is often more a result of historical accident than a carefully considered decision. When think tanks begin operations, the emphasis is on winning projects, completing them well, and getting the results used in the policy process. Worries about management and organizational decisions take a back seat to more pressing issues. While other management issues, particularly those of financial and staff management, are addressed later, the research organization question is often neglected because the work is getting done at an acceptable standard.

A think tank may be producing high-quality work under its current arrangements. But it may also be possible to do the work more efficiently and with greater staff satisfaction if management adopted an alternative structure for some or all of its research and policy analysis. Now may be a good time for managers to take a step back and reconsider their operation.

This chapter has three tasks: to outline alternative ways think tanks can structure their research operations; to present some information on the actual practices of think tanks in different environments; and to provide some guidance to senior think tank managers for assessing whether their current structure is best suited to their operations.

ALTERNATIVE MODELS

Perhaps not surprisingly, several distinct models for structuring analytical and policy work have emerged among think tanks over time. I have

183

identified these models from a series of interviews and on-site observations at about 30 think tanks in a half-dozen countries.[1]

These models result from a complex interaction of two distinct aspects of how think tanks conduct their research. The first aspect concerns the way research is organized. One can distinguish between the following two models:

- *The "solo star" model.* Under this model, notable and influential researchers basically work independently, with the aid of one or two research assistants. The research they produce is more often "soft," in the sense that it involves limited manipulation of large data sets and complex statistical analysis. The results are usually published under the star's name. In the United States, for example, institutions that conduct *solo star* work have senior researchers with strong connections to the government, Congress, and academia.
- *The team model.* Think tanks that rely on teamwork tend to conduct large-scale research projects, program evaluations, and demonstration and pilot projects. The work more often includes original data collection and other field work; statistical analysis is frequently complex and rigorous.

The second aspect that affects models is the staff structure. Think tanks rely either on full-time staff or on various forms of supplemental staff: associates, who are usually some type of part-time or full-time distinguished visiting fellow employed for a specific project; and consultants, who are engaged to work on specific projects, often with resident staff at the think tank. In this context I am restricting the use of the terms "associates" and "consultants" to projects on which they have a leading role over the life of the project; I am excluding cases in which consultants or associates provide specific, limited expert advice to a project (i.e., the classic short-term consultant role). Several variations in these arrangements can be distinguished:

- Very dominant resident staff; some supplemental researchers may be present but are not integral to the institute's operations;
- Resident staff working with consultants;
- Resident staff working with associates;
- Blend of resident staff, associates, and consultants.

A general idea of which models have been adopted by think tanks in quite different circumstances is provided in tables 7-1 and 7-2, which are based on information drawn from earlier studies. Table 7-1 shows the staffing arrangements at 10 "third-stage" think tanks in the United States and Western Europe. The *solo star* model, chosen by 5 of the 10 think tanks, is clearly dominant. The second most common model, chosen by three think tanks, is the joint *resident staff working with consultants and associates.* Under this model, work also tends to be organized according to the *solo star* rather than the *team* model.

Table 7-2 presents information for a selected group of 37 think tanks located in four countries in Eastern Europe and the Commonwealth of Independent States (CIS). Our focus is on the 21 with at least seven full-time researchers—a rough cut-off for "second-stage" institutions. These 21 think tanks clearly favor the full-time staff model over one with a small core staff and a large number of part-time researchers. Only two of these think tanks—both in Bulgaria—report having more part-time

Table 7-1 Organization of the Research Staff at Selected Third-Stage Think Tanks[a]

Think Tank	Solo Star	Teams	Staff and Consultants/ Associates	Staff and Foreign Fellows
U.S. think tanks				
American Enterprise Institute	X			
Brookings Institution	X			
Council on Foreign Relations	X			
Center for Strategic and International Studies			X	
Heritage Foundation	X			
Hoover Institution	X			
Institute for International Economics			X	
Urban Institute		X		
European think tanks				
Center for European Policy			X	
Stockholm International Peace Research Institute				X

Source: Struyk, Ueno, and Suzuki (1993), table 4.1.
a. Information is for the early 1990s.

Table 7-2 Hiring Status of Researchers at Selected Think Tanks in Eastern Europe and the Commonwealth of Independent States

		Number of Think Tanks With at Least Seven Full-Time Researchers		
Country	Number of Tanks Studied	Total	Number of Think Tanks with More Full-Time than Part-Time Staff	Average Number of Part-time Staff
Armenia	4	1	1	5
Bulgaria	11	6	4	18
Hungary	11	5	5	3
Russia	11	9	9	8

Source: Struyk (1999), appendix E-3.

than full-time researchers.[2] These two report a very large number of part-time researchers (70 and 30); this is the cause of Bulgaria's high average number of part-time researchers (last column in the table). In the other three countries, the average number of part-time researchers is about 4; in Bulgaria, it is 18. In short, in the Eastern Europe–CIS region, think tanks favor a model in which resident staff are dominant. No information on whether these organizations favor the *solo star* or the *team* model is available from the study used for table 7-2. But on-site observations at many of these think tanks suggest that the *team* model is dominant.

While the information just presented is helpful in describing current practices, it understates the variety of the models that exist in practice. In fact, think tanks combine the two sets of options for staffing research—*solo star* versus *team,* and varying emphasis on resident staff—in a variety of ways. Table 7-3 displays these options and presents my judgment on how frequently various models are adopted. The two most common models are the *very dominant resident staff* and the *resident staff with consultants.* But both of these have *solo star* and *team* variants. For example, among the *very dominant resident staff/solo star* third-stage institutions is the Brookings Institution in Washington, D.C. But the Urban Institute, also in Washington, D.C., employs the *very dominant resident staff/team* structure. Think tanks that employ the *solo star* structure are likely to have an associate or consultant only to lead his or her own project or to be a collaborator on a very large project.

Table 7-3 Alternative Staffing Models for Research at Think Tanks and Their Frequency of Adoption

Model	Solo Star	Teams	Use of Senior Associates/Consultants[a] Solo Star	Teams
Very dominant resident staff[b]	Common	Common	Separate or very large projects	Occasional
Resident staff with consultants	Common	Common	Separate or very large projects	Fairly common
Resident staff with significant number of associates	Occasional	Infrequent	Occasional	Infrequent
Blend of resident staff and associates/ consultants	Occasional	Infrequent	Occasional	Infrequent

Source: Interviews with think tanks, and author's observations.

a. Associates/consultants have major responsibility within the project and are not just providing limited expert advice.

b. Some visitors may be present but they are not integral to the institute's operations.

Many think tanks use the *resident staff with consultants* structure because it gives them greater flexibility in staffing specific projects and allows them to avoid the high fixed cost of a large permanent staff. Examples from the West include the Center for Strategic and International Studies and the Center for European Policy Studies. This model is used frequently in Eastern Europe, with consultants often leading project teams (e.g., the Center for the Study of Democracy in Sofia, a second-stage think tank). In other cases, leadership is provided by regular staff team leaders, and intermittent workers make up most of the other members of the team (e.g., the Expert Institute in Moscow, a second-stage think tank).

Of course, few think tanks offer a pure example of one of these models. The Urban Institute, which generally uses a team approach, also has senior fellows who typically conduct their research as solo stars. Similarly, the Brookings Institution forms research teams to execute exceptionally large projects—but the teams tend to be disbanded when the project is completed.

The final two models, involving the use of a significant number of visiting scholars in residence to conduct projects, are generally used less frequently. Matching the visitor's interests and schedule with the funded agenda of the think tank is consistently challenging. These models work well when the think tank has significant core funding from a government agency or other consistent source. I do not discuss them further.

WHICH MODEL TO CHOOSE?

There are six factors that managers should consider when determining the best arrangement for a particular think tank.

Type and Size of Projects

The larger the share of a think tank's workload that consists of program evaluations, demonstration and pilot projects, technical assistance projects, and other projects requiring significant primary data collection, the stronger the argument for a team model. The team model normally requires a core of resident staff to manage the projects and provide the necessary coherency and organization. For example, consider a pilot project that works with local governments to improve the targeting of locally administered social assistance programs. The project requires that a team work with local administrators to design and implement the pilot projects and then carry out rigorous implementation or process evaluations to determine whether pilots are successful. A team of six or more professionals could be engaged on such a project for more than two years.[3]

In contrast, when the emphasis is on policy analysis exploiting secondary data or a limited amount of qualitative information, the solo star model is more appropriate. When an analyst is addressing questions involving a country's foreign policy, typical tasks include reviewing a substantial literature and perhaps examining a volume of internal foreign ministry documents. Interviews with members of the policy elite may also be involved. An able research assistant may well be sufficient support for the senior researcher working on such a project.

While associates and consultants as well as resident staff can be solo stars, a core cadre of resident senior staff is necessary to give a think tank credibility. Hence, it is unusual to find a *solo star* model that is not mostly based on resident staff members.

Variability of the Work Load

The greater the variance (both positive *and* negative) in the total volume of an institution's activity or in the distribution of total activity among different topics over time, the greater the challenge to the institution's management to maintain a consistent core staff. Managers must try to keep full-time staff at work on appropriate projects during the troughs and to recruit and train needed additional staff in a timely way during expansions. Hence, the greater the variability, the stronger the case for having a comparatively limited full-time resident staff and relying more heavily on intermittent staff, associates, and consultants.

Flexibility of the Staff

An institute's agenda may change substantially on a year-to-year basis because of shifts in the country's policy priorities and interests of those funding the institute's work, even though the total volume of work may be significantly less volatile. Retaining a number of senior resident staff over time remains desirable even under these difficult conditions. The institutional knowledge and loyalty of these analysts and the continuity they provide are important assets.

A key question, however, is these people's willingness and ability to work effectively on new topics. A senior researcher's reluctance to shift the focus of his or her work away from a favored topic or line of analysis is often a greater problem than his or her ability to do so. Sensitive persuasion and guidance by senior management may be needed to convince a senior analyst to make the change and remain with the organization.

In general, the more flexible the senior staff in working on different topics, the better the case for having a larger resident staff. Still, senior management may well have to supplement their resident staff with short-term experts to maintain high-quality analysis on the new topics.

Tax and Social Fund Consequences

In a number of countries there are important differences in the cost to a think tank of hiring the same person as a staff member or as a consultant. This arises because of differences in the treatment of the two types of employment on the employer's responsibilities for withholding the personal income tax and/or remitting contributions to various social funds (e.g., health insurance, pension). Typically, consultants are relatively cheaper to the think tank in such situations. To be competitive, a think tank may have little choice but to hire a significant share of its total research staff through various kinds of consulting arrangements.

Institutional Reputation

A think tank's ability to choose among *resident staff, consultant,* and *distinguished visitor* models will depend substantially on the institution's reputation. The more prestigious the think tank, the easier it will be to attract a senior policy analyst or researcher to be a part-time staff member or a visiting fellow. If the institution has yet to establish itself in the first group of think tanks in its country, then hiring such senior people as consultants may be the right strategy, strengthening the resident staff and the institution's reputation.

Special Cases

Regardless of the principal model for organizing the research and analysis function a think tank's management selects, there are sometimes good reasons for making an exception to the rule. Consider a think tank with a strong tradition of using a team organization for its research. If it had the opportunity to attract a distinguished scholar in an area of particular importance to the think tank's longer-term agenda, but that researcher preferred to work in the *solo star* mode, it would seen reasonable for the think tank to accommodate the scholar. In another example, a think tank that generally employs a full-time resident research model might want to hire a part-time, or even intermittent, senior staff person when launching work in a new area. With the volume of work over the first few months being highly uncertain, this flexibility might be necessary to keep the initiative financially viable.

FINAL THOUGHTS

Most think tanks would do well to review their staffing and research structure strategy every few years. Preparing careful characterizations of the institution for each of the first five of the factors listed above would be a useful starting point for these deliberations. I have three further bits of advice.

First, think not only about the institution's current requirements but also about the goals the organization is striving to attain in the next few years. Is it trying to shift from being heavily concentrated on technical assistance projects to doing more policy research? Is it striving to make process or implementation evaluations of government programs a substantial part of its agenda? These plans should be reflected in the way the structure of the research operation evolves.

Second, be flexible. There is no need to adopt any single model as the sole structure for conducting research. As noted, major think tanks in the United States and Europe often employ more than one model, depending on the task to be done. When needed, different models should be adopted to fit particular circumstances. That said, it is probably nonetheless useful for a think tank to use a defined general approach to structuring its research—that is, a model that is believed to be effective in current operating circumstances—unless there are good reasons for changing.

Third, be creative. For example, some think tanks find that while the *resident staff/team* model generally works well, each team cannot be fully self-sufficient. One common problem is that the institution's research teams need help with econometric aspects of an evaluation or analysis, but no team needs a full-time econometrician. So think tanks employ an econometrician who acts as an in-house consultant to the teams, as well as carrying out his/her own projects. Sampling and survey experts can also work across projects.

NOTES

(Complete references can be found in the Reference Section at the end of this book.)

1. Most of this information is summarized in Struyk (1993; 1999).

2. The survey also asked about the number of "other staff," which was intended to record the number of workers involved in research (i.e., interviewers and consultants used from time to time). The information suggests that the question was not always understood as intended and that the answers in some instances refer to a wider range of staff than the types of groups just mentioned. Therefore, the information is not used in this discussion.

3. Note that while the team could conduct elite interviews, they would generally not carry out household or other large-scale surveys. Sampling and survey experts, along with interviewers, would have this responsibility. The team would, however, be responsible for managing the survey process to ensure that it met the needs of the project.

Raymond J. Struyk[1]

8

Communicating Results

Effective communication of results to the right audiences is just as important to a think tank's success as producing high-quality research and policy analysis. There is little point to conducting fine policy analysis if it is only to become a dust catcher on the analyst's shelf. A cottage industry has grown up around analysis of the link between research and policy development, and the outpouring of advice on how to conceptualize the effective dissemination of research results never stops.[2] The sheer volume of writing attests to the difficulty that most researchers and think tanks have in getting the results of their work used. After reviewing numerous reports and interviewing research contractors, Saywell and Cotton (1999) state, for example,

> It is a truism to say that research cannot be used unless it is available to those who might best use it, at the time they need it, in a format they can use and with findings that are comprehensible and adaptable to local circumstances . . . [D]issemination of research, as practiced by UK based research contractors . . . fail[s] to meet these fundamental criteria. (43)

Rather than try to summarize the voluminous literature on research dissemination to the policy and other communities, this chapter gives practical guidelines on how to establish an effective communication program. This discussion purposefully employs the term *communication* rather than dissemination. Dissemination indicates a process for distributing a product after it is developed. Here communication denotes a process that starts at the initiation of a research project with the identification of policy clients for the results, initially defines products to meet

193

the needs of the various audiences identified, and then updates this plan as needed as the research project evolves.

This discussion is organized in five parts. The first section reviews several principles about the nature of policy formulation that help guide the development of a concrete communications strategy. The second section takes a leaf from marketing literature to describe a seven-step process for developing a communication plan for a specific product. Each step is adjusted for the peculiarities of communicating in the public policy arena. In the third section I offer a series of pointers on how to make the seven-step process more effective. The fourth section outlines and compares the current practices of several of the most developed think tanks in Eastern Europe and the Commonwealth of Independent States; less complete information is presented for a group of African think tanks. The last section briefly discusses how the communications function can be organized within a think tank.

PRINCIPLES FOR COMMUNICATION

Bardach (1984), Stone, Maxwell, and Keating (2001), and many others have argued that the context in which research is produced fundamentally affects the utility of the results to policymakers—if the issue under study is a "hot" topic, the work may be influential, even if it is not packaged terribly well. On the other hand, great research, ably presented, may receive no attention if the policy question it addresses is not prominent on the agenda of the government or legislature.

Political scientists speak of "windows of opportunity" for policy changes (Hall, 1990; Kingdon, 1984). The early days of a new government are often cited as a moment of opportunity. There are similar windows for the effective use of research findings in the policy process—that is, when an issue is prominently on the nation's agenda and under active consideration (Garrett and Islam, 1998). In reality, there are multiple types and degrees of opportunity, as illustrated in table 8-1 for national-level policy issues. The opportunities in the table are differentiated by how prominent the issue is, whether the issue requires action by the government or legislature or by a lower-level government agency, and how timely the issue is (i.e., is it under active consideration?).

The most prominent public policy issues are the purview of senior government officials and the legislature. Within the legislature, its leaders constitute the key players. Members of the government and legisla-

Table 8-1 Types of Policy Issues from a Communications Perspective

Opportunity	Target Audience
Prominent policy questions under current discussion	Key members of the government and the legislature and their staffs; influential intermediaries[a]
Policy question that is likely to be prominent and to be taken up in the mid-term	Administration and legislative branch staff and intermediaries
Second-tier policy matters, for example, those addressing improved administration of a program, under active discussion	Key program administrators, interest groups, intermediaries
Second-tier policy matters likely to receive attention in the mid-term	Key program administrators, interest groups, intermediaries
Identification of a new potentially prominent policy issue	Senior members of government and legislators with responsibility for the area, relevant advocacy NGOs, intermediaries, the public

a. Intermediaries include relevant advocacy NGOs, think tanks and consulting firms working in the area, donor organizations, and individual experts and lobbyists.
NGOs = nongovernmental organizations

tive leaders are assisted by their staffs and by such intermediaries as advocacy nongovernmental organizations (NGOs), think tanks, and individual experts and knowledgeable lobbyists.[3]

One of the most famous examples of just-in-time policy recommendations from a Western think tank features the U.S. Heritage Foundation. Ronald Reagan was elected president in November 1980 and began immediately to assemble his cabinet and consider major policy directions for his new administration. Within weeks of the election the Heritage Foundation delivered to the government-in-waiting a several hundred page, comprehensive, and well-argued policy blueprint focusing on early actions the new government should take. The Foundation's recommendations, based on months of prior work, were unusually influential for the new government. This action also caught the imagination of the policy community and redefined the meaning of "timeliness" for the U.S. policy community. From then on the entire think tank industry has worked harder on timeliness and on clarifying its policy recommendations.

Naturally, analyses specifically commissioned from a think tank by a senior official can be extremely influential. An example of a significant success for a Russian think tank is given in box 8-1. But it is important to keep in mind that when work is commissioned in this way, the communications task is dramatically simplified because there is a ready-made audience.

Second-level issues will be dealt with by lower-level government officials, although the ultimate disposition of a question may require cabinet approval. Implementation of the results of many program evaluations are in this group. Regulatory changes are also often in this category.

Box 8-1 National Priority Issue with Timely Think Tank Input

Housing for Retired Russian Officers

In early October 1997, the highest officials of the Russian government decided that it was imperative to address the shortage of housing for retired military officers. Already about 150,000 recently retired officers were living either doubled up with friends or family or in makeshift arrangements. Another 50,000 officers would be retired as part of the structuring of the country's military forces. Neglect had already spawned a new conservative, military-oriented political party that was gaining national prominence. Legitimate grievances would fuel the party's appeal, which would pose a genuine threat to the country's liberal reforms in the next election.

First Deputy Prime Minister Boris Nemstov called up the Institute for Urban Economics (IUE), a local think tank, to draft a program within 15 days. Mr. Nemstov had worked with IUE previously testing a consumer subsidy scheme for retired officers when he was governor of Nizhni Novgoord Oblast. He and IUE agreed that this scheme would be the basis for the new program. IUE delivered the draft program on schedule; under it officers would receive grants covering 80 percent of the purchase price of a unit in the locality where they reside, with the subsidy paid by the bank acting as the government's agent directly to the seller of the unit. Ten days later the plan for financing the program with minimum public financing was delivered by the Institute. By the end of October 1997 President Boris Yeltsin had endorsed the concept. The program was subsequently formally created through a government resolution and implemented.

Source: Struyk (1999), p.1.

One example of effective research on a second-tier problem is an assessment done in four Russian cities of the quality of the administration of social assistance programs. In Russia, these programs are nearly universally administered through local government offices, sometimes with very precise regulations from national ministries but often not. The analysis of nine offices in four cities showed that administrative procedures were generally underdeveloped in such critical areas as staff training and supervision, quality control of eligibility and benefit determination, preparation of management reports, and monitoring program implementation. The results of this analysis were presented to senior staff at the Ministry of Labor and Social Welfare, who were motivated to agree to participate in the development of a program to improve the operations of local offices.[4]

On making use of policy results on second-tier issues, Platt (1987) points out the importance of networks, such as professional associations, in the process of informing administrators and generating a consensus for change. Worth stressing is that the involved policy communities are typically very well defined, often a comparatively small group with direct administrative responsibilities.[5]

Finally, there is a third class of policy topic—the newly identified issue. An extremely famous example in the United States was Michael Harrington's work publicizing substantial domestic poverty in the 1960s. Harrington's compelling description in *The Other America* made reducing the incidence of poverty a priority item on the nation's policy agenda. For new policy issues the audience may well be different from that for items already on the policy agenda, and achieving notice may require first engaging the public's interest in the issue.

Besides the prominence of the issue, a key dimension defining the relevant communication audience is the issue's place on the policy agenda—is it currently under consideration, on the agenda but unlikely to be considered before next year, or not on the agenda? In other words, is this the moment of opportunity? If it is a hot topic, then the think tank should design concise products and work hard to communicate results to the most senior policymakers and their advisers.

If the policy question is not current, it is still important to communicate analytic findings to relevant audiences for at least two reasons. First, strong early analysis of an issue can set the terms of the future debate. Experts in a field, in and out of government, may well come to think of the issue in the way it is depicted in early analyses. In this regard, a recent analysis by Andrew Rich (2001) on the influence of U.S. think tanks is insightful. While think tanks with a conservative perspective are much more active day-to-day in the national policy process than their more liberal counterparts, Rich does not see conservative organizations as necessarily more influential. The reason is that the liberal think tanks do more of the basic analysis and number crunching, while the conservative think tanks offer greater argumentation but less new information. In effect, the liberal think tanks are more successful at framing the way the issue will be considered—an extremely powerful advantage in a policy debate.

Second, it is extremely important to transmit analytic results to the key intermediaries for a particular topic—whether the advocacy NGOs, administration and legislative staff members, donor organizations, think tanks, or experts who will be consulted when the issue gains prominence. Bardach (1984) refers to these organizations and individuals as "information banks" or "storage cabinets." These are the resources that the key decisionmakers will consult once the issue matures. It is their job to be informed. So they will informally catalogue and store quality entries on a topic to have on hand when the issue does move up the agenda.[6]

Most think tanks do not differentiate among policy issues along the lines suggested in table 8-1; they have an undifferentiated communication strategy. They tend to use the same vehicles to disseminate their findings regardless of the prominence or timeliness of the issue. Yet the lesson implicit in both the research literature and prominent successes like Harrington's is that the first step in developing a communications strategy for a project is to understand the policy prominence and timeliness of the issue under analysis.

A STEP-BY-STEP PROCESS[7]

The development and implementation of a communications strategy for think tanks is a seven-step process. The steps listed in table 8-2 do not need to be followed slavishly for a good strategy to emerge, but they do structure the process in a way that is easily understood.

Step 1: Identify the Target Audience

As summarized in table 8-1, the target audience depends critically on who has responsibility for addressing the policy question and whether the issue is currently under consideration or may be later. In identifying

Table 8-2 The Seven Steps of Effective Communication

1. Identify the target audience.
2. Determine the communication objective for each audience.
3. Select the communication channels.
4. Design the message.
5. Establish the budget for communications for this project.
6. Decide on the communications mix.
7. Measure the communications results.

Source: Adapted from Kotler (2000), p. 552.

Box 8-2 Three Reasons Why the Intended Audience May Not Receive the Intended Message

Keep these pitfalls in mind and consider options that could minimize their adverse effects when designing the strategy to disseminate specific findings.

1. **Selective attention.** Key people in the policy community—policymakers, their staff, researchers at think tanks, advocates at NGOs—receive a huge volume of memos, reports, newspapers, magazines, and other documents, plus a high number of phone calls and e-mails. Even a well-crafted message may not be noticed in this maelstrom.
2. **Selective distortion.** Recipients will hear what fits into their belief system. As a result, they often add meanings to the message that are not there (amplification) and do not notice other components that are there (leveling). The communicator must then strive for simplicity, clarity, interest, and repetition to get the main points across.
3. **Selective retention.** People retain in long-term memory only a small fraction of the messages that reach them. Effectiveness in delivering the message is critical to retention. Messages with a positive reception are much more likely to be recalled later than those that make a negative first impression. The exception is that an effective negative message that causes the recipient to rehearse counterarguments is also likely to be remembered.

the target audience, be clear about the ultimate target. It is fine to target intermediaries who can carry the message to the ultimate decision-maker, but be aware of the distinctive roles of both parties.

Step 2: Determine the Communication Objective for Each Audience

The objective of communicating with a particular audience may be a *cognitive, affective,* or *behavioral* response. In other words, the think tank may want to put an idea or result in the person's mind, change his or her attitude toward an issue, or get the person to take an action. The marketing literature contains four main "response hierarchy models" that treat these three results as sequential events, that is, a person's natural thought process leads through a standard series of responses: cognitive → affective → behavioral.

So, according to the communications model described by Kotler (2000, 555) and reproduced here (see Table 8-3), in the cognitive stage the goal is to attract the target person's attention, get him or her to receive the information (pay attention to it), and digest the point intellectually; in the affective state, the information must influence the person's attitude toward the issue, at least enough to put it on his or her agenda, and then stimulate the recipient to form an opinion and an intention of action; then in the behavior stage, the person takes action.

Take the following example. If the research result is the identification of a new potentially prominent policy issue (e.g., under-servicing of rural infants' health care needs), one target audience is the broad population with an interest in improving the conditions identified. But to reach this audience, it is necessary to use mass media. So, in effect, there

Table 8-3 Three-Stage Model of Communication

Stage	Event
Cognitive stage	• Exposure
	• Reception
	• Cognitive response
Affective stage	• Attitude
	• Intention
Behavior stage	• Behavior/action

are two audiences—the ultimate (the population) and the proximate (mass media). To attract the attention of the reporters and editors, results must be expressed in vivid (but accurate) language, in a highly understandable way, and in a concise document that contains hard figures and, if possible, human interest vignettes from the project's field work. A briefing for the interested press could be held to follow up a press release that is embargoed until the day after the briefing. The goal is to grab reporters' attention and hold it long enough to make a convincing case about the problem's prominence and then move them to take action—first to acquire more information and consider writing the story and later preparing the story. The objective for the population is cognitive and affective—acceptance that this is a real problem and a predisposition to be sympathetic to calls for the government to address it.

On the other hand, for a second-tier policy issue that is likely to receive attention in the midterm, the objective may be strictly cognitive at this stage. The think tank seeks to get those concerned with the issue—NGOs, staff of the policy elite—to take note of the good work contained in the report so that it will be referred to when the issue surfaces later.

Step 3: Select the Communication Channels

How to communicate with the target audiences? This is certainly a critical question in developing a communications strategy for policy research results. Table 8-4 lists a number of platforms grouped under four headings used in the marketing community: promotion, public relations, personal "selling," and direct marketing. Which of these platforms or combinations of platforms is suitable for a particular policy research communication task depends critically on where the policy issue falls in the priority continuum shown in table 8-1. The following examples of possible mixes illustrate the possibilities.

For a "hot button" issue—a nationally prominent issue currently being addressed by the government or parliament—the team developing the strategy might decide on a combination of the following:

- Personal selling—having their most senior people meet with policymakers and with intermediaries, such as NGOs and staff of key policymakers;
- Preparation of short policy memos to support the visits and to distribute to other policymakers and intermediaries;

Table 8-4 Communications Platforms for Policy Promotion

Promotion	Public Relations	Personal "Selling"	Direct Marketing
Exhibits at conferences	Press kits and press conferences	Meetings with policymakers	Mailing documents
Exhibits at professional association meetings	Speeches at conferences and professional meetings	Meetings with intermediaries	Posting results on a web site
	Participation in seminars	Organizing roundtables with policymakers	E-mailing announcements
	Annual reports Publications[a] Short "policy memos" Newspaper articles		

Source: Adapted from Kotler (2000), table 18.1.
a. Includes short research reports, major research reports, and books.

- Production of a research report to complement the memos by providing technical backup and posting it on the institute's web site (direct marketing); and
- Presentations by senior staff at conferences and professional meetings where the issue is being discussed (public relations).

Depending on the prominence of the findings, a press conference might also be appropriate.

On the other hand, a quite different mix may be appropriate for a second-tier issue that is not yet on the action agenda of any responsible decisionmaker. In this case the mix could be

- Publication of a research report mailed to those intermediaries particularly interested in the issue and posting it on the web site;
- Meetings on a technical level between think tank staff and intermediaries;
- Presentations at professional conferences and presentation of seminars; and
- Publication of an article based on the research in a professional journal.

Seldom will a communications strategy employ a single vehicle. Rather, the kind of mixes illustrated above will be common.

Step 4: Design the Message

At this stage, the team working to design a dissemination strategy for the results of a policy research project have defined where the policy issue falls in the priority continuum shown in table 8-1: They know the results of the work (or can project them with some likelihood); they have identified the target audience; and they have decided which communications platforms to use to disseminate the findings. In step 4, the team determines the message to be delivered by defining three separate elements: message content, message format, and message source.

Message content. Content focuses on the principal points the team wants to make to the selected audience. Remarkably, researchers often find it difficult to summarize the heart of their findings in a few simple points. It is true that oversimplification can do a disservice to the richness of the findings and runs the risk of not fully informing the person receiving the information. But communication will not be successful if the points are not clear and straightforward. Sweeping generalities can be avoided without jeopardizing either objective. How streamlined the message must be depends on the target audience, message format, and the platform or vehicle picked (policy memo, TV appearance, scholarly journal, etc.).

Message format. Once content to be delivered and the platforms to be employed are identified, then the key issue is how the message should look or sound. Unfortunately, most think tanks devote their energy primarily to developing the message content at the expense of format.

In transitional and developing countries, a solid minority of think tanks work hard to have attention-getting yet tasteful layout for their policy memos. They consider the quality of the paper, colors for the banner and heading, whether quotations should be pulled out of the text and enlarged, as well as font size, margins, length of the article, and formatting questions such as whether to use bullets. The layout, including color, font size, and the heading, help to define how urgent the message being conveyed is and how the organization wants to be perceived. A more muted palate, high-quality paper, and moderate font size and language in the headings send a very different message from brassy colors, cheap paper, and headings that are clarion calls to action.

Numerous think tanks have developed unique banners and layouts for each policy memo series so that recipients quickly can identify the document as coming from a particular institute and dealing with a specific topic. Such customization raises the likelihood that a recipient heavily engaged on a specific policy question will pick up the document. Similarly, different formats are defined for series of reports on a particular topic or research area.

If the organization is trying to attract coverage in the print media, a good tactic is to begin the story with a brief, actual case in order to personalize the story for the reader. A story on improving the health system could begin with one or two paragraphs on how a particular person was poorly served by the present system, for example, no or poor service, high costs, etc. This will make the issue of immediate interest to the reporter and the reader. The balance of the article can then address the proposed reform.

Message format unquestionably has an impact on how a document—and the message it conveys—is received. For that reason, think tanks need to consider presentation issues very carefully.

Message source. The marketing literature points out that a credible message is based on how the person receiving the information perceives three aspects of it: expertise, trustworthiness, and likability. Expertise is the specialized knowledge the person or organization possesses to back a claim. Trustworthiness is related to how honest the information source is perceived to be. Likability, more prominent in in-person meetings and presentations, describes the source's attractiveness. Qualities such as candor, humor, and naturalness make a source more likable.[8] The tone of written documents serves something of the same role. Of course, for in-person communications, the staff member's skills as a presenter are also extremely important.

For written products, the institution's credibility is often paramount for implicit claims of expertise and trustworthiness. This is why think tanks must devote so much attention to controlling the quality of their output. For researchers who have yet to establish themselves in a field, the institution's name and logo on a publication or affiliation stated on a conference program is critical. For established researchers, institutional affiliation is less important, but the combination of a highly respected researcher and his or her affiliation with a preeminent think tank will most likely receive the policy community's full attention.

Whom the organization should select for in-person events should be carefully considered. Sometimes the researcher who has done the work is not the most effective presenter. A younger researcher may lack the credibility that the think tank's director or department head has established. The person may also lack experience in summarizing complex research findings so that a nontechnical policymaker can readily understand them. Often, a good solution is for a senior person and the researcher to call on key policymakers together. That way, the senior person lends his credibility to the researcher's statements, and the researcher begins building his own credibility. The researcher can "go solo" for more technical meetings and seminars, with, for example, intermediaries and staff of policymakers.

In-person events should be carefully organized. The team designing the communications strategy should work with senior management to define the events and determine who should do each of them. Clearly, the timing and sequencing of the meetings and seminars can be important. Key policymakers should be seen early in the process so that they are not miffed to learn about these new findings secondhand.

Step 5: Establish the Communications Budget

By this point, the communications strategy has been quite well defined on the target audience, the platforms to be used, and message to be delivered. Now the general ideas must be considered in light of the budget available. Keep in mind, though, that the final budget available for communicating the results of a policy research project will result from an iterative process—defining the strategy, computing its cost, revising the strategy to realize savings, etc. As the research project nears completion, the strategy designed near the start of the project should be revisited in light of the issue's current prominence. If the issue has risen sharply in importance, the institution may decide to devote more resources to communicating the results, including more time of the president or others to promote the position indicated in the findings.

The "available budget" is an elastic concept. In practice there are usually two separate sources of resources for implementing a communications strategy. The first is the line in the project budget for report writing and dissemination activities. Often, these resources are not exploited for executing the common strategy to the degree they might. Too frequently, the researcher writes the report for the client and then begins to think about a product for wider circulation. In fact, if the communications strategy is defined early in the project, then the researcher can make the products for the client more useful as products or sources of products for the communications strategy. For example, if the strategy calls for a policy memo to be distributed, then the executive summary of the report to the client could be given more attention than usual and written and formatted so that with small adjustments it could be used to communicate with a wider audience. Few clients are unhappy to receive a report with an exceptionally lucid and well-written executive summary. Similarly, if funds for publishing the report are available, the report can be organized and formatted from the beginning with the specific communications targets in mind.

Beyond the project resources are those of the institution—both money and in-house staff resources. Some staff resources are charged to overhead accounts and can be allocated to a communications task without additional funds, though their opportunity cost certainly should be recognized. If the think tank has a public relations person, how much time could he or she devote to marketing these results (i.e., lining up interviews with newspaper columnists, doing the layout for a policy memo, etc.)? How much time is the president prepared to spend telephoning and seeing senior policymakers? A comprehensive budget should list both dollars and contribution of in-kind resources.

Step 6: Decide on the Communications Mix

With the budget in hand and the messages and channels defined, the communications team can begin determining the mix of activities to be undertaken. The mix finally decided upon will depend on the cost of each marketing activity and its perceived effectiveness in realizing the communications objective.

Each think tank should define the cost or "internal price" for each activity. In making these calculations, consider the costs incurred at each step in carrying out an activity. Past experience is a very important source of information for determining how much staff time various tasks take and the cost of printing documents, etc. Some examples of the cost components of some activities follow.

- *Meetings with policymakers.* Cost of the staff time for the meetings and in arranging them.

- *Roundtable discussion*. Cost of staff time to organize the event, including (a) logistics, such as preparing and distributing invitations, sending reminders, and handling questions, and (b) inviting key participants. Cost of staff time to participate in the event, refreshments served, and, if necessary, renting a place to hold the event.
- *Policy memo*. Staff time to write and edit the memo, including senior management review; time of desktop publications person to do layout, etc.; printing; distribution, including staff time for preparing the mailing list and mailing labels and for stuffing envelopes.
- *Seminar participation*. Staff time to prepare the presentation and participate in the conference; travel costs; and costs of documents to be distributed.
- *Newspaper article*. Time of pubic relations staff to identify a reporter willing to do an interview; researcher time to prepare a customized write-up with an "angle" likely to appeal to the newspaper; and time to meet with the reporter and perhaps work further with him or her later.

With this "price list" developed, the total cost of activities can be defined. In computing these costs, distinguish between the set-up or fixed costs and the marginal costs. For example, once you have done all the work of preparing a policy memo, the cost of distributing it to fifty more people will be very low. In contrast, there are almost no economies of scale in conducting in-person meetings with policymakers.

Estimating the effectiveness of each communications platform or activity in reaching the communication campaign's objectives will be much more difficult. To a limited degree, the frequency with which think tanks in a country actually employ various platforms is a measure of their effectiveness. (Information of this sort is presented in the section on think tanks' practices.) But such aggregated information does not indicate how useful a channel is at reaching different audiences and for issues of varying degrees of policy prominence. For that reason, the think tank's own experience and sense of effectiveness of different activities will probably be paramount.

In scrutinizing the total cost of employing various platforms to various degrees and the effectiveness of each, the team designing the communications strategy will want to reconsider some of the decisions made in earlier steps. *In particular, steps 3 to 6 in table 8.2 should be reconsidered.*

Clearly, senior management and the researcher should be consulted closely throughout the development of the communication plan and be in agreement with the final product. This plan helps guide the researchers in the production of the products required under the grant or contract funding the project. It also gives all parties the chance to discover new opportunities to make presentations at conferences, etc., especially as the project draws to a close.

As the research findings crystallize near the end of the project, the strategy should be revisited to make sure that it accommodates the actual findings. Sometimes even well-conceived projects yield weak results. Sometimes the nation's policy priorities shift over the research period, especially if it is longer than six months. Changes such as these require that the strategy be fine-tuned or, in rare cases, completely rethought.

Step 7: Measure the Communications Results

Organizations that devote effort to monitoring the effectiveness of their past communications activities will do a much better job designing new ones. They will have critical information on the effectiveness of various platforms to use in deciding on the communications mix, as just discussed.

Different monitoring approaches are appropriate for different activities. The effectiveness of a press conference can be assessed by the resulting volume of newspaper and TV coverage, with due allowance made for what other newsworthy events occur on the same day. Another indicator of success is the number of follow-up of radio and TV appearances triggered by the press conference.

The effectiveness of mailing out or distributing documents (e.g., policy briefs and reports) can be assessed with a questionnaire distributed by mail three or four weeks after the initial distribution. It is extremely simple, taking only a minute to fill in. The number in the upper right hand corner is coded to the name of the respondent to give a sense of anonymity to the respondent and to save time. Linking the responses to the position of the respondent (e.g., government official, think tank staffer, policymaker, assistant to a policymaker, etc.) permits analysis of how the documents fare with various audiences. The questionnaire itself could be on a postcard addressed to be returned to the institute with postage already applied. An example of a survey of recipients is given in box 8-3, and a mini case study in box 8-4.

Box 8-3 Sample Mail Questionnaire for Measuring Effectiveness of Certain Types of Communications Activities

Dear Colleague, #225

About three weeks ago the Policy Institute sent you a *Policy Brief,* "Assisting Children of Poor Families," on the issue of whether the national government should change the housing allowance program so that benefits are targeted on low-income families. We would greatly appreciate your completing this short questionnaire and returning it to us. Circle the answers that apply.

Do you remember seeing this document?   Y   N
If you do not, do not answer the other questions.

Did you skim it?   Y   N   or

       read it?   Y   N

Did you find that the contents (1 = very positive response; 2 = OK; 3 = negative response)

• Provided you new information on the topic?   1   2   3

• Gave you a new perspective on the topic?   1   2   3

• Was well written and well presented?   1   2   3

Similar questionnaires could be sent to participants at roundtable events and seminars organized by the think tank. By carefully mining the results of surveys conducted on several reports or policy briefs, the organization can better decide which formats and layouts reach alternative audiences.

As promising as the survey approach may be, experience shows that response rates for such surveys are low. They can be increased somewhat by giving an incentive to respond, such as remaining on the mailing list or stating that the updated list will be used as the basis for invitations to future seminars and roundtable discussions. Still, the poor experience and the cost of such surveys discourages many think tanks, including those with sophisticated communications activities, from using them extensively.

Box 8-4 Checking the Effectiveness of a Policy Brief Series

The Urban Institute, in Washington, D.C., initiated the *Straight Talk* series of concise (one-page) policy briefs in 1999 on issues surrounding pension reform in the United States. Thirty-four briefs were produced and mailed to some 1,600 persons believed to be actively interested in the subject. The briefs were written by a senior fellow at the Institute who has a strong reputation in the policy community on this topic.

One year after the series began the Institute sent a mailing to those receiving issues of *Straight Talk* asking if they wanted to continue to receive the policy briefs. A space was also left on the self-addressed, pre-franked return postcard for the recipient to offer comments about the series. The overwhelming majority of those on the list responded with the request to be retained on the list. In addition, approximately 100 respondents offered comments—all positive—about the series and the author. A selection of these comments was later shared as part of the application for funds to continue the series.

Judging the effectiveness of meetings with policymakers or their staff is very demanding. The actual decision made by the policy participant, of course, is the ultimate indicator of success or failure. But the decisionmakers' predisposition on an issue and various political considerations often overwhelm even the most forceful and well-articulated arguments.

An idea for senior management to consider is to engage an outsider to look at the effectiveness of the institute's communication program. The simple idea here is that monitoring one's own activities may not be very fruitful if the whole program is weak. This person could be someone from the media, public relations, or a university communications faculty. They could do a simple review of the communications program or do that plus the kind of effectiveness surveys outlined above.

All of this said, the public affairs staffer could use the simple alternative of talking with counterparts at other think tanks about their experience. While more impressionistic, the information obtained is often valuable. Whatever the method used to monitor the effectiveness of communications activities, think tanks need such feedback if they are to avoid wasting scarce resources on unproductive activities.

TIPS ON MAKING THE PROCESS WORK

The presentation of our seven-step process may give the false impression that developing a strong communications program is like baking a tasty cake: follow the recipe and the result will be satisfying. Not true. Communications is both science and art. Below are several points of advice that, if followed, will dramatically enhance the step-by-step process.

Experience Matters

A novice to communications could work sedulously at following our seven-step process and still have disappointing results. Those charged with developing a communications strategy for the think tank and assisting in the structuring of plans for the results of specific policy research projects will benefit immeasurably from various kinds of experience. These include learning from other public relations professionals and workshops, developing relationships with journalists so that the public affairs staff does not have to guess at what journalists want, trading notes with other nonprofits working in the same area, mentoring, and staying abreast of communications technology developments. Senior management needs to encourage their public relations/communications staff to engage in these kinds of activities, and not just sit in the office.

Clear Language

The importance of lucid language, or even vivid language where necessary, was highlighted in the last section. The question is how to achieve such a clear message. Too often the process is for the public relations person to do some copyediting of the researcher's product. Nearly as often this step is insufficient to transform a research report into engaging writing that appeals to the media or public.

There are two ways to move beyond this situation, and think tanks should carefully consider engaging in both, at least for high-visibility/high-priority results. One is to augment the in-house communications staff by bringing a trained journalist to "translate" the findings into clearer, more effective format and language.

A second way to address this problem is to improve the quality of the staff's writing. Few researchers have a grasp of what effective communication means. If the researchers are not committed to producing writing for nonacademic audiences or do not understand what is being asked of them, the communications activities will be badly impaired. A proven approach is to have workshops for the research staff on good writing. At such workshops the principles of effective writing are presented and the attendees write short essays following the principles. The instructor provides feedback to the class on one or two of the essays by way of illustrating strengths and weaknesses. Sometimes the format varies with essays prepared between meetings of the group.

As strong as the need for better writing, the need for training for TV and radio appearances is often even greater. In response to questions from reporters or talk show hosts researchers tend to give thoughtful but often long statements embellished with conditionals. Such responses are deadly in this environment. Short, concise, well-phrased statements are the coin of the realm. Again, the researcher should clarify the two or three most important points he or she wants to communicate in advance of the interview. Saying this is easy; remembering to do it only comes with practice. Coaching sessions—including taping and reviewing mock interviews—can be extraordinarily productive.

Perhaps the organization's public relations person could conduct such writing and speaking classes, but it is often better to bring in someone from the outside with the relevant workshop experience.

Practice shows that it may be difficult to get some of those who most need to improve their writing to participate in such classes; in such cases senior management needs to encourage participation. More generally, senior management needs to establish a "culture of effective communication"—meaning that the managers emphasize frequently the importance of communicating results effectively to the think tank's various audiences. Even so they should be prepared for only a fraction of the staff showing genuine interest in working with the media or improving their communications skills.

Who Works for Whom?

An essential understanding for the communications function to be effective is that the communications staff works for the audience/readers on behalf of the authors. If they are doing the authors' bidding, they are not doing their jobs. Failure to understand this is at the heart of many of the differences between authors and communicators. Again, it is an important task for senior management to convey the idea that it is the task of the communications specialists to work for the audiences. This is not the kind of message that is well-promulgated with a directive; rather, management must on a case-by-case basis back the communications staff in improving the clarity and forcefulness of the results of policy research projects.

THINK TANK PRACTICES

What are think tanks in developing and transition countries doing already to communicate with policymakers and the public? Unfortunately, the available information is limited. A quite rich data set exists on the *kinds* of dissemination vehicles used—publications, personal contacts, public media—by think tanks in Eastern Europe, and indicator information for a sample of think tanks in Africa. Missing, however, is information on how these think tanks select communications vehicles and how the vehicles are matched to the different types of policy environments outlined in table 8.1. Nevertheless, the information at hand does provide a broad sense of current practices.

The presentation proceeds in two parts. The first gives the information on dissemination practices for a sample of think tanks in four countries in the former Soviet bloc as of 1997: Armenia, Bulgaria, Hungary, and Russia.[9] These practices are of particular interest because the organizations that use them were found to be highly active in policy development. The second part presents the information on the practices of a sample of African think tanks.

Practices in the Former Soviet Bloc[10]

The detailed survey of 37 think tanks in the four countries noted above yielded detailed information on how think tank researchers communicate with policymakers, the types of publications and other documents produced by think tanks, and think tanks' work with the media, mainly to educate the public about the issues of the day. Because of the way the questionnaire was structured, no information is available on how think tank directors view the comparative effectiveness of these various vehicles in influencing policy outcomes. That is, we do not know if directors think meeting with or telephoning policymakers is more effective than distributing short, hard-hitting memoranda in convincing policymakers of a particular position.

Communicating with Policymakers

How do think tanks in the region work with policymakers? Does it happen through structured opportunities, such as parliamentary committee hearings or a formal advisory panel created by a ministry? Or are personal, informal contacts more important? When asked about how they had access to the policy process, think tank leaders overwhelmingly signaled that personal contacts were the basis for their involvement. Practically speaking, only think tank leaders in Bulgaria and Russia reported that structured opportunities such as participating in a parliamentary working group figured at all in the advice-giving process.

Publications

Every think tank in the sample spends time writing books, articles, memoranda, training manuals, and other publications. The allocation of effort, as measured by time spent by professional staff on writing publications, varies substantially. Two-thirds of the organizations allocate 20 percent or less of professional staff effort to writing publications, with the balance going to research and consulting, seminars, and, in some cases, training. Several Russian and Hungarian institutes make such writing a higher priority, devoting between 21 and 40 percent of staff time to this purpose. At the extreme, one Armenian and one Bulgarian think tank reported allocating half of their staff time to writing publications.

Essentially all think tanks distribute some publications free of charge; about 37 percent distribute *all* publications free of charge. Others offer some of their publications by paid order or subscription. Publications are rarely noted as a significant source of revenue for think tanks in the region.

Targeting Strategy

The strategy and level of effort, but not the influence of these activities on policy, was recorded in the interviews conducted with think tanks. Some of the more academic institutes mainly publish books, while organizations more closely involved in policy practice primarily publish brief policy position papers. Many of the research publications are distributed and read within the group of think tanks and NGOs interested in the topics covered.

Over 80 percent of the think tanks had a targeting strategy for circulation of their free publications. Some clear patterns emerged:

- Sixty-eight percent send publications directly to policymakers, who are targeted by using a mailing list of officials interested in the topic of the publication, or distributing the publications at seminars policymakers attend.
- About three-quarters of Hungarian and Russian think tanks in the sample reported some targeting to policymakers, while only 55 percent of Bulgarian and half of the Armenian think tanks reported this approach.
- Several think tanks use a subscription list to target politicians.
- Several think tanks noted that the distribution and targeting of publications produced with grant monies are governed by conditions in grant agreements.

One Bulgarian think tank stated its strategy was to hand deliver "concise, topical materials" to policymakers who had expressed interest in the topic. Another singled out thirty to forty key figures to whom it distributed memoranda, books, and occasional papers at no cost to the recipient.

Bulletins, Newsletters, Journals, and Policy Position Papers

The think tanks interviewed generally considered short documents the best type of publication to reach policymakers, given their audience's time constraints and the wide range of information sources competing for that time. Short, specific policy memoranda, analysis or report summaries, journals, or bulletins were named by about two-thirds of think tanks. The other preferred method was to publish articles in newspapers and other periodicals. In the study year, bulletins and newsletters were produced by 75 percent of the think tanks. Over 90 percent of Bulgaria's think tanks produced a bulletin or newsletter, as did over 60 percent of the think tanks studied in Russia and Hungary.

About 17 percent of think tanks in the sample, mostly from Hungary, regularly publish an academic journal. Russia's Institute of Economic Transition, for example, makes a priority of publishing a journal up to four times annually in both English and Russian because it reaches politicians, economists, and the business sector with an independent analysis and update of economic and political reform. The journal is also directed to the public and aims to popularize economic reform ideas and the value of a "market democracy."

Books

Russians printed more book titles and distributed larger numbers of them than did the other countries in the study. Ten of the eleven Russian institutions published books and 90 percent of these had print runs between 1,000 and 50,000 copies, most at the lower end of the range. Over 80 percent of the Bulgarian think tanks published books in the survey year; together, these nine organizations published 36 titles, of which more than one-third were printed in runs of 1,000 to 5,000. Seven Hungarian think tanks produced a total of 34 books, and five of these titles were printed in runs of at least 1,000 copies.

The efforts of the Russians, Bulgarians, and Hungarians are striking because none of the think tanks in the sample chose books as the best type of publication to reach policymakers, and only four (two Bulgarian and two Russian) institutes chose books as one of the best types of publications to reach "interested nonexperts." Books are expensive and slow to produce and are more in the tradition of the academic-oriented research institutes than of think tanks active in policy development. Nevertheless, large, policy-active think tanks were prominent among organizations publishing several book titles with long print runs.

Think tanks have continued to devote resources to publishing books for various reasons. Simple prestige is one. Another reason is that in some cases books may be more impressive to policymakers. For example, EpiCenter in Russia targets books to various regions where it considers that format to be significantly influential in forming public opinion. It has also attracted private sponsors to publish a series of books. One more reason for publishing books, especially when the topics treated are not a high policy priority at the moment, is that the longer format permits fuller development of a position and presentation of the supporting evidence. Such treatment can frame the discussion of the issue when policymakers eventually address it.

Educating the Public. The study measured activity by levels and type of media events reported by think tank leaders. Nearly all think tanks said that educating the public on the issues of the day was a main objective and that they used the mass media in their efforts. Only four organizations, one in each study country, reported very little press contact or other outreach to the public. The interviews do not shed light on why these organizations adopted such a policy, or indeed whether it was an official policy at all. But the vast majority of think tanks were actively trying to reach the public. (See table 8-5.) Events include press conferences, press releases, work with individual reporters to get stories published, short public service announcements, and appearances on TV and radio talk shows. Two impressions emerge from the interview data: Think tanks on average work diligently to feed stories to the media and participate on TV and radio shows, but the variance among organizations is very large, for both the number of events and the type of event favored.

A strikingly lower rate of press activity among the Armenian think tanks was observed. The reason appeared to be more a case of limited supply of media opportunities—both print and electronic—than reticence on the part of think tanks to participate. Newspapers are few in number and circulation figures are low. TV is controlled by the government, except for one channel with limited programming, and these stations do not invite diverse viewpoints.[11]

A second pattern highlighted was that press conferences are used fairly infrequently. Only a half-dozen of the think tanks reported holding as many as eight such events a year. One reason is that the events can be expensive. If the institution does not have suitable space itself, a forum must be rented. Frequently, the major media outlets expect to be paid for carrying programming of the kind that would be aired at a press conference of this type. In some instances, the host organization must also provide high-quality refreshments to put the press in the right frame of mind. Expense aside, holding a press conference usually requires the host institution to have a substantial story to convey, one complete with hard figures and a compelling policy conclusion. This substantive deterrent may be more important than the financial one.

Table 8-5 Median Number of Media Events by Think Tanks in Eastern Europe, by Country

Type of Event	Armenia	Bulgaria	Hungary	Russia
Press conferences	2	4	2–3	4
Press release or work with reporters	6	25	30	30
Audio or visual public service announcements	0	1	0	8–10
Appearance on TV or radio program	4	10	15–20	5

Source: Struyk (1999), table 4.3.

By far the most consistently popular vehicles for the think tanks studied were press releases or stories in the press and appearances on radio
or TV programs. The median numbers in these categories are certainly
impressive. In both categories distributions around the medians are
wide. The most active think tanks churned out an impressive volume of
articles and press releases in a year, including the following:

- Economics 2000 (Bulgaria), 45 to 60 articles
- European Information Correspondents Center (Bulgaria), 300+
  articles and press releases
- Financial Research, Ltd. (Hungary), 150 to 200 articles and press
  releases
- Reforma (Russia), 600+ articles and press releases

The numbers of radio and TV appearances were lower but still indicated
a very high level of exposure for the principals of many of the think
tanks. In considering these figures, keep in mind that, according to
informed local sources, most of these articles and verbal presentations
were opinion pieces. In most cases, the results of careful research projects were not showcased. If original research results were required for
every media appearance, leaders of these institutions would not be able
to contribute to public commentary so often.

An intriguing question is how much work think tanks put into getting
their messages across to the public. One indicator of the level of effort is
the number of staff working on external relations. Each think tank leader
interviewed was asked if the organization had designated someone to
spend at least half their time on public relations and, if so, what the number of full-time equivalent staff formally involved in these activities was.
Responses to the question probably underestimated the resources going
to these tasks because many small organizations cannot afford to designate someone to specialize in public affairs. When everyone pitches in,
expect less professionalism in getting the task done and less impact.

Eleven think tanks, about 30 percent of those in the database, had
designated at least a part-time external relations person. Interestingly,
seven of the eleven are Russian. With two exceptions, the 11 with a designated external relations person were among the larger organizations,
ranging in size from 12 to 60 full-time professionals. The other two had
four professional staff each. But more than the size of organization and

the volume of media events determine success. A scan of the media activity of those with and without an external relations person suggested that organizations that had taken this step are more creative. A striking example was in Armenia, where the Armenian Center for National and International Studies had two external relations people. Its media program was much more comprehensive and aggressive than those of the other three think tanks in the country sample. Such differences may not have resulted solely from staffing, but the very presence of professional public relations people reflects the importance the organization's leadership places on reaching the public.

In summary, in the picture portrayed by think tank leaders their organizations were highly active in publishing their results, often in ways tailored to reach the busy policymaker. Similarly, most organizations worked actively with the media to educate the public on the important issues and to gain institutional recognition. Yet there were also pervasive questions about the effectiveness of many of the media events, where think tank staff were just playing the role of the bright commentator and not a technical expert.

On the surface, at least, the variance across think tanks in their public education activities is substantially larger than in their work directly with policymakers. More broadly, the study noted that the great majority of think tanks did not appear to have a communications strategy.

Practices in Sub-Saharan Africa

In 1998 Johnson (2000) surveyed and interviewed leaders of 24 leading think tanks in Sub-Saharan Africa on a number of topics, including their communications with policymakers and their interactions with the media. (Most data are for 1997.) Examining how these researchers communicated with policymakers, Johnson asked respondents to rate their preference for a particular way to present their views to policymakers, using a scale of 1 to 8 to rate each of eight options (the most preferred method is rated 1). As table 8-6 shows, policy memos and public conferences are rated higher than formal or informal meetings with the policymakers. This appears to be a distinct difference from the results for the former Soviet bloc, though the findings of the two studies are not comparable. In any case, it certainly emphasizes the importance of concise memos in the policy arena in Sub-Saharan Africa.

**Table 8-6 Methods Used by Think Tanks in Sub-Saharan Africa
            to Communicate with Policymakers**

Method	Score[a]
Policy memos	2.1
Public conferences	2.5
Formal meetings (with policymakers)	3.0
Informal conversations (with policymakers)	3.1
Policy issue papers	3.2
Issue briefings	3.6
Parliamentary hearings	4.3
Draft laws and white papers	5.2

Source: Johnson (2000), p. 469.
a. Respondents rated the importance of each method on a scale from 1 to 8, with 1 being the most preferred method.

Johnson also reports some interesting statistics for interactions with the media. In particular, he found the following:

- Press releases: 69 percent (11 of 16 respondents) issued press releases in 1997, with the average being 7.5 press releases and the highest number being 10.
- Press conferences: 60 percent (9 of 15) convened press conferences, with the average number being 4 and the highest number being 6.

In Johnson's view, the percentage of think tanks issuing press releases is strikingly low, given the centrality of communicating with the public a think tank's mission.

Johnson also found that 60 percent of these institutions had at least one full-time person assigned to communicate with the media. This is a distinctly higher rate than the 30 percent for think tanks in the former Soviet bloc.

ORGANIZING THE COMMUNICATIONS FUNCTION

This section briefly considers the who, where, and when of organizing the communications function within a think tank. Because think tanks differ so widely in their size, focus, mission, funding, and internal structure, it is extremely difficult to define a concrete structure that will be of use to more than a small fraction of all think tanks. Therefore, the following sets out some general propositions that each think tank can adapt to its specific situation.

Who and Where

Here we address the two closely related questions of *who* should be involved in developing a communications plan for disseminating findings from a particular policy research project and *where* the responsibility for the development and execution of the overall communications strategy as well as communications plans should be located within the organization.

For *where*, the high importance of this function and the fact that communications plans are needed by all of a think tank's divisions that are conducting policy research projects argue strongly for the overall communications function being centralized. In most large Western think tanks, there is a separate office for communications that typically is responsible for both public relations and publications. Placing publications and public relations under the same manager aims to foster coordination between the two types of activities. The director of this office usually reports directly to the institute's president.

In smaller think tanks where such specialization is not possible, the communications function could be shared by senior management and the public relations officer, if there is one. This team would usually decide on the organization's broad strategy—the level of the institute's own resources to devote to communications, the broad priorities in the area, and a general plan, that is, which communications platforms are preferred because they have been found in the past to be effective. The general strategy may well be a topic for discussion with the board of trustees. Regardless of the size of the organization and its "communications department," someone should be designated as having primary responsibility for the communications function.

In developing a communications plan for the findings of a given policy research project, the public relations officer, the principal researcher, the director of the division in which the project is located, and a member of senior management should participate. As team they should go through the seven-step process outlined above. The public relations person can cost out different mixes and levels of activities for the team. One should expect the whole process to take two or three meetings. This may seem like a large investment but it can ultimately result in major savings in communications costs because the researchers can prepare their reports and other products for clients knowing how they relate to the products that will be used in the broader communication of results.

When

The team designing the communications plan should meet near the beginning of a project. Some sponsors, particularly foundations, require a dissemination plan as part of a proposal or work plan for a new project. In such cases the team should convene to prepare this section of the proposal or work plan. In any case, as sketched above, the seven-step process should guide the preparation of the plan.

Near the end of the project, there should be an additional meeting among the same people to review the plan in light of developments that may have occurred during the time the research was being conducted. If there are significant changes to take into account, most likely the topic of analysis rising for falling on the country's policy agenda, this is the time to adjust the strategy. The likelihood of adjustments being appropriate increases sharply as the length of the research period extends beyond six months.

NOTES

(Complete references can be found in the Reference Section at the end of this book.)

1. I want to than Kathleen Courrier, vice president for communications at the Urban Institute, for excellent comments on a draft of this chapter.

2. On the general process of policy development see, for example, Dolowitz and Marsh (1996), Feulner (1985), and Kingdon (1984). Specifically for channeling research findings to policymakers, see, for example, Bardach (1984), Corwin and Louis (1982), Garrett and Islam (1998), Lomas (1993), Rich (2001), Saywell and Cotton (1999), and Stone, Maxwell, and Keating (2001). For channeling research findings to program administrators, see, for example, Huberman (1994), Platt (1987), and Stapleton (1983).

3. Saywell and Cotton (1999) and Lomas (1993) comment on the importance of such intermediaries in the policy development process. Stone (2000) specifically addresses the role of think tanks in this process.

4. The results of the office assessments are presented in Richman and Struyk (forthcoming).

5. Likewise, Huberman (1994) stresses the importance of researchers finding the right vehicle to reach frontline administrators (or in this case, teachers) to act upon research findings.

6. This formulation is consistent with the "knowledge utilization school" that views knowledge as cumulative. Accumulated research findings over an extended period change decisionmakers' views of both the causes of problems and the utility of alternative policy interventions. See, for example, Sundquist (1978).

7. This section draws heavily on Kotler (2000), chapter 18. The presentation there uses an eight-point sequence that I have modified to better correspond to the requirements of think tanks.

8. See Kotler (2000), p. 559.

9. The names of these think tanks are listed in the annex.

10. This section draws heavily on Struyk (1999).

11. Press freedoms were rated as restricted in the country in the Freedom House state-of-democracy report at this time. See Karatnycky, Motyl, and Shor (1997), p.45.

List of Think Tanks in Eastern Europe–CIS Included in Survey of Publications and Media Practices

List of Think Tanks in Eastern Europe—
CIS Included in Survey of Publications and Media Practices

Armenia

1. Armenian Center for National and International Studies
2. Magistros Physicians Association
3. Center for Health Services Research
4. Transformation Society Research Institute

Bulgaria

1. Access Association
2. Agency for Social Analysis
3. Center for Liberal Strategies
4. Center for Social Practices
5. Center for Strategic Studies— XXI Century Foundation
6. Center for the Study of Democracy
7. Center for the Study of Social and Political Change—Sofia Foundation
8. Economics 2000
9. European Information Correspondents Center for Bulgaria
10. Ianko Sakazov Foundation
11. Institute for Market Economy

Hungary

1. Agroconsult Economic Consulting
2. Center for Security and Defense Studies
3. GKI Economic Research Company
4. Institute of Central European Studies

Hungary (*Continued*)

5. Research Company
6. Foundation for Market Economy
7. Metropolitan Research Institute
8. Public Policy Institute
9. Foundation for Small Enterprise Economic Development
10. Szazadveg Political School and Policy Research Center
11. Association for Social Research and Information—TARKI

Russia

1. Center for Political Technologies
2. Center for Russian Environmental Policy
3. Center for Ethnopolitical and Regional Research
4. EpiCenter: Center for Political and Economic Research
5. Expert Institute of the Russian Union of Industrialists and Entrepreneurs
6. Institute of Economic Transition
7. International Fund for Economic and Social Reforms (Fund Reforma)
8. Fund of Efficient Politics
9. Institute for Urban Economics
10. St. Petersburg Center for Humanities and Political Science Strategy
11. Institute for Strategic Analysis and Development of Entrepreneurship (ISAPP)

Jeffrey Telgarsky 9

Financial Management: Sustainability and Accountability

Like any economic organization, think tanks operate in a market. Discussions about think tanks tend to focus on the aspect of this market that deals with ideas and policies: What problems and issues are critical to society and decisionmakers? What topics are in vogue with sponsors? There is also an economic aspect to this market: How much funding for research is available? What are the costs of carrying out that research? With the exception of those organizations with substantial endowments, most think tanks face a situation where they are required to compete for limited funding.

Assuming a think tank has the technical qualities to be competitive in the market for ideas and policies, being able to compete successfully for this limited funding also requires that the organization be able to demonstrate two other qualities: an understanding of its costs, and control of and accountability for its use of sponsor funding. The first quality is necessary to link the research it intends to carry out with the funding available from a sponsor. An organization that consistently underestimates the real costs of carrying out an assignment will soon either deplete its own resources or find that sponsors are reluctant to continue supporting work that is incomplete or requires additional funding. The second quality is necessary to demonstrate to sponsors that the funds provided were used for the purpose intended. Sponsors provide varying latitude on the use of research funds (for example, grants often allow more discretion on the part of the recipient than contracts), but most sponsors do require an accounting of the expenditure of funds to confirm their use for their intended purpose.

Despite the importance of these aspects of financial management to the sustainability of think tanks, understanding and accounting for costs

227

frequently pose problems for both the organizations themselves and their sponsors as the think tanks develop into more substantial organizations.

Outside of highly industrialized countries, think tanks often start in one of two ways: as a small group of professionals, often around a single strong technical leader or as an organization supported mainly by a single sponsor. In both of these cases, the systems of financial management usually adopted do not readily respond to the two qualities identified above. In the first case, the organization often operates on an ad hoc basis—staff are not salaried (or only paid nominal salaries), but are paid on a project basis (much like consultants) when funding is available; fixed costs (for items such as rent, utilities, and administration) are allocated to projects in an unsystematic manner; business development costs are either unpaid by the organization (through staff providing unpaid labor) or improperly financed from project funds; and record-keeping varies with the requirements of each project. In the second case, the other extreme often prevails—the organization's financial management is geared to meeting the requirements of the sponsor, not the organization. In such circumstances, sponsor funding often covers many of the fixed costs of the organization, leading to an underestimation of the real cost of developing and carrying out work for other sponsors.

As a think tank develops from these initial stages into a mature organizations, several situations naturally occur:

- Greater formality in staffing arrangements (payment of fixed salaries, payment of employee-related taxes and social insurance contributions, provision of paid leave, provision of support for staff training and professional development);
- More substantial fixed costs related to facilities (rent, utilities, equipment, and maintenance) and administration for the organization (personnel administration, meeting legal requirements for taxation and registration, internal organizational management);
- Greater costs for business development (staff time for collecting information on new funding opportunities and writing proposals) and fundraising.[1]

These changes all result in the organization incurring costs which either are not attributable to specific research projects or can only be attributed to specific projects with great administrative difficulty. These costs (typically referred to as "fringe benefits" when they relate to costs associated with staff and as "overhead" for the cost of facilities and administration; the term "indirect costs" typically refers to all of these costs in general) are vital inputs to the long-term sustainability of the think tank:

- If the organization cannot offer a competitive package of compensation and benefits, it will be difficult to retain and motivate staff;
- Without adequate facilities and equipment, staff will not be able to conduct their research in an efficient and effective manner;
- Without training and opportunities for professional development, staff will not maintain a level of technical knowledge necessary to remain competitive;
- Without funds to support business development and fundraising, the organization will be unable to continue obtaining new project work necessary to provide continuing support to the organization and its researchers.

Simply put, the full cost of a research project rightfully includes a share of the overall necessary costs of the organization. Knowing the full cost of a research project sets a baseline for financial analysis of the project (from within the organization) and provides a basis for requesting reimbursement from sponsors for the full costs of carrying out the research project.

Despite the importance of these costs to the vitality and sustainability of the think tank, sponsors are often reluctant to pay for these costs. From the narrower perspective as the supporter of a particular piece of research with limited funds, they naturally wish to limit their support to costs that can be most directly related to the research project. (Of course, this begs the question of who is left to pay for these indirect costs.) However, even taking a broader view of the sponsor as a supporter not only of the research but also of the think tank carrying out the research, the question naturally arises: In the long run, is all of this indirect cost necessary for the think tank to carry out this work? Given limited funds, the sponsor desires the greatest result for a given investment and therefore wishes to be assured that indirect costs are being limited to those costs reasonably necessary for the think tank to continue to survive and develop.

Sponsors, being the ones with the funding, have the upper hand here. One response on their part to this concern is the imposition of limitations on the amounts of indirect cost that sponsors will pay.[2] However, as will be more fully discussed below, the definition of what constitutes indirect cost is subject to interpretation, depending on the nature of the organization, the activities that it carries out, and the administrative ease or difficulty of allocating costs to individual projects. The issue is further complicated by the methods available for charging indirect costs to projects. These methods can validly use a variety of different bases of direct project costs over which indirect costs can be fairly allocated (usually expressed as a percentage of the base direct project costs). Thus, any limitation on indirect cost that seeks to describe an overhead rate of 30 percent as "too high" runs the danger of inadvertently penalizing organizations whose cost structures do not match that implied by the rate limitation.

The think tank with an eye on its future sustainability should seek to develop a means of accounting for its indirect costs that serves two functions: to provide an internal management tool for identifying and tracking costs crucial to the sustainability of the organization and to provide a clear and comprehensive statement of indirect cost recovery policies that address the concerns of sponsors to pay only for a fair share of the organization's necessary costs. In practice, this means developing a financial management system which segregates and tracks indirect costs against direct project costs. Ideally, this segregation of costs is done both prospectively (through the development of a planned budget for the organization's operations) and retrospectively (through a cost accounting system). This allows the organization to estimate what costs it is likely to incur (and thus what indirect costs it must build into its budgets for new projects) and what costs it has incurred (and thus what indirect costs its existing projects must bear).

Whether a think tank needs to go further in providing assurance to its sponsors that it is implementing its recovery of indirect costs consistent with its stated policies is a judgment that each organization needs to make. However, as an organization develops and its level of support by sponsor organizations increases, so too does the argument for having an annual external audit. The audit can confirm the consistent application of indirect cost recovery policies and validity of project direct costs. (Indeed, some sponsors make such an audit of project accounts a requirement once funding reaches a certain level. For example, the U.S. Government requires organizations receiving more than $300,000 in federal funds to undergo such an audit.) Incorporating such an audit into the financial management policies of a think tank, while adding expense to the organization's operations, also demonstrates a heightened sense of accountability for sponsor funds.

The balance of this chapter goes into greater detail about the principles concerning the development of indirect cost recovery systems and describes various models and approaches for the structure of such systems.

DEFINING INDIRECT COSTS

Within any think tank, all costs can be divided into two different types: direct and indirect. Direct costs are those which are clearly and easily attributable to a specific research project. For example, the cost of carrying out a survey to collect data for research on low-income households can clearly be related to that particular research project.

Indirect costs are those which are not easily identifiable with a specific research project, but are (as described above) necessary to the operation of the research project or the organization carrying out the project. These costs are shared among projects and, in some cases, among functions within the organization (direct research, management and general administration, and business development and/or fundraising). Costs are usually classified as indirect costs when either (or both) of two conditions exists: (1) the costs are of benefit to the entire organization and all projects carried out by the organization; or (2) the costs are attributable to specific projects, but the administrative cost of tracking and allocating these costs to individual projects outweighs the benefit of doing so.

An example of the first case is the cost of a personnel director who handles recruiting, develops and implements personnel policies, and ensures compliance with employment law. These necessary services are of benefit to the organization as a whole, rather than any particular research project. In the second case, the cost for local telephone service is difficult to attribute to individual projects because the costs are typically not tied to the number of calls or the calls are not itemized. Thus, allocating local telephone charges would require maintaining logs to list the number and duration of calls and then distributing the costs across the logged calls. Since the cost of local telephone service is small (relative to total costs) and the cost (in staff time) of creating such logs is significant, allocating such costs as an indirect cost across all projects is a sensible solution.

While there is general agreement on the division between direct and indirect costs, the specifics of what sponsors view as valid (or "allowable") direct and indirect costs vary widely. Two definitions in use for nonprofit organizations in the United States are provided by the

Financial Accounting Standards Board (FASB) and by the U.S. Office of
Management and Budget (OMB).

FASB Statement of Financial Accounting Standards No. 117 requires
nonprofit organizations to report expenses by "functional classification."
The two primary functional classifications are "program services" (direct
project costs) and "supporting activities"(management and general
administration, fundraising, and membership development); they are
defined as follows:

> Program services are activities that result in goods and services
> being distributed to beneficiaries, customers, or members that ful-
> fill the purposes or mission for which the organization exists.
> Supporting activities are all activities of a not-for-profit organiza-
> tion other than program services. Management and general activi-
> ties include oversight, business management, general recordkeep-
> ing, budgeting, financing and related administrative activities, and
> all management and administration except for direct conduct of
> program services or fundraising activities. Fundraising activities
> include publicizing and conducting fundraising campaigns; main-
> taining donor mailing lists; conducting special fundraising events;
> preparing and distributing fundraising manuals, instructions and
> other materials; and conducting other activities involved with solic-
> iting contributions from individuals, foundations, government
> agencies and others. Membership-development activities include
> soliciting for prospective members and membership dues, mem-
> bership relations and similar activities.[3]

OMB Budget Circular A-122, *Cost Principles for Nonprofit Organizations,*
provides the following definition of indirect costs for projects funded by
the U.S. Government:[4]

1. Indirect costs are those that have been incurred for common or
   joint objectives and cannot be readily identified with a particular
   final cost objective. [Any direct cost of a minor amount may be
   treated as an indirect cost for reasons of practicality where the
   accounting treatment for such cost is consistently applied to all
   final cost objectives.[5] . . . After direct costs have been determined
   and assigned directly to awards or other work as appropriate, indirect costs are those remaining to be allocated to benefiting cost
   objectives. A cost may not be allocated to an award as an indirect

cost if any other cost incurred for the same purpose, in like circumstances, has been assigned to an award as a direct cost.

2. Because of the diverse characteristics and accounting practices of nonprofit organizations, it is not possible to specify the types of cost that may be classified as indirect cost in all situations. However, typical examples of indirect cost for many nonprofit organizations may include depreciation or use allowances on buildings and equipment, the costs of operating and maintaining facilities, and general administration and general expenses, such as the salaries and expenses of executive officers, personnel administration, and accounting.

3. Indirect costs shall be classified within two broad categories: "Facilities" and "Administration." "Facilities" is defined as depreciation and use allowances on buildings, equipment and capital improvement, interest on debt associated with certain buildings, equipment and capital improvements, and operations and maintenance expenses. "Administration" is defined as general administration and general expenses such as the director's office, accounting, personnel, library expenses, and all other types of expenditures not listed specifically under one of the subcategories of "Facilities" (including cross allocations from other pools, where applicable).

In addition, Attachment B to OMB Circular No. 122 specifies categories of cost which are allowable, allowable under certain limitations or conditions, or unallowable for funding by U.S. Government grants and contracts. Table 1 below summarizes Attachment B.

Nonetheless, the above guidance still allows a range of differing practices and policies for allocating expenses among the indirect and direct cost categories. As a result, how expenses are allocated between categories varies widely from organization to organization. For example, time spent by the executive director developing and overseeing programs can legitimately be considered a program expense, yet some organizations will place the entire director's salary into the indirect cost category. Similarly, while rent, utilities, insurance, supplies, and other general expenses are typically included in the indirect cost category, there may be circumstances in which it may be more appropriate for an organization to allocate these costs directly to projects. Each organization needs to decide which expenses are legitimately programmatic and which are supportive in order to define its direct and indirect costs. The

Table 9-1 Allowability of Costs under OMB Circular No. A-122

Allowable Costs	Allowable Costs (Limited)	Unallowable Costs
Bid and proposal costs	Advertising and public	Alcoholic beverages
Bonding	relations	Bad debts
Communications	Defense/prosecution of	Contingency provisions
Compensation for staff	criminal/civil	Contributions/donations
Depreciation/	proceedings	to other organizations
use allowances	Equipment/capital	Entertainment
Employee morale/health/	improvements	Fines and penalties
welfare	Fringe benefits (including	Fundraising
Independent research	pensions)	Goods/services for
and development	Housing and personal	personal use
Insurance and	living expenses	Interest on borrowed
indemnification	Idle facilities/idle capacity	capital
Labor relations costs	Indirect costs associated	Investment manage-
Maintenance and repair	with donated labor	ment costs
costs	Interest on debt for capital	Lobbying
Materials and supplies	asset acquisition	Losses on other projects
Meetings and conferences	Overtime	Organization costs
Memberships, subscrip-	Patent costs	(in connection with
tions, and professional	Pre-award costs	establishment/
activity costs	Profits/losses on disposi-	reorganization)
Page charges in profes-	tion of depreciable	
sional journals	property or other	
Participant support costs	capital assets	
Plant security costs	Publication and printing	
Professional service costs/	costs	
consultant fees	Rearrangement/alteration	
Rental costs	costs	
Royalties/costs for use of	Reconversion costs	
patents and copyrights	Recruiting costs	
Taxes	Relocation costs for staff	
Training and education	Selling and marketing costs	
for staff	Severance pay	
Transportation costs	Specialized facilities	
	Termination costs	
	Travel costs for staff	
	Travel costs for trustees	

acceptability of these allocations by auditors and funders will depend on how reasonable and justifiable is the rationale for the decision.

Since the lack of standard practices in allocating indirect expenses means that there are no "standard" indirect cost rates against which an organization can evaluate its own indirect cost rates, it makes sense for an organization to track the trend of its indirect costs over time. Questions to be asked in reviewing these trends include: How has the relationship between direct project costs and indirect costs changed over time? If indirect costs are changing in relation to direct project costs, what is causing this change? If indirect costs are increasing in relation to direct project costs, is this increase in indirect costs affecting the ability of the organization to attract funding and if so, what can be done to reverse the trend? If indirect costs are decreasing in relation to direct project costs, are there investments in the organization (such as training for staff or improved management systems) that can be made without negatively affecting the ability of the organization to attract funding?

METHODS FOR ALLOCATING INDIRECT COSTS

Once an organization has identified its indirect costs, the next step is to develop a method for distributing or allocating these costs across the activities of the organization (since these indirect costs provide some benefit to all of the organization's activities). Although there are several methods for allocating indirect costs, this chapter will examine the two most common: case-by-case allocation and developing an indirect cost rate.

Case-by-Case Allocation

The case-by-case method of allocating indirect costs is to determine a rate of actual usage for each activity in the organization. In its simplest forms, this approach can be used to account for costs that can easily be tracked. Examples of this approach include keeping track of long distance telephone calls, using a counter or log for photocopying, or using timesheets as a means of allocating the salary cost of managers and administrative staff (such as the executive director, financial manager, or administrative assistant) whose work benefits more than one program or activity. As shown by the example above, a different method can be adopted for each type of cost.

The advantage of this method is that it creates a strong connection between activities and the indirect costs that support them. The disadvantage, however, is that this approach can require a great deal of time-intensive record keeping, even for costs which are relatively minor. Further, even if complete records are kept, there will still be shared costs that cannot be precisely allocated. (For example, office space costs can be allocated on the basis of the work being done by those occupying the space and the amount of space occupied. But how then should the cost of common space, such as hallways, be allocated? Similarly, local telephone service and Internet connections typically have fixed monthly costs, regardless of use, and so do not easily lend themselves to being tracked.)

As a result, most organizations do not rely solely on case-by-case allocation for distributing indirect costs. The choice as to whether to rely on case-by-case allocation or use of an indirect cost rate (as described below) depends on two factors:

- *Ease of record keeping.* Where automated systems can track costs by project with minimal effort (such as computerized tracking systems for long distance telephone calls or photocopies), using case-by-case allocation distributes costs more accurately.
- *Variability of cost across projects.* Where costs vary significantly across projects, case-by-case allocation helps limit cross-subsidization of indirect costs. For example, if the typical project of an organization requires only a nominal number of photocopies, but one project requires a large number of copies (because of a requirement for large-scale distribution of reports, for example), case-by-case allocation will ensure that the typical projects do not have to bear a disproportionate share of photocopy costs.

Because of the disadvantages outlined above, an indirect cost rate may be a more appropriate method for allocating those shared costs which cannot be easily allocated directly to specific activities or projects.

Indirect Cost Rate

An indirect cost rate is a means of proportionately distributing indirect costs across an organization's activities or projects. To do this, all of an organization's costs have to be divided into two groups: direct costs (which are typically project or program costs) and indirect costs. The indirect costs are then aggregated into a "pool" which is then allocated to project cost, usually in proportion to the ratio of indirect costs (the numerator in the ratio) to direct costs (either total direct cost or a component [such as direct labor expense] of total direct cost; the denominator in the ratio is known as the "base").[6]

The selection of an appropriate allocation method and direct cost base for an indirect cost rate should be based upon the commonality of indirect costs to all direct cost expenditures. For most organizations, there will be a strong correlation between indirect costs (which tend to be heavily weighted toward administrative labor and support costs and facilities costs) with direct labor costs. In most cases, a direct labor base will produce an equitable distribution of indirect costs. However, where the ratio of direct labor to total direct costs varies significantly from project to project (for example, where projects have widely differing costs for travel, consultants, subcontracts, or other direct costs), a total direct cost base is more appropriate for allocating the benefits of indirect costs to projects.

The balance of this chapter looks in more detail at how to develop an indirect cost rate.

TYPES OF INDIRECT COST RATES

As described above, the calculation of indirect cost rates is based on the ratio of indirect costs to a defined direct cost base. The actual ratio of indirect to direct costs can be known only after the accounting period (typically an organization's fiscal year) for which the rate is defined has been completed; this is typically called a "final" rate. However, because both the organization and funders typically cannot wait until the accounting period is over to bill expenses and pay these bills, indirect rate structures based on a prospective analysis of costs ("provisional" rates or "predetermined" rates) are often used. These different kinds of rates are described below:[7]

- *Final Rate.* A final indirect cost rate is established after an organization's actual costs for a given accounting period (normally its fiscal year) are known. Once established, a final indirect cost rate is used to adjust the indirect costs initially claimed through provisional rates (see below). The adjustment to actual costs is for the period in which the actual costs were incurred and thus cannot be determined until the end of the period.

- *Provisional Rate.* A temporary indirect cost rate is established for a future prospective period of time to permit budgeting and billing/payment of expenses to/by funders until such time as the actual indirect costs can be determined and a final rate is established. The provisional rate is usually based on the planned budget of an organization (based on expected expenses and activities). (Or a final rate for a particular year may be used as a provisional rate in the ensuing year, if anticipated changes in funding levels or costs are expected to be small.)

  Because the provisional rate is based on the expected activity of the organization (which is likely to be somewhat different than the actual outcome), a provisional rate is subject to later adjustment by issuance of a final indirect cost rate based on actual indirect costs incurred. The organization may then either need to seek additional payment from funders (if the provisional rate was too low and there was under-recovery of indirect costs) or provide refunds to funders (if the provisional rate was too low and indirect costs were over-recovered) for those agreements between the organization and its funders which are of the cost-reimbursement type.
- *Predetermined Rate.* A fixed rate is established for a specified current or future period and is not subject to adjustment. A predetermined rate may be used on contracts or grants where there is reasonable assurance that the rate is not likely to vary significantly from a rate based on the organization's actual costs. This type of rate would be used where the organization has a consistent indirect cost rate over time (for example, because it has a very stable cost structure and funding).[8]

The use of provisional and final rates is preferable for most organizations for the following reasons:

- Actual indirect costs are allocated to projects in the period incurred, creating accurate cost information;
- There are no prior period indirect costs carried into a future period to burden new or continuing funding;
- All indirect costs are properly funded in the period incurred, creating no profit or loss for the organization;
- The organization's accounting system must determine actual costs each year, a capability that ultimately must exist to synchronize accounting, budgeting, and cost allocation; and

- The actual cost of services or programs is determined annually and is therefore available for purposes of internal management and informed budgeting.

INDIRECT COST RATE DOCUMENTATION

To support a proposed indirect cost rate, an organization should develop a set of documentation that it can provide to funders. This documentation typically includes the information outlined below. Sample documents for an Example Organization (EO) are shown as exhibits.

- *Organizational Information.* This should include:
  - Information on the structure of the organization that describes the duties and/or responsibilities of all units that comprise the organization.
  - Financial data, such as financial statements (certified, if appropriate), budgets, or other accounting reports, upon which the proposed indirect cost rate is based.
  - If the proposed indirect cost rate is recognized by other funders, a list of contracts or grants, giving details on funders, value, period of performance, and any limitations on indirect costs.
- *Cost Policy Statement.* The Cost Policy Statement (CPS) states explicitly which costs the organization will charge directly and which costs the organization will charge indirectly. An example of a CPS for the EO is shown in the appendix to this chapter.
- *Statement of Salaries and Benefits.* This document should contain the estimated/actual costs of personnel salaries and fringe benefits. Personnel fringe benefits typically divide into two types: (1) those which are statutorily determined (such as social insurance contributions, unemployment insurance premiums, payroll taxes, and other required employer contributions or leave allowances [such as holidays or sick leave] on behalf of employees and other personnel); and (2) fringe benefits determined by the organization (such as annual leave, non-salary compensation [for example, performance bonuses], or health/life insurance). Organization-determined fringe benefits are usually evaluated by funders as part of the determination of the reasonableness of total compensation to personnel. A sample Statement of Salaries and Fringe Benefits for the EO is shown in exhibit 1.

Exhibit 1 Example Institute
Statement of Salaries and Fringe Benefits

	Total Annual Salary	Leave Component of Salary[1]	Non-Leave Component of Salary[2]
Salaries			
Executive Director	$ 60,000	$ 9,231	$ 50,769
Technical Staff (5 @ $40,000 each)	200,000	30,769	169,231
Financial Manager	30,000	4,615	25,385
Administrative Assistant	20,000	3,077	16,923
	$ 310,000	$ 47,692	$ 262,308

		Fringe Benefits Cost
Fringe Benefits		
Social/Health Insurance (Employer contribution)	15.00% of total salaries	$ 46,500
Retirement Fund (Employer contribution)	5.00% of total salaries	15,500
Annual Leave, Holidays, Sick Leave (40 days/year)	15.38% of total salaries	47,692
		$ 109,692
Fringe Benefits Rate[3]		41.818%

Notes

1. Leave component of salary is equal to 15.385% of total annual salary (i.e., 40 leave days divided by 260 paid days per year). These costs are paid as part of fringe benefits and are not considered part of salaries for the purposes of calculating fringe benefit and indirect cost rates.

2. Non-leave component of salary is equal to 84.615% of total annual salary (i.e., 220 non-leave work days divided by 260 paid days per year).

3. The Fringe Benefits Rate is calculated by dividing the fringe benefits cost by the non-leave component of salaries ($109,692 / $262,308 = 41.818%).

- *Statement of Labor Allocation and Total Costs.* A sample of this statement for the EO is shown in exhibit 2. This statement, when used to support a provisional indirect cost rate, is based on the planned budget of the EO. When a final indirect cost rate is being calculated, actual costs should be used in this statement.

  The sample statement reflects the estimated/actual direct salary costs (net of the portion of salary paid through fringe benefits) expended on either direct or indirect activities. The percentage of time per position should be spread under the appropriate cost category, making sure that 100 percent is allocated for each position.[9]

  The statement also shows (in conformance with the CPS) which costs are allocated as indirect, direct, or excluded/unallowable costs. The sum of these cost categories must match the total costs of the organization.

- *Indirect Cost Rate Calculation.* Exhibit 3 shows the calculation of two different types of indirect cost rates—Method 1 one uses direct labor as the direct cost base and Method 2 uses total direct cost as the base. The calculation of the indirect cost rate is done by (1) classifying the total cost for the base period (usually the organization's fiscal year) as either direct or indirect (as shown in the Statement of Labor and Total Costs); and (2) dividing the total allowable indirect costs by an equitable distribution base.

The result of this process is an indirect cost rate which is used to distribute indirect costs to individual projects funded by contracts/grants and for unallowable costs that benefits from indirect cost activities. The rate is expressed (in percent) as the ratio of the total amount of allowable indirect costs (the numerator) to the base selected (the denominator). This method may also be used where the organization has only one major function encompassing a number of individual projects or activities, and may be used where the level of Federal awards to that organization is relatively small.

Note that, despite the total amount of indirect cost being the same in each calculation, the rate varies depending on the choice of the direct cost base. Thus, the lower rate is not "better" than the higher rate; the different rates are simply the reflection of the distribution of the indirect cost pool over different direct cost bases.

Exhibit 2 Example Institute
Statement of Labor Allocation and Total Costs

	Column A Total Costs	Column B Indirect Costs		Column C Direct Project Costs		Column D Excluded/Unallowable		Column E = B + C + D = A Reconciliation	
	Costs	% Share	Cost	% Share	Cost	% Share	Cost	% Share	Cost
Salaries (Labor cost, Non-leave component only)									
Executive Director	$ 50,769	75.00%	$ 38,077	25.00%	$ 12,692	0.00%	$ -	100.00%	$ 50,769
Technical Staff (5 @ $40,000 each)	169,231	10.00%	16,923	90.00%	152,308	0.00%	-	100.00%	169,231
Financial Manager	25,385	100.00%	25,385	0.00%	-	0.00%	-	100.00%	25,385
Administrative Assistant	16,923	100.00%	16,923	0.00%	-	0.00%	-	100.00%	16,923
	$ 262,308	37.097%	$ 97,308	62.903%	$ 165,000	0.000%	$ -		$ 262,308
	Non-leave								
Fringe Benefits 41.82%	salaries $ 109,692	41.818%	$ 40,692	41.818%	$ 69,000	41.818%	$ -		$ 109,692
Non-Labor Indirect Costs									
Rent, Utilities, Cleaning $ 2,500 /month	$ 30,000		$ 30,000						$ 30,000
Office Supplies 300 /month	3,600		3,600						3,600
Local Telephone/Long Distance Telephone/Fax 200 /month	2,400		2,400						2,400
Postage, Courier, Delivery 200 /month	2,400		2,400						2,400
Copying 200 /month	2,400		2,400						2,400
Computer Support, Internet 500 /month	6,000		6,000						6,000
Lease of Equipment 250 /month	3,000		3,000						3,000

Exhibit 2 Example Institute
Statement of Labor Allocation and Total Costs

		Column A Total Costs	Column B Indirect Costs % Share	Column B Cost	Column C Direct Project Costs % Share	Column C Cost	Column D Excluded/Unallowable % Share	Column D Cost	Column E = B + C + D = A Reconciliation % Share	Column E Cost
Depreciation of Capital Equipment Owned	20.00% equipment value	5,000		5,000						5,000
Staff Training		4,000		4,000						4,000
Business Development		6,000		6,000						6,000
Board of Trustee Expenses		2,000		2,000						2,000
Insurance		3,000		3,000						3,000
Audit		3,000		3,000						3,000
		$ 72,800		$ 72,800		$ -		$ -		$ 72,800
Other Direct Costs										
Consultant Services/ Subcontracts		$ 20,000				$ 20,000				$ 20,000
Travel	$ 1,000 /month	12,000				12,000				12,000
Long Distance Telephone/ Fax	300 /month	3,600				3,600				3,600
Project Supplies/Materials	300 /month	3,600				3,600				3,600
Printing, Reproduction	500 /month	6,000				6,000				6,000
		$ 45,200		$ -		$ 45,200		$ -		$ 45,200
Unallowable/Excluded Costs[1]										
Capital Equipment Purchased	$ 25,000	$ 7,000						$ 7,000		$ 7,000
Undepreciated Value of Capital										
Bad Debts/Entertainment		3,000						3,000		3,000
		$ 10,000		$ -		$ -		$ 10,000		$ 10,000
Total Costs		**$ 500,000**		**$ 210,800**		**$ 279,200**		**$ 10,000**		**$ 500,000**

Notes

1. The cost of equipment purchases and major renovations (and in some cases [but not in this example], subcontract costs) may vary considerably from project to project which causes the indirect costs to be allocated in a disproportionate amount to the benefit derived. Therefore, such costs are typically excluded from the base when a total direct cost base is being used. Bad debts and entertainment are typical examples of unallowable costs.

Exhibit 3 Example Institute
Statement of Indirect Costs and Rate Calculation

Method 1 - Base: Direct Cost Labor (including Fringe Benefits)

Indirect Costs (from Exhibit 2)	$ 210,800
Cost Base (from Exhibit 2)	
Direct Cost Labor	$ 165,000
Fringe Benefits (41.818% of Direct Cost Labor)	69,000
Total Cost Base	$ 234,000
Indirect Cost Rate (Indirect Costs / Total Cost Base)	90.085%
Reconciliation with Total Cost (from Exhibit 2)	
Direct Cost Labor	$ 165,000
Fringe Benefits (41.818% of Direct Cost Labor)	69,000
Indirect Costs (@ 90.085% of Direct Salaries & Fringe Benefits)	210,800
Other Direct Costs	45,200
Unallowable Costs	3,000
Excluded Costs	7,000
Total Cost	$ 500,000

Method 2 - Base: Total Direct Cost

Indirect Costs (from Exhibit 2)	$ 210,800
Cost Base (from Exhibit 2)	
Direct Cost Labor	$ 165,000
Fringe Benefits (41.818% of Direct Cost Labor)	$ 69,000
Other Direct Costs	$ 45,200
Unallowable Costs[a]	3,000
Total Cost Base	$ 282,200
Indirect Cost Rate (Indirect Costs / Total Cost Base)	74.699%
Reconciliation with Total Cost (from Exhibit 2)	
Direct Cost Labor	$ 165,000
Fringe Benefits (41.818% of Direct Cost Labor)	69,000
Indirect Costs (@ 74.699% of Total Direct Cost)	210,800
Other Direct Costs	45,200
Unallowable Costs[a]	3,000
Excluded Costs	7,000
Total Cost	$ 500,000

Notes

  a. Unallowable costs are included in the cost base if they represent activities for which indirect costs are properly allocable.

COMMON INDIRECT COST PROBLEMS

This section presents examples of some of the more common problems related to indirect costs disclosed by audits of nonprofit organizations.

Timekeeping Systems

Labor costs, whether charged directly to grants/contracts or to the indirect cost pool, must be based on accurate time records reflecting the actual activities of personnel. The time records must account for all of the activity of the personnel. The most common problems are either the failure to use a timekeeping system to track personnel activity or using a timekeeping system solely for the purpose of calculating payroll (i.e., only to record time and attendance of personnel, but not activities of the personnel). Exhibit 4 shows a sample timesheet that records project activities as well as indirect labor costs such as proposal development, staff training, and fringe benefit costs such as annual leave and sick leave time.

Consistent Treatment and Specific Identification of Costs

Costs must be treated consistently on all projects of the organization. Some typical problems with this include directly charging particular projects with costs specifically identifiable with other projects or charging costs which were not treated consistently with other costs incurred for the same purpose in similar circumstance.

Costs of "Unallowable Activities"

If unallowable costs are improperly charged as indirect costs, then two problems result. First, the inclusion of unallowable costs in the indirect cost pool overstates the amount of indirect cost, resulting in an indirect cost rate that is higher than appropriate for the recovery of allowable indirect cost. Second, because not all such costs were directly charged to the "unallowable activities" cost category, an appropriate share of indirect costs was not allocated to these unallowable activities. As a result, direct cost projects are allocated a disproportionate share of the organization's indirect costs.

Even if an organization's own activities or certain direct cost projects funded under contracts/grants provide for little or no reimbursement of indirect costs, the full share of indirect costs must be allocated to such

Exhibit 4 Example Institute
Sample Timesheet

Employee Name: *Robert Smith*

Month / Year: *June 2002*

Project Name	Project Code	1	2	3	4	5	6	7	8	9	10	11	12	13	14	15	16	17	18	19	20	21	22	23	24	25	26	27	28	29	30	31	TOTAL
Social Assistance Review	10024			8	4													2	3								2						19
Housing Subsidy Reform	10031				4	8	8															6					6	8	8				48
Tax Study Proposal	90055																	6	5	8	8	2											29
Staff Training	00203																								8	8							16
Paid Holiday	00101																															8	8
Annual Leave	00102										8	8	8	8	8																		40
Sick Leave	00103							8																									8
				8	8	8	8	8			8	8	8	8	8			8	8	8	8	8			8	8	8	8	8			8	168

Employee Certification:

I certify that this timesheet is accurate regarding the allocation of work-related time and paid leave taken.

[Employee Signature]

Supervisor Approval:

I have reviewed this timesheet and to the best of my knowledge, the information is accurate in all respects.

[Supervisor Signature]

own activities and contracts/grants (i.e., indirect costs cannot be unfairly shifted to projects which do not have restrictions on indirect cost payment).

Credits

Credits generated through project activities, such as fees for conferences held for the benefit of a specific project, must be credited to that specific project. Similarly, applicable credits to indirect costs, such as subletting rental space included in the indirect cost pool, must be credited to the indirect cost pool.

Indirect Cost Allocation Base

The direct cost base must allocate indirect costs to all direct cost projects equitably. To ensure that objective is met, organizations must continuously evaluate whether the direct cost base is not disproportionately distributing indirect costs between projects. For example, an organization may have chosen a direct labor cost base because the organization originally had projects that had similar shares of labor and other direct costs. If the organization undertakes a new very large project (relative to the total activity of the organization) that has a much larger share of other direct costs compared to direct labor, then a switch to a total cost base may be appropriate in order to more equitably allocate the organization's indirect costs.

Inter-Organizational Transfers and Related-Party Transactions

Supplies and services acquired from affiliates, related parties, and organizations under common control must be based on the actual costs of the organizations providing the supplies and services. The "costs" of supplies and services from these related organizations must not include "profit" and/or other mark-ups added by the related organization.

Unsupported Costs

To be allowable, all direct costs and indirect costs must be adequately supported by source documentation which clearly shows the purposes of and circumstances under which the cost was incurred. For example, canceled checks, bank transfer records, or credit card receipts alone are insufficient as cost documentation because they do not establish the purpose of the expense, they simply record the payment of funds. Adequate supporting cost documentation should record the purpose and circumstances of the expense. For example, the supporting documentation for a travel expense should identify the expense incurred, by whom and when, and the project/activity for which the travel was undertaken (to determine whether it is a direct/indirect and/or allowable/unallowable cost).

CONCLUSION

Think tanks in developing and transition economies generally divide into two categories with regard to their institutional development in the area of financial management: (1) small organizations that operate in an ad hoc fashion; and (2) larger, more well-established organizations that receive substantial funding from international donors and foundations.

Most think tanks in the first category do not yet have financial management systems that can meet the standards outlined in this chapter. Most of them do not have a clear understanding of indirect costs. Their project budgets are either based solely on direct costs, which often means they are not truly including all of the costs of the organization in their requests for funding, or they include an ad hoc factor for "overhead," which is usually an arbitrary mark-up applied to total costs. This "overhead" rate is much more likely to be based on an educated guess about the level of resources the organization needs to survive than any financial analysis which can be defended to funders. As a result, these organizations seem to be constantly in a state of financial crisis, living from project to project, but with little financial stability for the organization or its staff.

The second group of tanks has a better understanding of the issues related to indirect costs, but their understanding seems to be rooted more in the requirements of their major funders than a careful examination of the organization's needs. These organizations usually have an established indirect cost rate, but it often has been developed years earlier as part of a major contract or grant and has not been reviewed to see if it still corresponds to the needs of the organization. Thus, it is unclear if many of these organizations could successfully defend their indirect cost structure to a funder that seriously questioned the organization's indirect cost rate.

There still remains considerable distance, then, for most research organizations in transition and developing economies to cover before their current financial management practices with regard to indirect costs and financial sustainability reach a level that will allow them to manage and assess their financial needs more clearly. Recognition by funders that indirect costs are a necessity for any viable organization's continued operation and greater emphasis on the ability of an organization to explain and defend its indirect costs, rather than implying that indirect costs are unproductive, would help encourage organizations to pay more attention to this aspect of their institutional development.

Model Cost Policy Statement

T he model Cost Policy Statement in this appendix is adapted from the U.S. Department of Labor *Indirect Cost Rate Determination Guide: Cost Principles and Procedures for Non-Profit Organizations.* It is provided here as an example of the kind of documentation organizations should develop in order to demonstrate to funders that they have a well-defined, reasonable, and justifiable method of allocating and recovering indirect costs. Of course, individual funders may have particular requirements with respect to indirect costs (such as a ceiling on the amount of indirect costs that can be reimbursed or particular types of costs that cannot be reimbursed) that may be in conflict with the example provided below. Each organization must decide how to structure its indirect cost recovery to reflect its own particular funding situation.

This model CPS assumes that the Example Organization (EO) uses the direct allocation method of charging costs (i.e., in addition to direct costs), EO has in place accounting procedures which enable it to direct charge some costs that would otherwise be considered indirect costs (see, for example, the description below on how the photocopy costs are charged).

251

COST POLICY STATEMENT
Example Organization

I. General Accounting Policies

A. Basis of Accounting   Accrual Basis

B. Fiscal Period   July 1 through June 30

C. Allocation Basis   Direct Allocation Basis

D. Indirect Cost Rate Allocation Base-Direct Salaries and Wages Including Applicable Fringe Benefits.

E. Example Organization (EO) Fringe Benefit Base-Direct Salaries.

F. EO maintains adequate internal controls to insure that no cost is charged both directly and indirectly to contracts or grants.

G. EO accumulates all indirect costs and revenues in accounts titled, "Indirect Cost-Expense" and "Indirect Cost-Revenue," respectively.

II. Description of Cost Allocation Methodology

A. Salaries and Wages

1. Direct Costs—The majority of EO's personnel direct-charge their salary costs since their work is specifically identifiable to specific grants, contracts, or other activities of the organization. The charges are supported by auditable labor distribution reports that reflect the actual activities of employees.

2. Indirect Costs—The following personnel charge 100 percent of their salary costs indirectly:

   Financial Manager

   Administrative Assistant

3. Mixed Charges—The following personnel may charge their salary costs to both direct and indirect activities:

   Executive Director

   Technical Staff

The distinction between direct and indirect is primarily based on the functions performed. For example, when the positions shown are performing functions that are necessary and beneficial to all programs they are indirect. When functions are specific to one or more programs they are direct because they do not benefit all programs.

Auditable labor distribution records that reflect the actual activities of employees are maintained to support the mix of direct/indirect charges. The time records are certified by the Executive Director.

B. Fringe Benefits

Leave time costs (vacation leave earned, sick leave used, and holiday pay) are considered fringe benefit costs. EO's accounting system records leave time as a fringe benefit cost in the same manner that salary costs are recorded. Vacation leave earned but not used during each fiscal period is recorded as a cost in the period earned.

EO contributes to the following fringe benefits for its personnel: social/health insurance (including unemployment insurance and worker's compensation) and matching contributions to retirement fund.

C. Travel

Travel costs may be charged as either direct or indirect costs depending on the purpose of the trip. For example, the Executive Director travels to a regional office to give employees a quarterly update. This trip is indirect in nature and should be charged as an indirect cost. However, if the Executive Director travels to a regional office to perform a specific task for a contract, the trip would be considered a direct cost.

D. Board Expenses

Board expenses charged on an indirect basis are for travel to/from Board meetings and an annual fee of $250 paid to each Board member. Other Board expenses are absorbed by EO and are not charged either directly or indirectly to contracts or grants.

E. Supplies and Material

To the maximum extent possible, office supplies and materials are direct-charged to the contract/grant that uses the supplies or materials. Supplies and materials used by personnel engaged in indirect activities will be charged on an indirect basis.

F. Facility Expenses

EO occupies space it leases from Lessor Corporation. The lease provides for equal monthly payments during the term of the lease. All rent is charged as an indirect cost.

EO's lease includes the cost of all utilities except electricity. The cost of electricity is charged as an indirect cost.

G. Communications

1. A log is maintained of all fax transmissions. The cost of fax services is charged either directly or indirectly based upon whether a direct or indirect activity benefits from the transmission.

2. Long distance telephone calls are charged either directly or indirectly based upon whether a direct or indirect activity benefits from the transmission.
3. Local telephone service costs treated as indirect charges.
4. EO uses a meter system for postage charges. The postage meter has been programmed to identify the specific project or activity to charge costs against. Express mail costs are also specifically identified to the project or activity incurring the cost.

H. Photocopying and Printing

EO maintains a photocopy activity log. From this log, EO is able to prorate its photocopy expenses to each project based on the specific volume of copies made for each program. Administrative personnel will record copies made to the benefiting project to the maximum extent practical. In situations where the photocopies being made by administrative personnel cannot be identified to a specific project and the matter being copied relates to the activities of EO in general, the cost of such copies will be charged to the "Indirect Cost-Expense" account.

Printing expenses are charged to the benefiting activity.

I. Outside Services

EO incurs outside services costs for its annual audit, legal fees, and for staff development specialists.
1. The cost of the annual audit is charged indirectly.
2. In general, legal fees are charged directly to the benefiting project or activity.
3. Legal fees that are not identifiable to specific direct projects are charged indirectly.

J. Capital Items

Capital expenditures are charged directly to projects only in cases where a contract or grant specifically authorizes such charges. No capital item is charged indirectly. The cost of capital items purchased with non-contract/grant funds is recovered through depreciation charges. EO's capitalization threshold is $500.

K. Depreciation

The cost of capital items purchased with non-contract/grant funds that are used in a manner that benefits projects is recovered through depreciation charges. EO recovers the cost of capital items using straight line depreciation methods in accordance with generally accepted accounting principles. Depreciation is charged indirectly.

L. Unallowable Costs

EO recognizes that the costs listed below are unallowable charges to contracts/grants and has internal controls in place to insure that such costs are not charged to contracts/grants:

- Advertising and public relations
- Entertainment/alcoholic beverages
- Capital expenditures
- Bad debts
- Interest
- Lobbying and fundraising

_____   _____

(Signature)   (Date)

_____

(Title)
Example Organization
(Address)

ENDNOTES

1. "Fundraising" is used here to mean funds solicited by the think tank for its own unrestricted use (as compared to "business development" which is used here to mean the solicitation of funds for specific research project activities).

2. The U.S. Government, for example, has a limit imposed by regulation on the amount of overhead costs it will pay to universities carrying out work under federal contracts and grants.

3. FASB statement No. 117, paragraphs 27 and 28.

4. OMB Circular No. A-122, Attachment A, Paragraphs C.1–C.3.

5. OMB Circular No. A-122, Attachment A, Paragraph B.2.

6. Although the base can be set in a variety of ways (for example, the number of hours expended by project staff, the number of persons working on or served by a project, by the size of facilities used for each project, or other methods which have a logical basis related to the nature of the activity or project), most organizations use direct labor cost or total direct costs as the base. Thus, there is no single "right" way to calculate an indirect cost rate, to determine what costs to include as indirect costs, or how much indirect cost is "fair." Under U.S. Federal Government guidelines, allowable indirect costs range from 3 percent to 70 percent, varying from agency to agency.

Although many funding organizations seem to operate from the perspective that a lower overhead rate is better, a lower rate does not necessarily imply a more efficient organization. For example, imagine a single organization implementing multiple projects where each project has its own accounting staff, purchases its own supplies, and has all its own equipment. Such an organization would have no indirect costs at all, but would be clearly less efficient than if the programs shared accounting costs, supplies and equipment.

7. These descriptions are based on information in the U.S. Department of Labor *Indirect Cost Rate Determination Guide* for contractors and grantees on its web site at http://www.dol.gov.

8. Another type of indirect cost rate is a "Fixed Rates with Carry-Forward." In this structure, a fixed rate is established for a period of time to permit budgeting and billing/payment of expenses to/by funders. Actual costs are determined by the organization's accounting system and the difference in indirect costs as calculated by the fixed indirect cost rate and actual indirect costs is carried forward to a future period (usually the organization's fiscal year) in order to adjust the fixed rate in the next period for any over- or under-recovery of indirect costs. This structure would only be used where the structure of funding for an organization remains stable over time; otherwise, the structure could result in inappropriate allocation of indirect costs to funders because of the

mismatch between a changing funding structure and the shifting of indirect cost recovery out of the period in which the costs were incurred.

9. The organization must maintain a time distribution system (such as timesheets) for documenting how salary expenses are incurred across indirect and direct cost activities and across projects for personnel whose time is charged to more than one cost activity or project.

References

Bacon, F.R., Jr., and T.W. Butler, Jr. 1998. *Achieving Planned Innovation: A Proven System for Creating Successful New Products and Services.* New York: Free Press.

Ban, C., S.R. Faerman, and N.M. Riccucci. 1992. "Productivity and the Personnel Process," in *Public Productivity Handbook,* edited by M. Holzer (401–23). San Francisco: Jossey-Bass.

Bardach, E. 1984. "The Dissemination of Policy Research to Policymakers," *Knowledge: Creation, Diffusion, Utilization,* vol. 6, no.2, pp. 125–44.

Bowser, J.E. 1998. *Revolutionizing Workforce Performance: A System Approach to Mastery.* San Francisco: Jossey-Boss, Pfeiffer.

Bruckner, S. 1996. "Policy Research Centers in Russia: Tottering Toward an Uncertain Future," *NIRA Review* (summer): 32–36.

Bryson, J.M. 1995. *Strategic Planning for Public and Nonprofit Organizations.* San Francisco: Jossey-Bass.

Bullen, P., S. Lawrence, P. Schwenke, A. Williamson, and S. Williamson. 1997. *Nonprofits in Busine$$.* Surry Hills, NSW Australia: WorkVentures, Ltd.

Burlingame, D.F., and W.F. Ilchman, eds. 1996. *Alternative Revenue Sources: Prospects, Requirements, and Concerns for Nonprofits.* San Francisco: Jossey-Bass.

Butteriss, M., ed. 1998. *Re-inventing HR.* New York: John Wiley.

Charan, R. 1998. *Boards at Work: How Corporate Boards Create Competitive Advantage.* San Francisco: Jossey-Bass.

Charan, R., S. Drotter, and J. Noel. 2001. *The Leadership Pipeline.* San Francisco: Jossey-Bass.

Clutterbuck, D., and D. Dearlove. 1996. *Charity as a Business.* London: Directory of Social Change.

Conger, J.A., and B. Benjamin. 1999. *Building Leaders: How Successful Companies Develop the Next Generation.* San Fransisco: Jossey-Bass.

Covello, J.A., and B.J. Hazelgren. 1995. *The Complete Book of Business Plans.* Naperville, IL: Sourcebooks.

Davis, Lee. 1997. "The NGO-Business Hybrid: Is the Private Sector the Answer?" Washington, D.C.: The Johns Hopkins University, Nitze School of Advanced International Studies.

Dees, J.G. 2001a. "Mobilizing Resources," in *Enterprising Nonprofits: A Toolkit for Social Entrepreneurs,* edited by J.G. Dees, J. Emerson, and P. Economy (63–102). New York: John Wiley.

————. 2001b. "Mastering the Art of Innovation," in *Enterprising Nonprofits: A Toolkit for Social Entrepreneurs*, edited by J.G. Dees, J. Emerson, and P. Economy (161–98). New York: John Wiley.

Dees, J.G., J. Emerson, and P. Economy, eds. 2001. *Enterprising Nonprofits: A Toolkit for Social Entrepreneurs*. New York: John Wiley.

Deschamps, J.-P., and P.R. Nayak. 1995. *Product Juggernauts: How Companies Mobilize to Generate a Stream of Market Winners*. Boston: Harvard Business School Press.

Dibble, S. 1999. *Keeping Your Valuable Employees: Retention Strategies for Your Organization's Most Important Resource*. New York: John Wiley.

Dolowitz, D., and D. Marsh. 1996. "Who Learns from Whom: a Review of the Policy Transfer Literature," *Political Studies*, vol.44, pp. 343–57.

Dotlich, D.L., and P.C. Cairo. 1999. *Action Coaching*. San Francisco: Jossey-Bass.

Fox, C.J. 1991. "Employee Performance Appraisal: The Keystone Made of Clay," in *Public Personnel Management: Current Concerns, Future Challenges,* edited by C. Ban and N. Riccorci (58–71). New York: Longman.

Freedom House. 1999. *Think Tanks in Central and Eastern Europe: A Comprehensive Directory.* Budapest: author.

Feulner, E.J. 1985. "Ideas, Think-Tanks and Governments," *Quadrant*, November, pp. 22–6.

Garrett, J.L., and Y. Islam. 1998. *Policy Research and the Policy Process: Do the Twain Ever Meet?* Stockholm: IIED, Gatekeeper Series no. 5A74.

Glen, R.M. 1990. "Performance Appraisal: An Unnerving Yet Useful Process," *Public Personnel Management* 19 (1): 1–10.

Hall, P. 1990. "Policy Paradigms, Experts and the State: The Case of Macro-economic Policy Making in Britain," in S. Brooks and A.-G. Gagnon (eds.), *Social Scientists, Policy and the State*. New York: Praeger.

Heneman, R.L. 2001. *Business-Driven Compensation Policies*. New York: American Management Association.

Herzberg, F. 1987. "One More Time: How Do You Motivate Employees?" *Harvard Business Review* (September–October): 109–20.

Heskett, J.L. 1987. "Lesson in the Service Sector," *Harvard Business Review* (March–April): 118–26.

Holland, T.P., and M. Blackmon. 2000. *Measuring Board Effectiveness: A Tool for Strengthening Your Board*. Washington, DC: National Center for Nonprofit Boards.

Huberman, M. 1994. "Research Utilization: The State of the Art," *Knowledge and Policy: The International Journal of Knowledge Transfer and Utilization*, vol. 7, no.4, pp. 13–33.

Johnson, E. 2000. "Think Tanks in Sub-Saharan Africa," in J.G. McGann and R.K. Weaver, eds., *Think Tanks & Civil Societies*. New Brunswick: Transaction Publishers, pp. 465–90.

Karatnycky, A., A. Motyl, and B. Shor. 1996. *Nation's in Transit 1997*. New Brunswick, NJ: Transaction Publishers.

Kingdon, J. 1984. *Agendas, Alternatives and Public Policies*. Boston: Little Brown & Co,

Kingsley, T. 1993. "Ideas for Managing a Japanese Think Tank," in *A Japanese Think Tank: Exploring Alternative Models*, edited by R. Struyk, M. Ueno, and T Suzuki (appendix D). Washington, D.C.: Urban Institute.

Kitzi, J. 2001. "Recognizing and Assessing New Opportunities," in *Enterprising Nonprofits: A Toolkit for Social Entrepreneurs*, edited by J.G. Dees, J. Emerson, and P. Economy (43–62). New York: John Wiley.

Kotler, P. 2000. *Marketing Management*. Upper Saddle River, NJ: Prentice Hall, Tenth Edition.

LaPiana, D. 1997. *Beyond Collaboration: Strategic Restructuring of Nonprofit Organizations*. Washington, D.C.: National Center for Nonprofit Boards.

Ledford, G.E. Jr. 1995. "Designing Nimble Reward Systems," *Compensation and Benefits Review* (July–August): 46–54.

Lee, C. 1996. "Performance Appraisal," *Training* 33 (5): 44–59.

Leigh, A., and M. Maynard. 1995. *Leading Your Team: How to Involve and Inspire Teams*. London: Nicholas Brealey Publishing.

Letts, C.W., W.P. Ryan, and A. Grossman. 1999. *High Performance Nonprofit Organizations: Managing Upstream for Greater Impact*. New York: John Wiley.

Light, P.C. 2000. *Making Nonprofits Work: A Report on the Tides of Nonprofit Management Reform*. Washington, D.C.: Brookings Institution.

Light, P.C. 1998. *Sustaining Innovation: Creating Nonprofit and Government Organizations that Innovate Naturally*. San Francisco: Jossey-Bass.

Liner, B., H. Hatry, E. Vinson, R. Allen, P. Dusenbury, S. Bryant, and R. Snell. 2001. *Making Results-Based State Government Work*. Washington, D.C.: Urban Institute.

Langsford, J.W., and K.L. Brownsey, eds. 1992. *Think Tanks and Governance in the Asia-Pacific Region*. Halifax, Nova Scotia: Institute for Research on Public Policy.

Lomas, J. 1993. "Diffusion, Dissemination, and Implementation: Who Should Do What?" *Annals New York Academy of Sciences*, pp. 226–37.

Majeska, K. 2001. "Understanding and Attracting Your 'Customer'," in *Enterprising Nonprofits: A Toolkit for Social Entrepreneurs*, edited by J.G. Dees, J. Emerson, and P. Economy (199–250). New York: John Wiley.

Maxwell, M.M. 1996. "New Ventures in a Nonprofit Environment," in *Alternative Revenue Sources: Prospects, Requirements and Concerns for Nonprofits*, edited by D.F. Burlingame and W.F. Ilchman. San Francisco: Jossey-Bass Inc.

McAdams, J.L., and E.J. Hawk. 1994. *Organizational Performance and Rewards*. Scottsdale: American Compensation Association.

McGann, J. 1999. "Think Tanks: Catalysts for Ideas in Action —An International Survey." Philadelphia: Foreign Policy Research Institute.

McMurtry, S.L., F.E. Netting, and P.M. Kettner. 1991. "How Nonprofits Adapt to a Stringent Environment," *Nonprofit Management & Leadership* 1 (3) 235–52.

Quigley, K.F.F. 1997. *For Democracy's Sake: Foundations and Democratic Assistance in Central Europe*. Washington, D.C.: The Woodrow Wilson Center Press.

Perry, J.L. 1991. "Linking Pay to Performance: The Controversy Continues," in *Public Personnel Management: Current Concerns, Future Challenges*, edited by C. Ban and N. Riccorci (73–86). New York: Longman.

Platt, J. 1987. "Research Dissemination: A Case Study," *The Quarterly Journal of Social Affairs*, fol. 3, no.3, pp. 181–98.

Rabin, J., C.E. Teasley III, A. Finkle, and L.F. Carter. 1985. *Personnel: Managing Human Resources in the Public Sector*. San Diego: Harcourt Brace Jovanovich.

Rees, F. 2001. *How to Lead Work Teams.* San Francisco: Jossey-Bass, Pfeiffer.

Rich, A. 2001. "U.S. Think Tanks and the Intersection of Ideology, Advocacy, and Influence," *NIRA Review* 8 (1): 54–59.

Richman, B., and R. Struyk. Forthcoming. "Local Administration of Social Assistance in Russia," *International Journal of Public Administration.*

Robinson, M.K. 2001. *Nonprofit Boards that Work: The End of One-Size-Fits All Governance.* New York: John Wiley & Sons.

Rothwell, W.J., and H.C. Kazanas. 1994. *Improving On-the-Job Training.* San Francisco: Jossey-Bass.

Saywell, D., and A. Cotton. 1999. *Spreading the Word: Practical Guidelines for Research Dissemination Strategies.* Leicestershire, UK: Loughborogh University, processed; available at www.lboro.ac.uk/wedc/publications.

Shultz, S.F. 2001. *The Board Book: Making Your Corporate Board a Strategic Force in Your Company's Success.* New York: American Management Association.

Singer, M.I., and J.A. Yankey. 1991. "Organizational Metamorphosis: A Study of Eigthteen Nonprofit Mergers, Acquisitions, and Consolidations." *Nonprofit Management & Leadership* 1 (4): 357–69.

Slesinger, L.H. 1995. *Self-Assessment for Nonprofit Governing Boards.* Washington, DC: Center for Nonprofit Boards.

Smith, J.S. 1991. *The Idea Brokers: Think Tanks and the Rise of the New Policy Elite.* New York: The Free Press.

Stapleton, B. 1983. "Disseminating Social Services Research," *Research, Policy and Planning,* vol. 1, no. 2, 1983, pp. 14–7.

Stone, D. 2000. "Non-Governmental Policy Transfer: The Strategies of Independent Policy Institutes," *Governnance: An International Journal of Policy and Administration,* vol.13, no.1, pp. 45–62.

Stone, D., with S. Maxwell and M. Keating. 2001. "Bridging Research and Policy." Coventry, UK: Paper presented at An International Workshop, processed.

Stone, M.M., B. Bigelow, and W. Crittenden. 1999. "Research on Strategic Management in Nonprofit Organizations: Synthesis, Analysis, and Future Directions," *Administration & Society* 31 (3): 378–423.

Stone, D., A. Denham, and M. Garnett. 1998. *Think Tanks Across Nations: A Comparative Approach.* Manchester: Manchester University Press.

Struyk, R. 1993. "Learning from the U.S. and European Experience," in *A Japanese Think Tank: Exploring Alternative Models,* edited by R. Struyk, M. Ueno, and T. Suzuki (31–55). Washington, D.C.: Urban Institute.

Struyk, R. 1999. *Reconstructive Critics: Think Tanks in Post–Soviet Bloc Democracies.* Washington, D.C.: Urban Institute Press.

Struyk, R., M. Ueno, and T. Suzuki. 1993. *A Japanese Think Tank: Exploring Alternative Models.* Washington, D.C.: Urban Institute Press.

Sundquist, J.L. 1978. "Research Brokerage: The Weak Link," in L.E. Lynn (ed.), *Knowledge and Policy: The Uncertain Connection.* Washington, DC: National Academy of Sciences.

Telgarsky, J., and M. Ueno, eds. 1996. *Think Tanks in a Democratic Society: An Alternative Voice.* Washington, D.C.: Urban Institute Press.

Tschirbart, M. 1996. "Maintaining Legitimacy and Reputation Through Impression Management," in *Alternative Revenue Sources: Prospects, Requirements and Concerns for Nonprofits*, edited by D.F. Burlingame and W.F. Ilchman (75–86). San Francisco: Jossey-Bass.

Ulrich, D. 1998. "A New Mandate for Human Resources." *Harvard Business Review* (January–February): 125–34.

Wernet, S.P., and S.A. Jones. 1992. "Merger and Acquisition Activity Between Nonprofit Social Service Organizations: A Case Study," *Nonprofit and Voluntary Sector Quarterly* 21 (4): 367–80.

Wheeler, T.L., and J.D. Hunger. 2000. *Strategic Management and Business Policy.* Upper Saddle River, NJ: Prentice Hall, 7th edition.

Wilson, T. 1994. *Innovative Reward Systems for the Changing Workplace.* New York: McGraw-Hill.

About the Authors

Raymond J. Struyk is a senior fellow at the Urban Institute, Washington, D.C. He holds a Ph.D. in economics from Washington University (St. Louis). Before joining the Institute in 1972, Mr. Struyk was a staff member at the National Bureau of Economic Research and taught at Rice and Rutgers Universities. His career has been at the Institute, except for an appointment as the Deputy Assistant Secretary for Research and Evaluation at the U.S. Department of Housing and Urban Development.

Mr. Struyk created the Institute's international program in 1983 and directed it until 1992. He has concentrated his work on developing and transition countries for the past 20 years. From 1992 through 1998 he was the resident director of the Housing Sector Reform Program in Russia. He was the founding president of the Transitional Policy Network, a group made up of several of think tanks in the former Soviet bloc and of the Urban Institute; he served as president from 1997 to 2000. He continues his work in Russia on housing and social assistance reform issues and collaborates closely with the Institute for Urban Economics in Moscow, as well as serving on the IUE's board of trustees.

Mr. Struyk has published extensively. Among his recent publications are *Reconstructive Critics: Think Tanks in Post-Soviet Democracies* (Urban Institute Press, 1999); *Making Aid Work: Lessons from Successful Technical Cooperation in the Former Soviet Bloc* (Urban Institute Press, 1997); and the report *Homeownership and Housing Finance Policy in the Former Soviet Bloc: Costly Populism* (Urban Institute, 2000).

Jeffrey P. Telgarsky is the Director of the International Activities Center at the Urban Institute, Washington, DC. He holds an MSc in Development Economics and an MA in Politics, Philosophy, and Economics from Oxford University. Mr. Telgarsky joined the Institute in

265

1987 as a research associate and from 1987-1992 worked on urban development issues in Asia, Latin America and the Caribbean, and Eastern Europe. He became Director of the Institute's international programs in 1993.

As Director, Mr. Telgarsky's responsibilities include managing the Institute's portfolio of projects in Eastern Europe, the former Soviet Union, and elsewhere overseas. In this role, he works closely with foreign organizations collaborating with the Institute on its research projects. His previous publications include *Think Tanks in a Democratic Society: An Alternative Voice* (with Maiko Ueno, editor; Urban Institute Press, 1996) and *Towards a Market-Oriented Housing Sector in Eastern Europe* (with Raymond J. Struyk, Urban Institute, 1990).